NEUE
CUISINE

A GIFT FOR
THE WINE TASTING 2012 ATTENDEES

Compliments of:

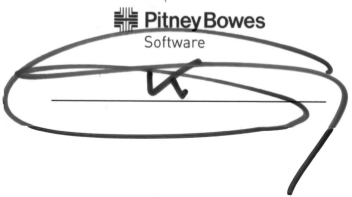

NEUE CUISINE

THE ELEGANT TASTES ∙OF VIENNA∙

RECIPES FROM WALLSÉ, CAFÉ SABARSKY AND BLAUE GANS

KURT GUTENBRUNNER

WRITTEN WITH JANE SIGAL

RESEARCH BY HELEN FREUND • PHOTOGRAPHY BY ELLEN SILVERMAN

IN ASSOCIATION WITH NEUE GALERIE NEW YORK

RIZZOLI
NEW YORK

New York ∙ Paris ∙ London ∙ Milan

First published in the United States of America in 2011
by Rizzoli International Publications, Inc.
300 Park Avenue South
New York, New York 10010
www.rizzoliusa.com

Text copyright ©2011 Kurt Gutenbrunner
Written with Jane Sigal

Photography copyright ©2011 Ellen Silverman
Styling by Susie Theodorou and Noemi Bonazzi

2011 2012 2013 2014 / 10 9 8 7 6 5 4 3 2 1

Printed in China

ISBN 13: 978-0-8478-3562-1

Library of Congress Control Number: 2011 927 547

Project Editor: Sandra Gilbert
Book Design: Richard Pandiscio, William Loccisano/Pandiscio Co.

PAGE 2 Brook Trout with Cauliflower, Raisins, and Almonds (page 98) on 1938 *Urania* plates by Trude Petri, with 1917 *Patrician* stemware by J. & L. Lobmeyr and 1906–1907 *Rundes Modell* cutlery and a 1912–1913 crystal flower bowl, both designed by Josef Hoffmann, and sterling silver napkin cuffs by Biscaye Frères, create an early twentieth-century-inspired lunch at Café Sabarsky. All items provided by Neue Galerie Design Shop.

OPPOSITE Even with a demanding schedule, I always try to have dinner with my children. Here, Ben, the girls—Romane, Tess, and Lou—and I share a Viennese breakfast at Café Sabarsky, featuring Austrian Doughnuts (page 169), Lemon-Poppyseed Cake (page 188), and a soft-boiled egg in a martini glass. My children eat really, really well.

This book is dedicated to
my loving parents, and to my children, Benjamin, Romane, Tess, and Lou,
who provide so much inspiration and endless laughter.

CONTENTS

A Gustav Klimt print makes a sensual background for luscious Caramel-Cream Layer Cake (page 196).

PREFACE

When the Neue Galerie opened in 2001, New York welcomed its first museum devoted to early twentieth-century German and Austrian art and design. Situated in a landmark mansion built in 1914, the museum immediately attracted a loyal following, drawn to the refined atmosphere and to the extraordinary artworks on view. Paintings and drawings by Gustav Klimt, Egon Schiele, Max Beckmann, Otto Dix, and their contemporaries fill the galleries.

However, there was another crucial factor in the success of the Neue Galerie: Café Sabarsky, located in the elegant wood-paneled former dining room on the ground floor. Café Sabarsky is an important part of our mission, in that it draws its inspiration from the great Viennese cafés that have long served as important centers of intellectual and artistic life. The setting, with furnishings by Josef Hoffmann, Adolf Loos, and Otto Wagner, is a celebration of Viennese café atmosphere. Best of all, the dishes served here are as delicious as they are authentic.

Chef Kurt Gutenbrunner has done a magnificent job in establishing Café Sabarsky, making it a favorite spot for New Yorkers. Through his work there and at his other restaurants, Wallsé and Blaue Gans, Kurt has revitalized the entire tradition of Austrian cuisine. He has made Café Sabarsky a proud upholder of the Viennese café tradition, and an inseparable part of the Neue Galerie. Just as we will always display the works of Gustav Klimt and Egon Schiele in our galleries, we will always be pleased to serve the cuisine and preserve the ambience and hospitality of the great cafés of Vienna.

Ronald S. Lauder
President and co-founder, Neue Galerie New York

Installation view *Gustav Klimt: The Ronald S. Lauder and Serge Sabarsky Collections*, Neue Galerie New York, October 18, 2007–June 30, 2008, showing *Adele Bloch-Bauer I* (1907) by Gustav Klimt flanked by *Kneeling Youths* (ca. 1898) by George Minne. Photograph by Raeanne Giovanni.

FOREWORD

Cafés have always captivated me. They seem to provide the perfect backdrop for romance and intrigue. In them one hears lovers quarreling, sees lonely souls pretending to read the newspaper while eavesdropping on their neighbors. During the Cold War, cafés served as a common meeting place for spies, with trenchcoat-wearing operatives hiding microphones in the salt and pepper shakers. In sum, cafés are a magnificent stage on which to observe the human comedy.

The Viennese café has a centuries-old history. The first one was opened in 1685 with the introduction of coffee beans to the city, a legacy of the Turkish invasion. The new drink—always served with a chaser of water—was well-received, and the number of coffee houses increased quickly. By the late nineteenth century, the café had become the preferred meeting place for writers and artists. The literary journal *Die Fackel* (*The Torch*), edited by Karl Kraus, is said to have been written, to a large extent, in cafés. The writer Peter Altenberg even had his mail delivered to his favorite haunt, the Café Central. Starting around 1950, many well-known Viennese coffee houses began to close. However, some of the finest cafés are still thriving, and it is these places that served as our inspiration in creating Café Sabarsky.

Our café, led by America's premier Austrian chef, Kurt Gutenbrunner, is named for the co-founder of the Neue Galerie, Serge Sabarsky (1912–1996). Born in Vienna, Serge led a colorful life. He worked as a clown and set designer for Simplicissimus, the leading cabaret of the era. He fled his native city in 1938 and settled in New York, where he worked successfully as a contractor before establishing a gallery for Austrian and German art. In partnership with his friend Ronald S. Lauder, he established the Neue Galerie. Although Sabarsky died five years before the museum came to fruition, his passion, expertise, and generosity have informed every aspect of the institution, including our ever-popular café.

It was Serge who wisely instructed us, "If the coffee is no good, you may as well forget the museum." Chef Gutenbrunner's menu includes such Viennese specialties as a tempting selection of aromatic coffees, strudels, and tortes, along with classic sausages and goulash. We also honor Serge's love of music by hosting a marvelous cabaret series in the café, featuring top performers such as Ute Lemper and Max Raabe interpreting the classic cabaret repertoire. I know Serge would be pleased with the café bearing his name.

Renée Price
Director, Neue Galerie New York

Café Sabarsky's marble mantelpiece displays irresistible Viennese pastries and confections, left to right:
Caramel-Cream Layer Cake (page 196), Hazelnut Torte with Chocolate Ganache (page 192), Chocolate-Cherry Torte (page 190),
Quark Cheesecake (page 200), Linzertorte (page 186), Austrian Doughnuts (page 169), Dark Chocolate Almonds (page 207),
Chocolate Hazelnuts (page 206), Chocolate-Almond Loaf Cake (page 202), Marble Cake, Sabarskytorte, Black Forest Cake,
Sachertorte (page 194), Apple Strudel (page 176), and Lemon-Poppy Seed Cake (page 188).

Gasthof Sengstbratl in Wallsee

MY AUSTRIAN TABLE
FROM WALLSEE TO WALLSÉ

In my head, I'm still a boy from a village of two thousand on the Danube. Sure, I've worked in kitchens in Salzburg, Vienna, the Swiss Alps, and Munich, and I've created an expanding family of Austrian restaurants in New York. In fact, as much as I adore Austria, I probably could not live there anymore. I love the United States, my children are here, and I feel at home here.

But little me, a New York restaurateur? It's the most incredible thing. Yet, here I am with Wallsé in the West Village, Café Sabarsky in the Neue Galerie on the Upper East Side, and Blaue Gans in Tribeca. It's hard to believe that my restaurants have been so warmly accepted. More than that, people have really understood and appreciated what I'm trying to do. What a mind-blowing journey!

WALLSEE: IF YOU WANT TO EAT IT, YOU HAVE TO GROW IT

I grew up in the 1960s in Wallsee, a small fifteenth-century town with a Habsburg castle about eighty miles west of Vienna. It was a tight-knit community, and if I didn't say hello to a neighbor, my mom would hear about it. On the way home from school, we'd be invited to pick the fruit in a friend's yard. Everybody was so proud of what they were growing. Taste, the cherries are fantastic this year!

The Danube literally flowed through our lives. My father helped build hydroelectric plants along the river, and our house was so close that we were often flooded when the snow melted in the mountains. We never knew how high the water was going to be in the living room.

We weren't farmers, but we raised chickens, rabbits, and pigs. Everybody did. In the winter, our sandstone cellar was stocked with apples and pears from our trees; celery root, horseradish, and beets from the kitchen garden; homemade red currant, raspberry, and blueberry jams; apricot and plum syrups; pickled ramps and other vegetables; and cured hams and sausages. Our milk came from the cows next door; every morning and afternoon, we boys went to collect it.

OPPOSITE Austrians celebrate *Fasching* Tuesday (Mardi Gras) by wearing costumes
and eating *Krapfen* (doughnuts). I'm aptly suited up in a chef's toque and apron, alongside my brother.

ABOVE Traditional inns like Gasthof Sengstbratl in Wallsee serve nostalgic fare such as
Pork Schnitzel with Bacon, Chanterelles, and Cream Sauce (page 125).

THIS PAGE AND OPPOSITE Kitchen snapshots of skillets,
salt and pepper shakers, and onions by Peter Medilek.
The photo of charred onions reminds me of my apprenticeship;
I learned they bring deep flavor and color to stocks.

Wallsee had only a few food shops, a bakery, and a butcher's shop, where we bought items like bread, sugar, coffee, and paprika. We couldn't buy bananas if we wanted to—they weren't local. Anyway, my mother would have said, "Why do you need bananas? We have apples. We have peaches." We grew or made almost everything else, including apple and pear wine (*Most*, in German), cider, and vinegar. We cultivated peas, strawberries, salad greens, herbs, beans, tomatoes, peppers, potatoes, cauliflower, cabbage, and kohlrabi. If we wanted to eat it, we had to grow it.

The animals dictated our menus. If the chickens didn't lay eggs, we didn't have omelets. If a rabbit got to be a certain size, my mother let my father know it was time to kill it. If there was no bacon, it was time to kill a pig.

It was an uncomplicated life. I played soccer, went fishing in the Danube, rode my bike in the Habsburg park. My brother, Fritz; my sister, Christiane; and I pitched in around the house. There was no "I don't want to help—" it didn't exist. Whatever had to be done, we did. We learned how to plant seeds. We dug up potatoes. We gathered apples and loaded them into the cider press. We weren't told we had to do these chores; we wanted to help. It was just what you did to be part of a family, part of a larger community.

We ate nature and were surrounded by it—its beauty, like the sun setting over the river, and its dangers, like the storms that came. Even though I live in a skyscraper now, I still sleep with the windows open. The Hudson is not the Danube, but I sometimes think I can hear the frogs and the crickets.

CHOPPING ONIONS AND SWEEPING: THE EDUCATION OF A CHEF

When it came to my future, there was no question of me climbing around on construction sites like my father. I didn't feel comfortable with heights. (I have no trouble skiing, though!) I preferred to go pick tomatoes. Also, I grew up watching the boats go by on the river and I was curious to know about where they went. I thought that cooking would allow me to travel anywhere I wanted to go.

So, when I was fifteen, I was enrolled in a two-year hotel-and-restaurant school about an hour from Wallsee. Externships were required during the summer vacation, and I worked at the luxury hotel-restaurant Richard Löwenherz, which was an incredible experience. Named after Richard the Lionhearted, it was in the medieval village of Dürnstein in the beautiful Wachau Valley, where winemakers produce Austria's most exclusive Grüner Veltliner and Riesling wines.

I worked the front of the house. There was no doorman. We had to take up the luggage. We had to work the breakfast service. We swept the yard. We'd change our clothes to be in the dining room for lunch. We had an hour or two in the afternoon to relax, and then it was back to work until 11 p.m. It was a lot of work for a sixteen-year-old, but I wanted to do it. I absorbed so much at this weekend retreat for the rich and famous of Vienna.

After Richard Löwenherz, I continued my apprenticeship at another hotel closer to home, where I worked mostly in the kitchen. There was no full-time person washing up. It was us, the apprentices. If you washed the dishes the right way and you did it fast enough, you got a chance to help out at the appetizer-and-salad station. If you were good enough and lucky, somebody else arrived to wash the dishes and you moved up the ladder.

I learned many things during my apprenticeship, including how to cut an onion. I was told, "Here's a bucket of onions, why don't you cut them until you know what you are doing?" I learned to hold my fingers the right way, to stand the right way, to use a knife the right way.

These things never left me. Every single day I spent in those kitchens put a stamp on me. Consciously or unconsciously, I was filling my pockets with pebbles of knowledge. Then when it was needed, I put my hands in my pockets and grabbed.

MAKING IT ON THE HOT LINE IN EUROPE

Growing up at home, I had to work hard; it wasn't a choice. But then it became my decision. Nobody told me, "Hey, finish your apprenticeship. Go find a job in Salzburg, then in Switzerland. Get your butt kicked every single day. Go live in Europe, share a room with two people, shower in a bathroom down the hall, work six days a week." I wanted to.

At twenty, I had completed my military service. I said, "I'm leaving. Time to get away." I signed on to work a summer season in Switzerland at a hotel all the way up in the Alps, in Crans Montana, because I believed the greatest chefs worked in Switzerland. It was a beautiful place, I met a lot of people, and I learned new techniques, but the sun wasn't shining as brightly as I had expected. I wasn't sure what I was looking for, but I wanted something more.

At Wallsé, Julian Schnabel's *Monkey Painting* (detail) is a cheeky backdrop for a trio of classic strudels, left to right: Quark Custard Strudel (page 180), Apple Strudel (page 176), and Cherry Strudel (page 178).

When I returned to Austria, opportunity knocked. One of my teachers from culinary school called. "There's a chef who's opening his own restaurant near Wallsee," he said. "His name is Erich Schuller. He is phenomenal, and he needs help."

Erich had worked at the legendary Rotisserie Prinz Eugen at the Hilton Hotel in Vienna with chef Werner Matt, an early adopter of nouvelle cuisine, and at the Michelin-starred Tantris in Munich, one of Europe's most innovative restaurants. So Erich was one of the big guys. His passion for food, enormous knowledge, and contacts galvanized my life. But I also wanted to study with the chefs who had mentored him.

After working with Erich at the Allhartsberger Hof, I followed in his footsteps to the Hilton Hotel. It was tough: seventy chefs, five restaurants, room service, banquets. In 1986, the Rotisserie Prinz Eugen was one of Austria's finest restaurants. We had a Michelin star. And Werner Matt pushed us hard.

He once said to me, "I'm here to do my job. I'm not here so people love me." The sous chefs were just as tough—and talented. It was like being a goldfish in a sea of sharks. I had to fight for my job every single day. It was grueling dues-paying, but it was also fun. I started out as a young chef and worked my way up. I learned to handle foie gras, to deal with caviar, to carve ice sculptures and butter sculptures, to butcher fish the best and fastest way.

I could have worked at the Prinz Eugen for years. I was happy there. With my increasing expertise, however, my expectations grew. The next step had to be Tantris. I went to Munich five or six times on my day off to ask the chef, Heinz Winkler, for a job. He had two hundred applications a year for ten slots. But I didn't want to work anywhere else.

Finally, in July 1986, I landed a spot in the kitchen. We weren't frying Wiener Schnitzel, as thrilling as the classic golden cutlet can be in the right hands. We steamed turbot with cabbage and Champagne sauce. Or we wrapped it in spinach and served it with *beurre rouge*. We did foie gras with apples, a terrine of salmon, and caviar with vegetables in a tomato gelée. Exceptional ingredients arrived from Rungis, the extraordinary food halls outside Paris, two or three times a week. We were cooking with the same squabs, the same langoustines as chefs in Paris.

I feel that any aspiring chef who has a chance to do so should work at Tantris. The place is magical. I still get inspiration from many of the things I learned from Mr. Winkler. For instance, I use his Tomato Water (page 45) to make one of Wallsé's signature cocktails, Tomato Pepper Martini (page 44). It also serves as the broth for Tomato Consommé with Salmon (page 75). I think of him every time I prepare Pheasant Roasted in Salt Dough à la Heinz Winkler (page 114), moist pheasant breasts wrapped in bacon and baked in a simple dough. It's amazing.

Josef Hoffmann, Cabaret Fledermaus,
view of the foyer and bar, Vienna 1907,
as reproduced in *Deutsche Kunst und Dekoration*,
Vol. 23 (1908-09), page 159.

PICKING UP A NEW YORK ACCENT

Working at Tantris was the most fantastic two years of my life. Yet I wanted another experience. Where do you go next, though? To the other side of the city? "I can't play for one team, then play for the competition," I thought. "I have to show some loyalty." Anyway, no place else was as good.

Every time I spoke to Mr. Winkler about it, he said, "You have to go to a restaurant with a future." I was lucky. Hermann Rainer, another Austrian chef who had trained with Werner Matt and was then the executive chef at Windows on the World, gave me the chance to work in New York. So in 1988, I started as a sous chef at Windows on the World's Cellar in the Sky, 107 stories above the Financial District.

Hermann gave me so much control over the menu. If I wanted turbot, he got me turbot. But I was still adding pebbles of knowledge to my pockets. At that time, my friend Walter Krajnc had a little coffee shop in the South Street Seaport called Café Fledermaus. He had been the maître d' at Vienna '79, and David Bouley a cook there, when *The New York Times* restaurant critic Mimi Sheraton awarded the nouvelle Austrian restaurant four stars. Walter suggested I talk to David at his own four-star French restaurant, Bouley, on Duane Street in Tribeca.

Instead of looking at my résumé, David took me to his walk-in refrigerator and showed me the chicken he was using. I knew instantly that this would be like cooking at Tantris again and I wanted to be part of his team.

RETURN TO GERMANY

Bouley was a great experience. I stood at David's side cooking fish. Bill Yosses, now at the White House, was the pastry chef. The blazingly talented Greg Shelton worked the meat station. But in 1990, my son, Benjamin, was on the way, and I thought it would be better for him to grow up in Europe. I went back to Munich and found a place at a small new restaurant, called Bistro Terrine, that was a little sister to Tantris. The owner, Fritz Eichbauer, had taken apart an authentic Paris bistro and reassembled it in Munich. I was the executive chef and had a lot of freedom, along with exquisite ingredients. I was able to buy from the same vendors as Tantris.

But I was not done with New York. At Bistro Terrine, I was using the light vegetable purees and scented herb oils I had discovered at Bouley. I returned every year on my vacation to see David. I even brought a few of my cooks with me. Yes, I loved Munich. I had a lot of friends. I had a good job. But New York was like an unfinished book, and I wanted to keep reading.

"NEUE CUISINE" IN NEW YORK

In 1996, after six years in Germany, I returned to New York as culinary director of David's growing enterprise. We opened Bouley Bakery, but our other projects were delayed, and I didn't want to delay my life. When I got an offer from restaurateur Peter Glazier to become the executive chef at the Monkey Bar in midtown, I took the job.

It was my first chance to make a name for myself in New York, and I began, tentatively, to find my own style, putting a Viennese spin on the menu. Ruth Reichl, then the restaurant critic at *The New York Times,* awarded the Monkey Bar two stars, but she also chided me for not fully embracing Austrian food when I could have been in the forefront of a movement.

Given the restaurant's roots in the New York of the 1930s and '40s, my Austrian accent had never been quite right at the Monkey Bar. Also, I wasn't ready to define myself by my passport. It's what I hated the most, when people brought up waltzes and schillings. But I didn't forget what Ruth had said. When I started imagining my own place, I realized Wiener Schnitzel and strudel *were* me and that that was what people wanted. It might have been old for me, but it was new for New York. And elegant. I thought, "If I can give a pretty lady a Wiener Schnitzel that is as elegant as she is, that's an accomplishment."

What really allowed me to set my own course was the support I got from my business partner, Jack Desario. It's funny the way I met Jack and his wife, Yvonne. Our boys were in the same downtown soccer league, and I was the coach. Jack said to me, "If you ever want to open a restaurant, let us know." They not only backed me financially, they've left me alone to do what I wanted. I've never been controlled, never micromanaged.

What I wanted was my own interpretation of the cooking I had grown up with—a *neue* cuisine that was half Mozart, half Lou Reed. My idea was to take Austrian flavor combinations that have been around for centuries and riff on them.

Americans think very few Austrians live in the United States. But 30 to 40 million Americans have their roots in the Austrian and Austro-Hungarian Empires, because their domains were so expansive. Americans with Swiss, German, Czech, Slovakian, Hungarian, Croatian, Slovenian, Italian, Romanian, Russian, Bohemian, and Bulgarian backgrounds can all claim Austrian heritage.

I created a menu at Wallsé that reflects these diverse culinary influences plus the contributions of many others, including French, Turkish, and Jewish, with such dishes as Beef Goulash (page 134) inspired by Hungary, Crème Fraîche Panna Cotta with Strawberries (page 172) from Italy and France, and Poached Apricot Dumplings (page 170) from the Czech Republic.

What are the main characteristics of Austrian food? Aside from the intricate pastries like Sachertorte (page 194) and Dobostorte (page 196), it is hearty, simple cooking, with lots of sausage, cabbage, and potatoes. Austria has no ocean, only lakes and rivers, so naturally cooks prepare trout, pike perch, and carp. There are woodlands for hunting wild mushrooms,

In the Wallsé kitchen, I put the finishing touch on Steak with Crispy Potato Cakes (page 129) before sending it out to the dining room. Photograph by Maike Paul.

berries, and game, and Austrians cook dishes like Braised Venison Shoulder with Red Wine and Vegetables (page 140) in the cold months. Famously, Austrians are pig farmers, and you can find classics like Pork Schnitzel with Bacon, Chanterelles, and Cream Sauce (page 125) at every country *Gasthaus*.

Once you understand the basics, you can update them, as I do. Take dill cucumbers, which are classically added to a béchamel as an accompaniment to boiled beef. To make my Halibut with Cucumber-Dill Sauce and Chanterelles (page 104), I replace the flour and cream with cucumber juice, onion puree, and dill oil and pair the sauce with steamed halibut. I still have dill cucumbers, but I use them in a different way.

The first setting for my new cooking was a corner space on West 11th Street with huge windows that flooded the rooms with light. When we opened in 2000, the West Village was a residential frontier, and there was no other place around to eat. I named the restaurant Wallsé after my hometown, but with a French spelling to make it easier to pronounce. The logo echoes the signature of the painter Egon Schiele, who inspired me with the balance he struck between invention and respect for tradition.

We hired the architect Constantin Wickensburg to help create a *Gesamtkunstwerk*, in this case a totally integrated dining experience, inspired by early twentieth-century Austrian minimalism. In 2000, how many Josef Hoffmann lamps were there in the entire city? But it had to be this light fixture. It had to be the Adolf Loos chair with its *Jugendstil* wiggle. Constantin believed that the strong masculine lines in the rooms needed a feminine touch. I said, "I can't afford this chair." He said, "You can't have a faked one."

CREATING AN AUSTRIAN EMPIRE IN AMERICA

I ordered the bentwood chairs from Gebrüder Thonet Vienna, which is how I connected with the Neue Galerie New York. The businessman, philanthropist, and art collector Ronald S. Lauder was renovating a 1914 Beaux Arts mansion on Fifth Avenue, designed by Carrère & Hastings, to house a new museum of fin-de-siècle Austrian and German art, and Renée

Price, the director, was buying the same Adolf Loos chairs for its café. The president of Thonet said to Renée, "I don't know what's going on in New York, but there was just a young man here who bought some Thonet chairs and now you are here."

Wallsé had not yet opened when I met Mr. Lauder and Renée. "We want you to create the best Viennese coffeehouse for us," they said. One year after Wallsé debuted, we opened Café Sabarsky.

Where Wallsé is intimate and elegant but not stiff—you don't have to be afraid if a fork falls to the floor—Café Sabarsky is opulent and genteel. My goal was to offer the most classic coffees and the most traditional cakes, strudels, sandwiches, and other little dishes, which together make you believe that you are sitting in a Viennese *Kaffeehaus*. Of course, the marble tabletops and banquettes upholstered with a 1912 Otto Wagner fabric helped. Again, the key notion was *Gesamtkunstwerk*, a completeness, which at Café Sabarsky resulted from a blending of the menu, spectacular setting, even the free newspapers, and the buzz of conversation in the room.

The Neue Galerie was a good fit for me. I was already focused on art, hanging first black-and-white photographs by Alexander Vethers, then works by such contemporary international artists as Julian Schnabel and Albert Oehlen, at Wallsé. The museum seemed like an extension of the same aesthetic. There was so much I had never seen before. I became totally fascinated by the self-portrait of Egon Schiele with the red eye, then by Gustav Klimt's portrait *Adele Bloch-Bauer I.*

In addition, there was a natural connection between Vienna 1900 and my *neue* cuisine. The Vienna Secession ethic flouted tradition, and I like to take liberties with the classics. Another aspect of the movement was a purity, a paring down. The architect Adolf Loos wrote that ornament is a crime, and my food is never head-scratchingly complicated. I don't have fifteen elements on the plate. Everything is straightforward. Turn-of-the-century Viennese artists also incorporated foreign influences into their work. In much the same way, although I didn't have seafood when I was growing up in Wallsee, because the ocean was far away, now I do a Lobster with Cherries, Fava Beans, and Béarnaise Sauce (page 106).

Four years later, in 2005, I had the opportunity to take over the Le Zinc space in Tribeca. The walls there were already plastered with posters—it was like living wallpaper—creating the perfect backdrop for a traditional *Wirtshaus,* an Austrian-style bistro. Called Blaue Gans (blue goose), the restaurant gave me an outlet for serving draft beers, sausages, pretzels, and other cozy fare.

Everyone should know what a wonderful piece of apple strudel tastes like, or a crunchy, light Wiener Schnitzel. To have created a home for this kind of food—and wine and culture—at Wallsé, Café Sabarsky, and Blaue Gans just makes me happy. I never would have imagined that Austrian cooking could interest so many people in New York. And even so far away, I don't feel so far away from my hometown on the Danube.

The painter Julian Schnabel is a regular at Wallsé, and his portrait of me hangs in the dining room.

Wiener Werkstätte Postcard Number 597 by Adalberta Kiessewetter, Vienna: Ringstrasse, 1912. Leonard A. Lauder Collection, Neue Galerie New York.

VIENNA 1900: CITY OF DREAMS

Janis Staggs

Associate Curator, Neue Galerie New York

Mein Herz und mein Sinn
schwärmt stets nur für Wien,
für Wien, wie es weint, wie es lacht,
da kenn ich mich aus, da bin ich halt z'haus
bei Tag und noch mehr bei der Nacht,
und keiner bleibt kalt,
ob jung oder alt,
der Wien wie es wirklich ist, kennt.
Müßt einmal ich fort
von dem schönen Ort,
da nähm' meine Sehnsucht kein End.

My heart and my mind
are so full of Vienna,
for Vienna as it weeps, as it laughs,
that's where I know my way, that's where I'm at home
at day and at night,
and no one is untouched,
be he young, be he old,
who knows Vienna as it really is.
Would I have to leave
this beautiful place,
my yearning would never end.

Rudolf Sieczyński
"Wien, du Stadt meiner Träume" (Vienna, You City of My Dreams), 1914

INTRODUCTION

Vienna 1900 occupies a significant place in our collective psyche. The era, which spans the years from the founding of the Vienna Secession in 1897 to the outbreak of World War I, has been termed a golden age. All of the arts and sciences made great strides during this brief period. The City of Dreams became a wellspring of extraordinary innovations. The achievements of the period continue to fascinate and inspire to this day.

The creative outpouring touched every aspect of life and led to the birth of a modern city. The era saw the rise of both the femme fatale and the liberated woman. Advances in the sciences, arts, music, literature, architecture, and decorative arts reshaped the way people lived and how they envisioned their place in the world.

THE VIENNA SECESSION AND ITS LEGACY

In 1897, the Vienna Secession launched a revolution in the arts. More properly known as the Vereinigung bildender Künstler Österreichs (Austrian Association of United Artists), the Secession was established under the leadership of the artist Gustav Klimt (1868–1918), who served as its first president. Klimt, along with the nineteen other founding members, had several goals. Despite being one of the largest cities in Europe in 1900, Vienna was in many ways provincial. The artists of the Secession hoped to make the Viennese art world more cosmopolitan by exhibiting avant-garde work from other countries. Their aim was to provide a forum to enable artists, collectors, and the public to study contemporary developments from abroad. The aesthetics of an installation was central; paintings were hung at eye level rather than stacked salon-style.

The first Vienna Secession exhibition was held from March to June 1898. The group initially rented space at the Society of Horticulture. Over fifty-seven thousand visitors came to see the exhibition, including the emperor of the Austro-Hungarian Empire, Franz Josef I. Of the more than five hundred objects on view, remarkably almost half sold. One of Vienna's leading critics, Hermann Bahr (1863–1934), described the show as "a résumé of modern painting . . . a marvel."

The poster for the first Secession exhibition was designed by Klimt, and it caused a scandal. It depicted a scene from Greek mythology showing Theseus slaying the Minotaur, chosen to symbolize the struggle of the new gener-

ation in revolt against the old. The initial design was censored because Theseus was nude. Klimt had to modify his poster and insert strategically placed tree trunks to ensure that no delicate sensibilities would be offended.

The artists of the Secession were rebelling against Vienna's leading exhibiting group, the Künstlerhausgenossenschaft (Austrian Artists Cooperative), a private and conservative male society established in 1861. Almost all artists

in Vienna belonged to the Künstlerhaus. Prior to the establishment of the Secession, the cooperative was the only place to exhibit artwork in Vienna. Critics of the Künstlerhaus objected to its intolerance of progressive art and the overt commercialism of its exhibitions. Klimt and his followers resigned from this group and formed a rival organization, the Vienna Secession.

The Secession soon had its own building on the Karlsplatz. The cost of construction was

financed by industrialist and art collector Karl Wittgenstein (1847–1913), father of the philosopher Ludwig Wittgenstein (1889–1951). The building, designed by architect Joseph Maria Olbrich (1867–1908), with some collaboration from painter and designer Koloman Moser (1868–1918), was completed in 1898. The façade bore the group's motto, *Der Zeit ihre Kunst, der Kunst ihre Freiheit* (To every age its art, to art its freedom), Ludwig Hevesi's quote. Reaction to the build-

ing itself was mixed. It was dubbed "the golden cabbage head" because of its golden cupola, an openwork semi-dome constructed to resemble laurel leaves and berries. Other sarcastic nicknames were "Mahdi's tomb," and "the Assyrian outhouse," and it was viewed by some as "a cross between a glasshouse and a blast-furnace."

Fortunately, reaction to the Secession's exhibitions was more favorable. The Secession played a seminal and defining role in the de-

Vienna Secession artists at the opening of the Fourteenth Vienna Secession exhibition (*Beethoven* exhibition): Seated on the "throne," Gustav Klimt: immediately in front of him wearing a hat, Koloman Moser; reclining on far right, Carl Moll. Photograph by Moritz Nähr, April 1902. Neue Galerie New York.

velopment of Modernism in Vienna in the early twentieth century. It held twenty-three major exhibitions in the first seven years. The shows included a wide range of international works that represented various styles, from the Arts and Crafts movement, and Art Nouveau (known as *Jugendstil*, or "Youth Style" in German-speaking countries), Post-Impressionism and the arts of Japan.

In September 1894, just a few years prior to the founding of the Vienna Secession, Klimt had received his most important public commission to prepare paintings for the new Vienna University that had been built on the Ringstrasse. He worked on the project for a decade, producing nearly three hundred preparatory sketches and three oil paintings—*Philosophy*, *Jurisprudence*, and *Medicine*—each became controversial. The oil paintings were to be installed on the ceiling of the Great Hall of the new University building in Vienna. His collaborator on the project was Franz Matsch (1861–1942), a fellow graduate of the Kunstgewerbeschule (School of Applied Arts). Although it may have seemed natural to pair Matsch and Klimt for the painting commission because they had worked together previously, from the outset the duo was at odds. While Matsch provided a decorative treatment for his painting *Theology* that was traditional in its allegorical allusions and ornate in style, Klimt approached his subjects in a radical fashion. Critics objected, purportedly not to the nudity, nor to Klimt's right to exercise artistic freedom, but to what they called "art that is ugly."

The first of Klimt's faculty paintings, *Philosophie* (*Philosophy*, 1900), was exhibited at the Vienna Secession in 1900. Thirty-five thousand people attended the exhibition, undoubt-

Joseph Maria Olbrich, Poster for the Second Vienna Secession exhibition, 1898, colored lithograph with bronze dust. Serge Sabarsky Collection, New York, Courtesy Neue Galerie New York.

edly attracted to the scandal associated with the commission rather than to the work itself. He fared better outside his homeland. When *Philosophy* was displayed at the Austrian Pavilion at the *Exposition Universelle* in Paris in 1900, Klimt received a gold medal (*Grand Prix*). When the remaining two paintings, *Medizin* (*Medicine*, 1901) and *Jurisprudenz* (*Jurisprudence*, 1903), were shown in Vienna in the following years, though, furor arose again. Klimt became disillusioned and decided to withdraw from the commission. In 1905, he repaid the funds he had received, and the paintings were returned to him. The paintings subsequently entered the collections of August Lederer and Koloman Moser. Unfortunately, they and other major canvases by Klimt were destroyed by fire during World War II.

After the University cause célèbre, Klimt devoted himself primarily to portraits of wealthy society women. His sitters included Adele Bloch-Bauer, Margarete Wittgenstein, and Sonja Knips, among others. He was also an avid draftsman and his studio was frequented by female models, whom he captured in endless erotic poses.

During the summer, while vacationing in the Salzkammergut lake region of Austria, Klimt painted landscapes for his own pleasure. He also enjoyed the company of Emilie Flöge, one of the founders of Schwestern Flöge (Flöge Sisters), a fashion salon in Vienna favored by the city's elite. It was outfitted by the Wiener Werkstätte, or Vienna Workshops, in 1904, one of the firm's earliest commissions. Schwestern Flöge, the Wiener Werkstätte, and Klimt had many patrons in common. Flöge and Klimt shared a lifelong friendship, exchanging postcards, going to concerts, and even taking French lessons together. During their summer vacations on the Attersee, Klimt and Flöge wore caftan-style clothing that allowed for complete freedom of movement. Although they never married, she was his muse. He gave her Wiener Werkstätte jewelry as a token of his affection, and she inherited many of his drawings and other personal items upon his death.

Klimt also played an important role in recognizing the talent of a younger generation. He helped both Oskar Kokoschka and Egon Schiele, the two leading figures of the Austrian Expressionist movement, at pivotal moments, by promoting their work through exhibitions and introducing them to important patrons.

The fourteenth Vienna Secession exhibition, mounted in the spring of 1902, was a major milestone. Josef Hoffmann was responsible for the installation design. At the heart of the show was a sculpture of Beethoven by the German artist Max Klinger (1857–1920). The exhibition provided an immersive experience that combined various art forms, including music, and was intended to demonstrate the uplifting and transformative power of art.

The Vienna Secession remained vital until 1905, when a coterie of artists centered around Klimt, left due to a dispute over how the exhibitions were hung and promoted. Some members saw a conflict of interest, and a violation of the Secession rules, when a few of the members centered around Klimt, exhibited at the Galerie Miethke, a commercial venue in Vienna. The dissenting members thought that too much emphasis was placed on decorative art and design. Klimt and his followers, known as the "Klimt group," left the Secession, and mounted two important exhibitions, one in 1908 and one in 1909, both of which had a significant impact on the arts in Vienna.

WIENER WERKSTÄTTE Nº 412

OPPOSITE Emilie Flöge and Gustav Klimt rowing on the Attersee, ca. 1910. Photograph by Richard Teschner. Neue Galerie New York.

ABOVE Wiener Werkstätte Postcard Number 412 by Gustav Kalhammer, View from the Café Heinrichhof of the Imperial and Royal Court Opera Theater, 1911. Leonard A. Lauder Collection, Neue Galerie New York.

"KUNSTSCHAU WIEN" 1908

The first "Klimt group" exhibition was held in the summer of 1908 and was entitled the *Kunstschau Wien 1908*, or Art Show Vienna 1908. It was the largest exhibition devoted to contemporary Austrian art held in Vienna to date. Temporary buildings designed by the architect Josef Hoffmann (1870–1956) were erected on the Schwarzenbergplatz. Approximately fifty-five rooms were constructed and about two hundred artists participated. A wide array of contemporary art, ranging from painting, sculpture, prints, and decorative arts to art for children, garden art, theatrical design, and even a modern cemetery was shown. The highlight of the exhibition was a gallery devoted to Klimt's work. The room included his most renowned canvases from this period, including *The Kiss* (1907–1908) and the portraits *Margaret Stonborough-Wittgenstein* (1905), *Fritza Riedler* (1906), and *Adele Bloch-Bauer I* (1907).

Oskar Kokoschka also participated in the *Kunstschau Wien*. Kokoschka was dubbed the *Oberwilding*, or "super savage," and his room became known as the "wild gallery." Most of Kokoschka's art from this exhibition has been lost. Parodies of the work suggest that critics objected to his candid portrayal of adolescent sexuality and his unorthodox use of materials. Like Egon Schiele, Kokoschka preferred young, nonprofessional models, often children. Kokoschka's illustrated book, *Die träumenden Knaben* (*The Dreaming Youths*), was included in the *Kunstschau 1908* exhibition and serves as an example of his work from the period. It was published by the Wiener Werkstätte in 1908 with a dedication to Klimt. Although described as a children's fairy-tale, both the text and its accompanying color lithographs have erotic

overtones. It includes depictions of a nude adolescent boy and girl, meant to be Kokoschka and the girl Lilith or Li, whom he had a crush on at the time, posing in dance-like postures. The book was intended as a love letter to fellow student Lilith Lang but Kokoschka soon got over his crush. The critics largely ignored the book, and it proved a financial failure for the Wiener Werkstätte.

Soon after the *Kunstschau 1908*, the architect and writer Adolf Loos (1870–1933) recognized Kokoschka's talent and convinced him to sever his ties with the Wiener Werkstätte to pursue painting. Kokoschka painted his first oil portrait in 1909, and Loos assisted the young artist in finding clients. Loos also acquired the paintings that Kokoschka's sitters did not accept. Between 1909 and 1925, he purchased twenty-nine canvases, twenty-six of which were portraits. Kokoschka's patrons clearly had a difficult time accepting his "images of the soul," favoring instead more traditional, idealized portraits. But the shift in Austrian painting at this time reflected the search by both artists and psychologists to expose the soul of the person rather than the façade typically displayed in public.

In 1909, the *Internationale Kunstschau Wien* was held. This was the second major exhibition organized by the Klimt group. For this renowned show, artists outside of Austria were also invited to contribute, including Pierre Bonnard, Lovis Corinth, Maurice Denis, Paul Gauguin, Max Klinger, Charles Rennie Mackintosh, Henri Matisse, Edvard Munch, Félix Vallotton, Vincent van Gogh, and Édouard Vuillard, among others. In addition, a new generation, including Egon Schiele, was given the opportunity to show their avant-garde work in a prominent public setting.

WIENER WERKSTÄTTE

Just as the fine arts were undergoing dramatic changes at the turn of the century, the decorative arts were experiencing a period of revival. The Wiener Werkstätte was founded in 1903 by architect Josef Hoffmann and graphic designer Koloman Moser, with the financial support of the textile industrialist Fritz Waerndorfer (1868–1939). It was one of the most important outgrowths of the Secession. The Wiener Werkstätte founders wished to elevate the role of the decorative arts. The *Gesamtkunstwerk*, translated as "total work of art," a theory that took root in architecture and decorative arts at this time, was an integral concept. The notion of the total work of art was been pioneered in the late nineteenth century by composer Richard Wagner (1813–1883), who sought to integrate music and set and costume designs. By the early twentieth century, the term *Gesamtkunstwerk* had come to refer to the integration of all art forms. The goal, utopian in nature, was that everything—from fine art and furnishings to table settings, fashion, accessories and jewelry should harmonize.

One important school for the decorative arts was Vienna's Kunstgewerbeschule (School of Applied Arts). Established in 1867 as an adjunct institution to the Österreichisches Museum für Kunst und Industrie (Austrian Museum for Art and Industry, it is known today known as the MAK-Austrian Museum of Applied Arts/Contemporary Art, Vienna). The school had a decisive impact on Vienna's contribution to the development of modern decorative arts. Director Felician von Myrbach (1853–1940) instituted a series of reforms. Emphasis was placed on the link between art and craftsmanship. Study was made of contemporary developments in the applied arts, particularly advances by the British Arts and Crafts movement. Myrbach added new faculty, including fellow members of the Secession, Hoffmann was named a professor of architecture in 1899, and Moser received his appointment as a professor of painting in 1900.

In 1901, ten graduates from the Kunstgewerbeschule banded together to form a group known as Wiener Kunst im Hause (Viennese Art in the Home). Their aim was to design objects for domestic use that could be commercially manufactured. The group's goals anticipated much of the program of the Wiener Werkstätte.

The founders of the Wiener Werkstätte may have discussed their plans for an artists' collaborative as early as 1900. In 1902, Hoffmann and Moser were engaged by Waerndorfer to assist with remodeling his villa. In March 1903, Waerndorfer corresponded with the Scottish architect and designer Charles Rennie Mackintosh, who was also involved in remodeling the villa's interiors, soliciting his advice for their plans to establish a metal workshop in Vienna. Mackintosh was supportive but replied unequivocally: "If one wishes to achieve artistic success with your program . . . then every object which you release must be most definitely marked by individuality, beauty, and the utmost accuracy of execution."

By May 1903, the Wiener Werkstätte was registered with the Vienna Trade Ministry as an artisan production cooperative, and it began modestly in a three-bedroom apartment in Vienna's fourth district. According to its roster, the firm had only six members at the beginning: Hoffmann and Moser served as

Exhibition room of the Wiener Werkstätte, Neustiftgasse 32-34, Vienna 1904, as reproduced in *Deutsche Kunst und Dekoration*, Vol. 15 (1904–1905), page 4.

directors (and the designers); Waerndorfer served as the first treasurer; and they hired three craftsmen—Karl Kallert, a silversmith, and Konrad Koch and Konrad Schindel, both metalworkers.

By late 1903, the apartment had proved too small and the company moved to larger premises in Vienna's seventh district, at Neustiftgasse 32–34, where the business expanded. In addition to the metal workshop (which had already been enlarged to include gold and jewelry), they added workshops for bookbinding, lacquerwork, and leatherwork and an area to display their products and to receive clients. They also established an architectural office. Hoffmann and Moser consciously modeled the Wiener Werkstätte after Charles Robert Ashbee's Guild of Handicraft, which had been established in Britain in 1888 to foster a collaborative working environment for artists and craftsmen. Industrialization was seen as undermining the role of the craftsman in Britain. By reintroducing a guild type of manufacturing system, the founders aimed to infuse pride in production and to create better-quality goods for the masses so that daily life would be touched and uplifted by art.

But circumstances in the Austro-Hungarian Empire, were somewhat different from those in Great Britain. Industrialization was not as widespread. The goals of the founders of the Wiener Werkstätte did not mirror those of their British counterparts. Ashbee's guild hoped to produce well-crafted items that would be affordable to the masses. While the founders of the Wiener Werkstätte did wish to create a wide array of domestic requisites, they recognized that quality and fine craftsmanship came at a price. In their *Work-ing Program* published in 1905, Hoffmann and Moser wrote, "We neither can nor will compete for the lowest prices—that is chiefly done at the worker's expense. We, on the contrary, regard it as our highest duty to return him to a position in which he can take pleasure in his labor and lead a life in keeping with human dignity."

However, the idealism that drove the firm proved difficult to maintain. Insisting on artistic perfection without concern for economic profitability meant the Wiener Werkstätte's coffers were soon depleted. In late 1906, Waerndorfer approached Moser's wife, Editha (Ditha) Mautner von Markhof (1883–1969), for a loan of 100,000 crowns. When Moser learned of the request, he objected and claimed that the firm's lack of attention to commercial considerations was unsustainable. Moser resigned from the firm in 1907 and focused his energies on painting, although he continued to provide designs to the Wiener Werkstätte until 1910.

The Wiener Werkstätte began producing textiles in 1905, focusing on hand-printed and hand-painted silks. The firm Johann Backhausen & Söhne was responsible for manufacturing the woven and machine-printed fabrics. In 1911, the firm established a fashion branch headed by architect and designer Eduard Josef Wimmer-Wisgrill (1882–1961), who was quickly dubbed "the Poiret of the Viennese," after the French fashion designer Paul Poiret. Over time, the fashion department would become one of the most profitable branches of the Wiener Werkstätte.

Architect Dagobert Peche (1887–1923) joined the Wiener Werkstätte in 1915, although he had been contributing designs to

WIENER CAFE: DER LITTERAT.

the firm since 1911. A talented designer in all media, he infused the firm with renewed artistic vigor and made the overtly decorative fashionable once again. Peche's involvement signaled a dramatic shift from the early designs of the Wiener Werkstätte, which were marked by geometric restraint and linear clarity. Peche was invited to head the new branch of the Wiener Werkstätte in Zurich in 1917, where he remained until 1919. He returned to Vienna at that time and died at age thirty-six in 1923. With his passing, Hoffmann remarked, "Peche was the greatest ornamental genius Austria has produced since the Baroque."

The Wiener Werkstätte would endure for almost a decade after Peche's death, although it struggled to remain economically viable after the war. During its nearly thirty-year existence, the firm added many new products and locations. Besides Vienna, it opened branches in the fashionable spa city of Karlsbad (now Karlovy Vary) (1909), as well as in Marienbad (1916), Zurich (1917), New York City (1922), and Berlin (1929). At its high-point, it employed nearly three hundred artists and craftsmen, who designed everything from hat-pins and corncob holders to entire place settings and suites of furniture. Despite the wide range of products, the firm never developed a broad base of clients. Rather, it was supported over the years by a small group of wealthy investors. In fact, a few of their financial benefactors saw their fortunes depleted by their attempts to keep the firm afloat. Waerndorfer lost a substantial sum, and in 1914 he was forced to leave the firm. He had to sell his collection of Klimt paintings and he moved to the United States, settling in Florida, where he started a coconut plantation. The Wiener Werkstätte found new backers, including the Primavesi family. But even their resources, drawn from banking, did not last forever, and the firm was liquidated in 1932.

VIENNESE COFFEEHOUSES

It has been reported that Hoffmann, Moser, and Waerndorfer laid plans for the Wiener Werkstätte while sitting together at the Café Heinrichshof in Vienna. Waerndorfer was evidently so enthusiastic about the idea of starting a workshop along the lines of what he had seen in England, he immediately put money on the table so the project could get under way. This story exemplifies the role of the coffeehouse in fin-de-siècle Vienna: much important business was conducted in these popular establishments.

Coffee drinking was de rigueur with the Viennese and there were coffeehouses throughout Vienna by the late nineteenth century. At the time, it was not unusual for patrons to linger in coffeehouses for hours, reading, talking, socializing, and managing business affairs. Some patrons even received their mail at their regular coffeehouse, including writer and satirist Peter Altenberg (born Richard Engländer, 1859–1919). He practically lived in Vienna's coffeehouses, sleeping in cheap hotels, where he stored his prize collection of postcards, mostly of young girls.

Individuals became patrons at their *Stammcafé*, or regular coffeehouse, based on their preferences. Some were frequented by writers, others by artists and musicians, and politicians became habitués at their cafés of choice. Newspapers and magazines, kept on long wooden poles, were available for patrons. Most coffeehouses were also equipped with billiard tables, cards, and other games, such as chess, and they were open to anyone.

The rise of café culture was sparked in part by a change in people's habits. There was an increased desire to spend more time outside the home and to be more socially active—a somewhat voyeuristic wish to see and be seen. There was an acute shortage of housing in Vienna at the time caused by a dramatic increase in the population. Thus, the coffeehouses provided much-needed outlet. But, most of all, they were places for lively discussion and good company.

One such establishment was the Café Griensteidl, a popular meeting spot for writers, including the literary group known as Jung Wien (Young Vienna). Among its habitués were such talents as Hermann Bahr (1863–1934), Arthur Schnitzler (1862–1931), Hugo von Hofmannsthal (1874–1929), Richard Beer-Hofmann (1866–1945), and Felix Salten (1869–1945).

Just as it is today, coffee could be made to suit any patron's taste preference. One popular choice was the so-called *Wiener Mélange*, which is made by blending black coffee with hot frothy milk. All coffees were accompanied by a small glass of water served as a chaser, and the beverages were often presented on a small silver tray. Coffeehouse patrons typically sat at small round marble-topped tables on upholstered banquets or bentwood chairs, which were produced by Gebrüder Thonet or by J. & J. Kohn. These bentwood chairs became ubiquitous during the mid-nineteenth century, as they were easy to assemble, elegant, and inexpensive to produce. Michael Thonet's Model No. 14 has become one of the most popular chairs throughout the world.

In 1899, Adolf Loos designed a chair for the Café Museum, another popular coffeehouse of the era. It was painted red and had a woven cane seat. This was the first time that an architect had collaborated with an industrial firm, but soon other designers, such as Hoffmann, followed suit and created objects that bore their names and were mass-produced. Most are scarce today.

Loos designed the interiors of the Café Museum, which were considered stark in comparison to the more traditional coffeehouses of the day. Due to the spartan interior treatment, it was nicknamed Café Nihilismus. Numerous prints of Gibson Girls by the American illustrator Charles Dana Gibson hung in one area. Loos had lived in America briefly and was an ardent Anglophile. He chose the Gibson Girl because she represented an American ideal. Her voluptuous figure contrasted sharply with the waifs favored by Klimt and the Secession artists, whom Loos mocked in his acerbic writings.

In addition to coffee, coffeehouses also served pastry and alcohol, but rarely an extensive offering of food. Entrées did not become regular items on the menu until after World War I. Coffeehouses are still popular in Vienna, although they do not hold the same prominence that they once did. Among the most popular today are Central, Demel, Diglas, Hawelka, Landtmann, Sacher, Sperl, and Tirolerhof.

CABARET

Nightlife in Vienna was modeled after its counterparts in Berlin, Munich, and Paris. Evening entertainment typically consisted of a variety of shows that combined musical and literary performances with dance, and

Wiener Werkstätte Postcard Numbers 74 and 75 by Josef Hoffmann Bar Room, Cabaret Fledermaus, Vienna, Kärntnerstrasse 33, 1907.
Leonard A. Lauder Collection, Neue Galerie New York.

sometimes circus or revue acts. One of the most important and ambitious cabarets to emerge in the early twentieth century was the Kabarett Fledermaus, or Cabaret Fledermaus (*Fledermaus* means "bat" in German, an appropriately nocturnal animal for a nighttime venue). Many of the company's programs incorporated images of bats, playing on its name. Opened in October 1907 at Kärntnerstrasse 33, the Cabaret Fledermaus was a true *Gesamtkunstwerk*, where every detail was carefully planned. All of the interior furnishings were designed by Josef Hoffmann of the Wiener Werkstätte. The table settings, also Hoffmann designs, included dishes for goulash and gravy and his popular "Round" flatware service of 1906. Various artists affiliated with the Wiener Werkstätte and the Vienna Secession assisted with the decoration of the interior and also helped to design the programs, sets, costumes, posters, and other items. The small cabaret was divided into two spaces, a bar area and an auditorium. The auditorium could seat approximately three hundred people. The much smaller bar area was famous both for its drinks and for a wall comprised of several thousand brightly colored majolica tiles fabricated by the Wiener Keramik firm, founded in 1906 by Bertold Löffler (1874–1960) and Michael Powolny (1871–1954). The cabaret was one of the greatest artistic spaces in Vienna in the early twentieth century.

IMPERIAL HISTORY: EMPEROR FRANZ JOSEF I

Emperor Ferdinand I of Austria (1793–1875) abdicated in 1848, and his eighteen-year-old nephew Franz Josef I (1830–1916) ascended the throne. During his sixty-eight year reign, Franz Josef I was known for his meticulous personal habits. Corruption was not tolerated under his regime. Famously hardworking, he rose at 5 a.m., spent eight to ten hours a day on government business, and retired at 11 p.m. He was admired for his punctuality and for his deep devotion to affairs of state. For lunch, the emperor preferred *Tafelspitz* (boiled beef), which had to be so tender that it could be cut with a fork. It was always accompanied with vegetables and a single glass of champagne. The no-frills emperor not only slept on an iron field bed, he was resistant to change and refused to travel by automobile or train. He did not allow electricity or modern plumbing to be installed in the imperial palace, and he distrusted telephones, typewriters, and other technological advances.

Nevertheless, he ruled over an empire that stretched from present-day Italy to Romania. Although this domain was called the Dual Monarchy of Austria-Hungary, twelve official languages were spoken across the empire. In a population census taken prior to the outbreak of World War I, citizens identified themselves as Croat, Czech, German, Hungarian, Italian, Pole, Ruthenian, Serb, Slavic, Slovak, or Slovene.

The tragic upheaval of Franz Josef's personal life is legendary. His brother Maximilian, archduke of Austria and emperor of Mexico, was executed by Mexican nationalists in 1867. In January 1889, the emperor's son, Rudolf, archduke and crown prince of Austria (1858–1889), killed his mistress, seventeen-year-old Baroness Maria Vetsera (1871–1889) at the royal hunting lodge in Mayerling and then turned the gun on himself. Franz Josef's beloved wife, Empress Elizabeth of Austria (1837–1898), was assassinated in Geneva in September 1898 by an Italian anarchist,

Luigi Luccheni. Afterward, he found some consolation in his close friendship with court actress Katharina Schrattt (1855–1940).

One of the most significant occurrences during the reign of Emperor Franz Josef I was the razing of the medieval ramparts that surrounded Vienna's inner city. This marked the beginning of modern Vienna. In 1857, plans were made for the Ringstrasse, a grand circular tree-lined boulevard, which was erected in its place. Soon both public buildings and grand private residences went up, interspersed with parks and monuments. Critics and architects attacked the buildings because of the mishmash of styles employed, from Greek, medieval, Gothic, and Renaissance to Baroque. There was no stylistic unity among the buildings and no master plan for the Ringstrasse redevelopment project.

During the same period, Vienna's first modernist architect, Otto Wagner (1841–1918), was awarded an important project, to develop the city's transit system, or Stadtbahn. Wagner reconceived the city's infrastructure—bridges, tunnels, viaducts, and railway stations—from a functional perspective. His use of contemporary *Jugendstil* (Youth Style) motifs was a secondary concern. A professor of architecture at Vienna's Akademie der bildenden Künste (Academy of Fine Arts), he outlined his ideas about how function should dictate form in his book *Moderne Architektur* (*Modern Architecture*, 1896). The concept was beautifully realized in one of his most famous commissions, the Postsparkasse (Post Office Savings Bank) 1904–1906. Wagner designed a building that was clad in thin slabs of white marble, which were bolted to the façade with thousands of aluminum rivets. By using structural elements as part of the decorative treatment, he demonstrated a new approach to function, known as *Nutzstil*—"usefulness-style." His work, employing new materials such as aluminum, was a path to Modernism that others would emulate.

While Wagner used the classroom to promote reform in architecture, his contemporary Adolf Loos, wrote essays that were published in newspapers. These expressed his views about not only architecture, but also fashion, design, theatre, and even food—typically his criticism was biting. Loos's work as an architect also attracted notoriety, particularly the Haus am Michaelerplatz (1909–1911), a building he designed for the tailors Goldman & Salatsch. Both a commercial and residential building, it was erected across from one of the entrances to the Hofburg, the imperial residence. The grain-elevator-like building sparked controversy during its construction because of its unadorned façade, which was seen as radical at the time. It was dubbed "the house without eyebrows." To mollify his critics, Loos added flower boxes. It was said that Emperor Franz Josef I refused to have the curtains open in rooms in the palace that faced this building after it was constructed, as he could not bear to look at it.

A DEVELOPMENT IN THOUGHT: PSYCHOANALYSIS

Another radical breakthrough at this time was made by Sigmund Freud, who recognized the link between the subconscious and human behavior. Although he completed one of his most important works in 1899, *Die Traumdeutung* (*The Interpretation of Dreams*), it was published with the date 1900, as this was seen as more auspicious. In his treatise, Freud argued that many desires were expressed during sleep. He concluded his text by stating that, "dreams really have a meaning . . . and we perceive a dream is the fulfillment of a wish."

Although Freud is well-known now and associated with the period, he struggled to find an audience. By contrast, Otto Weininger (1880–1903), who published *Geschlecht und Charakter* (*Sex and Character*) in 1903, found a wide readership and notoriety. His book was avidly read and admired, despite his misogynistic and anti-Semitic ideas. Weininger disliked the attention he received, and committed suicide at age twenty-three, the same year the book was published, by shooting himself in the heart in the room where Ludwig van Beethoven died.

Weininger was not alone in his impulse toward self-destruction. Other famous Viennese who committed suicide during this period were painter Richard Gerstl (1883–1908), poet Georg Trakl (1887–1914), critic Ludwig Hevesi (1843–1910), and at least two members of the Wittgenstein family, to cite a few of the better known.

The empire was crumbling. With the outbreak of World War I, the Austro-Hungarian Empire and its monarchy were waning. The war was precipitated by the assassination of heir to the throne, Archduke Franz Ferdinand (1863–1914), and his wife Sophie, Duchess of Hohenberg (1868–1914) by Gavrilo Princip, a Serbian nationalist, in Sarajevo in June 1914. On the death of Franz Josef I in 1916, his grandnephew, Karl ascended to the throne and became the last emperor of Austria, reigning for only for two years. Although Karl (1887–1922) participated in secret negotiations with the Allied powers to find a peaceful end to the war, he failed in his efforts, as he was reluctant to cede territory from the empire. When his plans were made public, his reputation was tarnished.

Much was lost in the final years of the war. With the outbreak of the so-called Spanish influenza epidemic, a number of talents were lost, including Egon Schiele. Others died in 1918 as well, including Gustav Klimt, Koloman Moser, and Otto Wagner, and the war claimed numerous lives and fortunes.

With the conclusion of World War I, the centuries-old Austro-Hungarian Empire came to an end. Austria became a democracy and lost most of its territory. Perhaps the City of Dreams had long been more an illusion than a reality. The art, however, remained. The Secession building survived, although it later had to be rebuilt after suffering severe damage during World War II. It remains an important exhibition space in Vienna to this day. Other cultural institutions preserve the legacy of Vienna 1900, such as the Albertina; the Belvedere; the Leopold Museum; the MAK—Austrian Museum of Applied Arts/Contemporary Art, Vienna, and the Wien Museum. In the United States, the Neue Galerie New York is dedicated to the art of Austria and Germany from this period. It features two cafés that serve Austrian cuisine in an environment that authentically re-creates a Viennese coffeehouse.

Today there is much to be enjoyed from this vibrant period of unprecedented splendor. There is great food and wine to be savored and magnificent art to appreciate and contemplate. The yearning to recapture the spirit of Vienna 1900 continues to fuel our imagination.

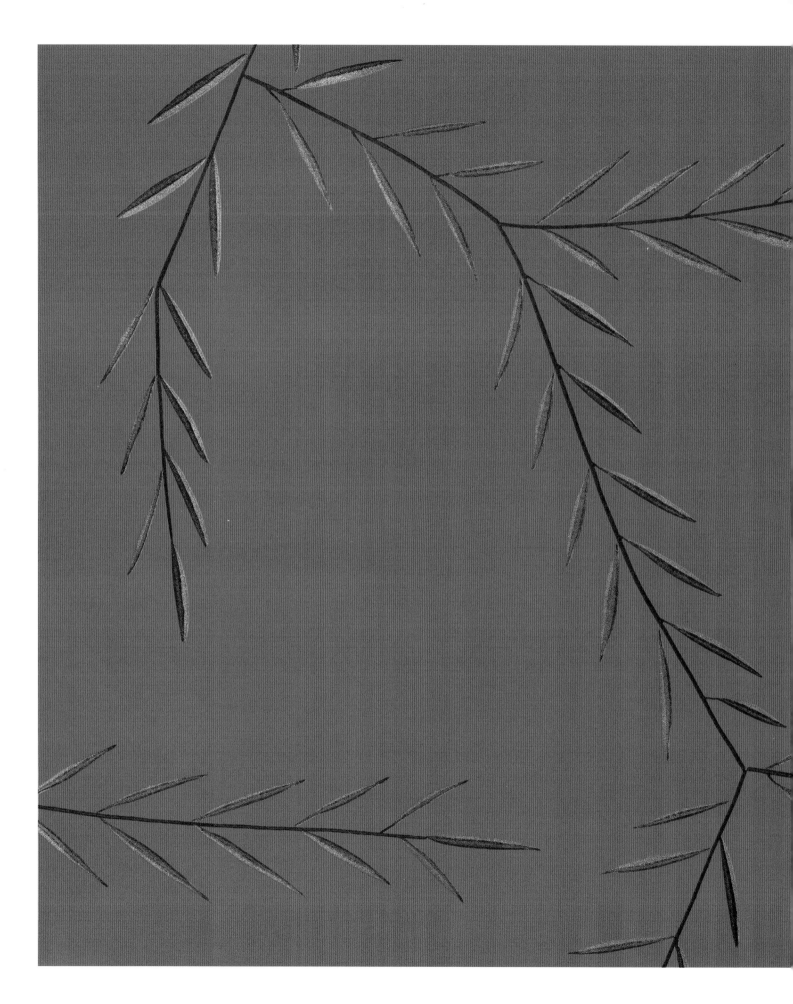

COCKTAILS

AND

STARTERS

THE VIENNA 1900

Wien 1900

1 SERVING

Ice cubes

1 tablespoon fresh lemon juice

Tonic water

1 tarragon sprig

1 lemon slice

Tea-infused gin

1 cup loose Viennese Earl Grey tea (see Tips)

1 quart gin

Simple syrup

1 cup sugar

1 cup water

I love the Viennese Earl Grey we get from our tea purveyor, Harney & Sons. It's a black tea similar to the regular Earl Grey—it has the same bergamot taste—but Darjeeling is added to the base blend. We serve it as a simple tea at Café Sabarsky and, at Wallsé, we use it to flavor sorbets and desserts. In this cocktail, it infuses gin for a delicious highball.

1 Make the tea-infused gin: In a quart container, combine the tea and gin. Let stand overnight to infuse, then strain through a fine sieve.

2 Make the simple syrup: In a small saucepan, combine the sugar and water, bring to a simmer, and cook, stirring, until the sugar dissolves. Let the syrup cool slightly, then refrigerate.

3 Fill a cocktail shaker with ice. Add ¼ cup of the tea-infused gin, the lemon juice, and a splash of the simple syrup and shake well. Fill a highball glass with ice. Strain the drink into the glass and top off with tonic water. Garnish with the tarragon sprig and lemon slice, and serve.

Tips

Viennese Earl Grey is available at harney.com, but you can substitute another variety of Earl Grey tea.

The leftover simple syrup can be used to sweeten other drinks, like iced tea and lemonade, without the graininess of granulated sugar.

Variation

You can make a Viennese gin and tonic by mixing tea-infused gin with tonic water and garnishing the drink with an orange twist.

Make ahead

The gin needs to infuse overnight, and the simple syrup must cool completely before it's used, so plan accordingly. The leftover syrup can be refrigerated for up to 1 month. The gin keeps indefinitely.

My signature drinks, left to right: Tomato Pepper Martini (page 44), Pomegranate Fizz (page 42), and The Vienna 1900 (above), are presented on a shiny 1904 tray by Josef Hoffmann, matching the mirror in two large mixed media paintings (detail) by Albert Oehlen. The radically modern tray was designed for the Waerndorfer family, co-founders of the Wiener Werkstätte.

THE CARLOTTA COCKTAIL

"Carlotta" Cocktail

1 SERVING

1 tablespoon raw light brown sugar,
    such as turbinado
1/4 teaspoon crushed red pepper flakes
1 lime wedge
    Ice cubes
1/2 ounce (1 tablespoon) St-Germain liqueur
2 ounces (1/4 cup) tequila
2 tablespoons fresh grapefruit juice
1 tablespoon fresh lime juice

Tequila isn't something that comes to mind when you think of Austria, but this drink is named for Charlotte of Belgium, who married Maximilian of Austria and became Carlotta of Mexico when the couple reigned briefly as emperor and empress of Mexico in the 1860s. The cocktail gets nuanced elderflower sweetness from St-Germain liqueur, which marries well with the drink's citrus and spice. It's an intriguing alternative to a margarita.

1 On a small plate, mix the sugar with the pepper. Rub the lime wedge around the rim of a chilled rocks glass and dip the rim in the sugar mix to coat lightly. Reserve the lime wedge.

2 Fill a cocktail shaker with ice. Add the St-Germain, tequila, and grapefruit and lime juices and shake well. Fill the rimmed glass with ice. Strain the drink into the glass. Garnish with the lime wedge, and serve.

POMEGRANATE FIZZ

Granatapfel "Fizz"

1 SERVING

    Ice cubes
2 tablespoons pomegranate juice
1 ounce (2 tablespoons) gin
1 tablespoon fresh lemon juice
    Splash of elderflower syrup (see Tips,
        opposite page)
1 ounce (2 tablespoons) Sekt or other
    sparkling wine

An Austrian take on the classic gin fizz, this colorful cocktail is prepared with pomegranate juice and a splash of elderflower syrup, which makes the drink both sweeter and tarter than the original.

1 Fill a cocktail shaker with ice. Add the pomegranate juice, gin, lemon juice, and elderflower syrup, shake well, and strain into a tall Champagne flute. Top off with Sekt, and serve.

CUCUMBER DELIGHT

Gurken-Birnen Cocktail mit Sekt

1 SERVING

2 slices peeled cucumber

1 ½ ounces (3 tablespoons) pear vodka
   (see Tips)

1 tablespoon fresh lemon juice
   Splash of elderflower syrup (see Tips)

1 ounce (2 tablespoons) Sekt
   or other sparkling wine
   Strip of cucumber peel

This spritzy cocktail is similar to the classic French 75, but muddled cucumbers and pear vodka stand in for the standard gin or Cognac base. Finished with Sekt, Austrian sparkling wine, the result is a delectable drink to serve year-round.

1 In a cocktail shaker, muddle the cucumber slices. Add the vodka, lemon juice, and elderflower syrup and shake well. Strain into a chilled martini glass and top off with the Sekt. Garnish with the cucumber peel, and serve.

Tips

I like Grey Goose's La Poire vodka, but other brands, such as Absolut and Smirnoff, also offer pear vodka. Elderflower syrup is a floral-scented sweetener made from extract of elderflower blossoms. In northern Europe, it's often diluted with water to make refreshing drinks or added to cocktails, such as this one, for a fragrant touch.

APEROL SOUR

Aperol Süss "Sour"

1 SERVING

Ice cubes

2 ounces (¼ cup) Aperol

2 tablespoons fresh lemon juice

1 tablespoon confectioners' sugar

1 thin lemon slice

1 small tarragon sprig (optional)

Similar to Campari, Aperol is a bright orange Italian liqueur. It's incredibly refreshing in a spritzer, simply poured over ice and topped with fizzy club soda. (Try a one-to-four ratio.) My cocktail pairs the bittersweet orange flavor with tart lemon juice and confectioners' sugar—perfect as a cocktail on a summer afternoon or as an aperitif before dinner.

1 Fill a rocks glass with ice. In a cocktail shaker, combine the Aperol with the lemon juice and sugar. Shake well and strain into the glass. Garnish with the lemon slice and tarragon sprig, if using, and serve.

Tip

The result won't be exactly the same, but Campari can be substituted for the Aperol.

TOMATO PEPPER MARTINI

Paradeiser-Pfeffer Martini

1 SERVING

Gegenbauer tomato vinegar
(optional; see Tips)
Ice cubes
2 tablespoons Tomato Water (recipe follows)
½ teaspoon celery salt
2 dashes of Tabasco
1 ounce (2 tablespoons) pepper-flavored
vodka
1 ounce (2 tablespoons) plain vodka
1 cherry tomato

This is one of Wallsé's most beloved cocktails. People often look at the name and think it's some kind of Bloody Mary hybrid. It's not. Pepper vodka is mixed with a dash of Tabasco and homemade Tomato Water, then strained into a chilled glass. The result is a fantastic, icy martini with a delicate tomato flavor and a touch of spice.

1 Using a spray bottle, spritz a chilled martini glass with the vinegar, if using.
2 Fill a cocktail shaker with ice. Add the Tomato Water, celery salt, Tabasco, and both vodkas and shake well. Strain the cocktail into the glass. Garnish with the cherry tomato, and serve.

Tips
Gegenbauer is an Austrian producer of high-quality unusual vinegars like asparagus, apricot, cucumber, and tomato. Their tomato vinegar is available at some specialty markets and at gegenbauer.at/englisch/start.aspx.

Spray bottles are available at hardware stores and drugstores.

Variation
You can leave out the hot sauce for a less spicy martini.

TOMATO WATER

Paradeiserwasser

MAKES 2 CUPS

5 pounds very ripe tomatoes, chopped
(see Tips)

1 teaspoon salt

¼ teaspoon cayenne pepper

1 teaspoon sugar

½ ounce (1 tablespoon) gin

1 tablespoon white wine vinegar
Dash of fresh lemon juice

Making Tomato Water is a great way to distill the essence of tomatoes into a limpid liquid. It can be used in a variety of dishes, sauces, and drinks, but I especially love it in the Tomato Pepper Martini (opposite). The cocktail is light but fragrant with tomato flavor.

1 In a blender, combine the tomatoes with the salt, cayenne, sugar, gin, vinegar, and lemon juice and puree until smooth.
2 Line a colander with a large piece of cheesecloth and set the colander over a large bowl. Pour the tomato puree into the colander. Using kitchen string, tie the cheesecloth into a loose bundle. Transfer to the refrigerator and let the tomato water drip into the bowl overnight.
3 Pour the Tomato Water into a bowl and reserve the puree, if desired.

Tips
Juicy, ripe tomatoes are essential, or you won't get enough liquid out of them. The beefsteak variety works really well.
Pressing the tomato puree through the cheesecloth would be quicker, but the water would be murky. To get a clear liquid, let it drip slowly.
The tomato puree in the cheesecloth doesn't have to be discarded; save it to make tomato sauce.

Variations
We also serve Tomato Water as a warm consommé; see Tomato Consommé with Salmon (page 75). If you omit the gin and sugar, you can use it as a *nage* (broth) for poached white fish fillets like striped bass.

Make ahead
The Tomato Water can be refrigerated for up to 2 weeks.

OPPOSITE Ernst Ludwig Kirchner, *Gentleman with Lapdog at the Café*, 1911, colored woodcut. Serge Sabarsky Collection, Courtesy Neue Galerie New York.

RIGHT Wiener Werkstätte Postcard Number 288 by Egon Schiele, Portrait of a Woman, 1910. Leonard A. Lauder Collection, Neue Galerie New York.

GLASSWARE

The Wiener Werkstätte never manufactured glass, but its members worked with a number of glass-producing firms. They designed both unique objets d'art and pieces for daily use. Most glass-producing firms within the Austro-Hungarian Empire were located in Bohemia, today part of the Czech Republic. It was one of the world's most important glass-producing regions, with nearly two hundred manufacturers by the late nineteenth century. Among the most important was Johann Lötz Witwe, based in Klostermühle (now Klášterský Mlýn), renowned for its iridescent glass.

On occasion, Wiener Werkstätte artists such as Josef Hoffmann and Otto Prutscher were commissioned to create designs for Lötz products. Typically they produced designs for one of the major distributors of the time, E. Bakalowitz & Söhne; the objects were manufactured by Lötz. The collaboration of significant artists and designers of the era with one of the major firms of the empire was intended to add cachet and enhance the market for these products.

Another key producer of the era was Johann Oertel, located in Haida. Oertel often collaborated with the Wiener Werkstätte, with Oertel providing the glass forms and artists of the Wiener Werkstätte painting the enamel decoration. During the war, many of the artists were women.

The Wiener Werkstätte sold lattice-style wine and Champagne glasses produced by Meyr's Neffe in Adolf near Winterberg after designs by Otto Prutscher. These glasses, from around 1907, represented a dramatic shift away from the curvilinear forms associated with the *Jugendstil* or "Youth Style," which had been popular around the turn of the century. They were available in various colors and were not intended for use at the table but for *après le dîner*. They were exhibited at the *1908 Kunstschau Wien* (1908 Art Show Vienna).

In 1920, Josef Hoffmann created what is arguably his most famous service for J. & L. Lobmeyr, the *Patrician* stemware set. Made from muslin glass, the glasses are almost as thin as a sheet of paper yet remarkably strong. Fellow architect and rival Adolf Loos also designed a series of drinking glasses for Lobmeyr in 1931. Loos reduced the glass to its essential form. Ideal proportions and superb execution provided a sense of luxury. The only decoration, a type of crosshatching at the base, is known as *Steindelschnitt*, diamond diaper cutting. It requires the skills of a master craftsman to execute it with precision. The thick base ensures a stable grip with the surface that it rests upon and the diamond facets reflect light and color like a prism, offering an unexpected nuance in this pristine form.

Josef Hoffmann's *Patrician* Service, designed 1917, produced by J. & L. Lobmeyr, blown, hand-polished, muslin crystal. Neue Galerie Design Shop.

SABARSKY SANDWICHES

Served at Cafe Sabarsky and at our cocktail receptions, these open-face sandwiches (*Brötchen*) were inspired by those at the famous Trzesniewski in Vienna. Started by Polish immigrants in 1902, this tiny spot is one of my all-time favorite places to get a snack when I'm in town. The twenty-two different varieties of sandwiches with spreads are displayed in neatly aligned rows, which makes perusing a delight. Patrons usually pick one or two sandwiches to eat with a small glass of beer, and stand, not sit, at the bar.

For parties, I cut the sandwiches into bite-size squares and serve them as canapés. With a glass of Champagne, they make elegant hors d'oeuvres. Surprisingly for something so refined, they're easy to prepare. You lightly slather an egg or other spread on thin, crustless slices of bread—I like dark wheat bread (*dunkles Hausbrot*)—and then add a topping, which can be as simple as sliced cornichons, sliced hard-boiled eggs, or sliced cured meat or fish. Here are the fundamentals for assembling your own sandwiches.

To make Basic Egg Spread: In a food processor, puree 5 hard-boiled eggs with 2 tablespoons of mayonnaise, 2 tablespoons of Dijon mustard, 6 cornichons, and 1 tablespoon of drained capers (optional). (Makes 1 cup.)

For Spicy Egg Spread: In a food processor, puree 5 hard-boiled eggs with 3 tablespoons of mayonnaise, 2 tablespoons of Dijon mustard, 8 cornichons, 1 ½ teaspoons of Hungarian sweet paprika, ½ teaspoon of cayenne pepper, and 1 tablespoon of drained capers (optional). (Makes about 1 cup.)

For Salami Spread: In a food processor, puree 5 ounces of salami, preferably spicy, with 5 hard-boiled eggs, 2 tablespoons of mayonnaise, 2 tablespoons of Dijon mustard, and 5 cornichons. (Makes about 1 cup.)

Feel free to get creative with the toppings. I also like olive tapenade; smoked salmon with cream cheese and thin cucumber wedges; sliced ham with pickle and horseradish; Matjes herring with sliced hard-boiled eggs and apples; smoked trout with pears; and salami with cornichons and capers. Garnish the sandwiches with tiny herb sprigs, sprouts, or edible flowers, if you like.

For a cocktail party, I dressed up a table with a hand-loomed table runner inspired by the Wiener Werkstätte. Sabarsky sandwiches are lined up on Josef Hoffmann's 1904 silver-plated tray. His facet-cut crystal dishes are elegant holders of Liptauer spreads (page 52), and the 1912 *Series B* decanter with black bronzite décor, also by Hoffmann, pairs beautifully with *Patrician* wine glasses. All of these items are from the Neue Galerie Design Shop. A detail of two large mixed-media paintings by Albert Oehlen provides a contemporary foil.

BAVARIAN-STYLE PRETZELS

Laugenbrezen

MAKES 5 PRETZELS

4 teaspoons table salt

3 ½ teaspoons sugar

3 ⅔ cups all-purpose flour

1 ½ cups bread flour

1 tablespoon instant yeast (see Tips)

2 ⅓ cups warm water

3 tablespoons olive oil

1 tablespoon baking soda

Pretzel salt (see Tips) or kosher salt

In the fall months at Blaue Gans, I join in the German celebration of Oktoberfest by serving these big pretzels. Made from a simple yeast dough, they are soft inside from being poached in water, and then they're baked to develop a crust. With just the right amount of crunchy salt, they make a terrific companion to a bratwurst fresh off the grill and a frothy stein of beer.

1 In the bowl of a stand mixer, combine the table salt, sugar, and both flours. Sprinkle the yeast on top.

2 In a separate bowl, combine the water and olive oil. Add the liquid ingredients to the dry and mix at low speed until fully incorporated, about 4 minutes. Increase the speed to medium and mix until the dough forms a ball, about 2 minutes.

3 Transfer the dough to a baking sheet and press into an 8 ½-by-11-inch rectangle. Loosely cover with plastic wrap and let rise in a warm place for 1 hour. Gently press down the dough, and refrigerate overnight.

4 Remove the dough from the refrigerator. Line a large baking sheet with parchment paper. Cut the dough rectangle lengthwise into 5 equal strips, 1 ½ inches wide. Lightly flour a work surface (a large kitchen table is best for this).

5 Transfer 1 strip of the dough to the work surface. Using your fingers, roll and stretch the dough into a rope 1 yard long. Pick up the ends of the rope and make a U shape. Holding the ends of the rope, cross them over each other and press onto the bottom of the U to make a pretzel shape. Transfer to the prepared baking sheet. Repeat with the remaining strips of dough. When all the pretzels are shaped, cover them loosely with plastic wrap and let rise in a warm place until the dough springs back when touched, about 30 minutes.

6 Meanwhile, heat the oven to 325 degrees. Line another baking sheet with parchment paper.

7 Bring a large pot of water to a simmer and add the baking soda. Working in batches, add the pretzels to the water, without crowding, and cook, turning once, until they float and expand slightly, about 30 seconds on each side. Using a large slotted spoon or a skimmer, carefully transfer the pretzels to the prepared baking sheet.

8 Sprinkle the pretzels with pretzel salt. Bake the pretzels until they are golden brown, about 25 minutes. Remove from the oven and let cool slightly on the baking sheet.

9 Serve warm or at room temperature.

Tips

I like the SAF brand of instant yeast, available at many specialty supermarkets.

I let the pretzel dough rise in a warm spot (90 to 95 degrees; try next to the stove or oven), which speeds up the proofing. In a cooler spot, the dough will likely take an additional 30 minutes to rise fully.

Pretzel salt is a highly compressed form of salt, and the crystals are often much whiter than table salt. It is available at specialty supermarkets and online gourmet food retailers, such as americanspice.com.

The baking soda added to the pretzel cooking water gives the pretzels a slight tang and helps them develop a crust during baking.

Serve with

All you need to accompany a pretzel is a good dollop of mustard, but for a quick meal, I enjoy eating them with a bratwurst or a bowl of Goulash Soup (page 84).

Make ahead

The pretzel dough is refrigerated overnight before shaping, poaching, and baking, so plan accordingly.

The pretzels are best served the day they are baked, but they will keep, covered with plastic wrap, for up to 1 day. If the pretzels seem a little tough, reheat in a 350-degree oven for 5 minutes to soften.

Wiener Werkstätte Postcard Number 490 by Gustav Kalhammer, Hütteldorf Brewery, A. Brussati, 1911.
Leonard A. Lauder Collection, Neue Galerie New York.

PAPRIKA AND HERB CHEESE SPREAD

Liptauer

The time after lunch and before dinner is known as *Jause* in Austria (and *Brotzeit*—bread time—in Germany). If you're hungry for a late-afternoon snack, you're likely to have a *Zwischenmahlzeit*. This meal between meals usually consists of an assortment of small cakes or crackers, a cup of coffee, sliced breads, and savory spreads like Liptauer. This rich, piquant blend of quark cheese, spices, and herbs is also served at parties and wine tastings, accompanied by sliced dark rye bread and chilled rosé or crisp Grüner Veltliner.

MAKES ABOUT 2 CUPS

1 cup quark cheese (see Tip)

8 tablespoons (1 stick) unsalted butter, softened

2 tablespoons sour cream

1 tablespoon Hungarian sweet paprika

1 tablespoon finely chopped onion

2 teaspoons caraway seeds

1 teaspoon dry mustard

1 teaspoon chopped capers

1 teaspoon kosher salt
  Freshly ground pepper

3 tablespoons finely snipped chives

1 baguette, thinly sliced and toasted

1 Using the back of a spoon, press the cheese through a fine sieve into a small bowl.

2 In a medium bowl, beat the butter until smooth. Add the cheese, sour cream, paprika, onion, caraway seeds, mustard, capers, salt, and a generous grinding of pepper and beat until smooth.

3 Line a small bowl with plastic wrap. Scrape in the cheese mixture. Cover and refrigerate until firm, at least 3 hours.

4 Unmold the cheese mixture onto a platter and remove the plastic. Sprinkle with the chives, and serve with the toasts.

Tip
Quark is a soft, tangy cheese with a consistency similar to that of Greek-style yogurt. Quark can be found at specialty food shops.

Serve with
A crusty loaf, pumpernickel bread, or crackers are often passed alongside this party staple. Bavarian-Style Pretzels (the large, puffy kind; page 50) are also an excellent and typical accompaniment, as are Semmel rolls—the white bread rolls with a crispy crust and chewy crumb that are ubiquitous in Austrian bakeries.

Variations
Instead of unmolding the Liptauer, you can omit the plastic wrap and serve the spread in the bowl.

To make a Liptauer dip, add an extra $\frac{1}{2}$ cup of sour cream in Step 2. This doesn't need to firm up in the refrigerator, but it is nice lightly chilled. Sprinkle with the chives, and serve with crudités.

Make ahead
Liptauer can be refrigerated for up to 5 days.

ARTICHOKES BRAISED IN WHITE WINE AND OLIVE OIL

Artischocken in Weisswein und Olivenöl

This is a classic French preparation with distinctly Mediterranean flavors (olive oil, thyme, rosemary, basil). I love the way it can easily be made vegetarian—simply omit the pancetta or bacon. With no butter and no cream, it's really quite healthy.

4 SERVINGS

2 lemons, halved

12 medium artichokes

1 cup olive oil

¼ pound thick-sliced pancetta or bacon, cut crosswise into ¼-inch-thick strips (optional)

2 onions, thinly sliced

1 large leek, white and light green parts only, cut into ¼-inch dice

  Salt and freshly ground pepper

2 carrots, peeled and thinly sliced

4 thyme or rosemary sprigs

1 cup dry white wine

8 basil leaves, coarsely chopped

1 Fill a large bowl with cold water and squeeze in the juice of 1 ½ lemons; add the lemon shells to the bowl. Working with 1 artichoke at a time, snap off the stem and all the dark green outer leaves. Using a sharp knife, slice off the remaining leaves even with the top of the base. Peel and trim the base. Using a spoon, scrape out the choke. Rub all over with the remaining lemon half and drop the artichoke into the lemon water.

2 In a large saucepan, heat 1 tablespoon of the olive oil until shimmering. Add the pancetta and cook over medium-low heat until just beginning to brown. Add the onions and cook, stirring occasionally, until slightly softened, about 3 minutes. Add the leek, season with salt and pepper, and cook until slightly softened, 3 to 4 minutes. Add the carrots and thyme and cook until softened, about 4 minutes.

3 Drain the artichokes and add them to the saucepan. Season with salt and pepper and add the wine and remaining olive oil. Bring to a boil, cover, and simmer over medium heat until the artichokes are tender, about 20 minutes.

4 Remove the pan from the heat and add the basil. Transfer the artichokes to warmed soup plates, ladle some of the broth and vegetables over them, and serve.

Tip

Rubbing the cut artichokes with lemon and adding them to a bowl of lemon water before cooking keeps them from turning brown.

Serve with

Serve before a nice fillet of fish, such as halibut or monkfish, or pan-seared scallops. This dish also makes a light lunch on its own with a piece of crusty baguette.

Variation

You can easily change the recipe according to the season and, instead of artichokes, add whatever is fresh, such as green beans or asparagus.

Make ahead

The artichokes can be refrigerated in the broth for up to 3 days.

WHITE ASPARAGUS WITH FRESH MORELS AND PEAS

Weisser Spargel mit Morcheln und Erbsen

4 SERVINGS

5 tablespoons unsalted butter
Salt
1 tablespoon sugar
1 ½ pounds white asparagus (24 spears), peeled, 1 inch of bottom ends reserved (see All About White Asparagus, page 77)
2 cups shelled peas (about 12 ounces)
½ pound fresh morels (see Tips)
3 tablespoons dry sherry
Freshly ground pepper
2 shallots, finely chopped
1 cup heavy cream
Chervil leaves, for garnishing (optional)

This appetizer highlights some of spring's best flavors. Because you can get really fresh white asparagus, morels, and peas for only a brief period, I'm especially devoted to this dish. The asparagus makes a delicate foil for the rich morel and sherry sauce, and bright green peas add great color to the plate.

1 Bring a large pot of water to a boil. Add 3 tablespoons of the butter, 1 ½ tablespoons of salt, and the sugar, then add the asparagus and cook until tender, about 8 minutes. Using tongs, transfer the asparagus to a kitchen towel and pat dry. Reserve 2 cups of the asparagus broth for the sauce.

2 Bring a medium pot of water to a boil. Fill a medium bowl with ice water. Add the peas to the boiling water and cook until just tender but still bright green, 30 seconds to 1 minute. Drain the peas and add to the ice water to cool as quickly as possible, 1 to 2 minutes. Drain again and pat dry.

3 In a medium bowl of water, swish the morels, draining them and adding fresh water as necessary until the water remains clear. Lift out, leaving any grit behind, and pat dry with paper towels.

4 In a medium sauté pan, melt 1 tablespoon of the butter over medium-high heat. Add the morels and cook, stirring frequently, until the water they release has evaporated, about 3 minutes. Add the sherry and peas, season with salt and pepper, and cook for 2 minutes. Remove from the heat and keep warm.

5 In another medium sauté pan, melt the remaining 1 tablespoon of butter over medium-high heat. Add the shallots and reserved asparagus ends and cook, stirring frequently, for 3 minutes. Season with salt and pepper and add the reserved asparagus broth and the cream. Bring to a boil, then reduce the heat and simmer for 20 minutes. Pour the sauce into a blender and puree until very smooth. Strain through a fine sieve into a bowl.

6 Mound the asparagus on plates and top with the morels and peas. Spoon the asparagus sauce on top, garnish with chervil leaves, if desired, and serve.

Tips

Morels, fresh or dried, are notoriously sandy. Generally, the rule is to wash them in two or three changes of water, although it may be more or less depending on the size and quality of the mushrooms. The determining factor is the water after they are washed: it should be clear. Dried morels can be used in this recipe, but they must be soaked first. In a large heatproof bowl, soak 5 ounces of dried morels in boiling water to cover until softened, about 20 minutes. Lift the morels out of the soaking water and proceed. Reserve the soaking liquid for a soup, sauce, or stew; it's delicious.

Serve with

I like to serve this as a starter and follow it with a hearty, seasonal entrée such as Roasted Leg of Lamb (page 133). It also makes a terrific vegetarian lunch.

Variation

You can swap green asparagus for the white. See Variations for White Asparagus with Home-Smoked Salmon, Sour Cream, and Chives (page 56) for cooking directions, and skip to Step 2.

WHITE ASPARAGUS WITH HOME-SMOKED SALMON, SOUR CREAM, AND CHIVES

Weisser Spargel mit geräuchertem Lachs, Sauerrahm und Schnittlauch

4 SERVINGS

4 tablespoons unsalted butter
   Salt
1 tablespoon sugar
1 pound white asparagus (16 spears),
      peeled and trimmed (see All About
      White Asparagus, page 77)
1/3 cup sour cream
1/3 cup crème fraîche
1/4 cup fresh lemon juice
2 tablespoons finely snipped chives,
      plus more for garnishing
1 tablespoon vodka
   Freshly ground pepper
One 1-pound skinless salmon fillet,
      cut crosswise into 4 equal pieces
2 tablespoons olive oil
1/2 cup hardwood chips

Smoking your own salmon is remarkably easy to do at home using wood chips and a large wok with a rack and lid or a stovetop steamer. Just remember to turn on the exhaust fan! The smoky salmon fillets have a natural affinity for white asparagus and this tangy chive cream. It's a sophisticated appetizer.

1 Bring a large pot of water to a boil. Add the butter, 1 1/2 tablespoons of salt, and the sugar, then add the asparagus and cook until tender, about 8 minutes. Using tongs, transfer the asparagus to a kitchen towel and pat dry.

2 In a small bowl, combine the sour cream with the crème fraîche, lemon juice, chives, and vodka. Season with salt and pepper. Cover with plastic wrap and refrigerate.

3 Using a pastry brush, generously coat the salmon pieces on both sides with the olive oil. Season all over with salt and pepper.

4 Line a large wok with foil. Lightly oil the wok rack and place it in the wok. Set the wok over high heat for 3 to 5 minutes. Add the wood chips, cover, and heat the chips, tossing them frequently, until they are slightly burned on the edges and smoke starts billowing out, 8 to 10 minutes.

5 Set the salmon on the wok rack, quickly cover with the lid, and remove the wok from the heat. Smoke the salmon, uncovering the wok every few minutes to release some of the smoke, until the fish is smoked but moist and still pink on the inside, about 10 minutes. Transfer the salmon to a platter and let cool slightly.

6 Arrange 4 of the asparagus spears on each warmed plate. Top with a piece of salmon and dollop some of the chive cream on top. Garnish with the chives, and serve.

Tips

If your wok doesn't have a lid, cover it tightly with a sheet of heavy-duty foil instead.

While smoking the fish, turn the pieces occasionally so they cook more quickly and evenly. Just be careful not to let too much of the smoke escape when you lift the wok lid.

If the smoke is not strong enough or the fish is not cooking in the residual heat, set the wok back over low heat to finish smoking.

Serve with

The dish makes a light lunch alongside a fresh, green salad such as the Boston Lettuce Salad with Spicy Radishes, Pumpkin Seed Oil, and Lemon Vinaigrette (page 88) and a glass of Grüner Veltliner.

Variations

You can substitute trout or sturgeon fillets for the salmon. Green asparagus can replace the white. Bring a large saucepan of salted water to a boil. Add the asparagus and cook until just tender, 4 to 5 minutes. Drain and transfer to a bowl of ice water to cool down as quickly as possible, 1 to 2 minutes. Drain again and pat dry. Proceed with Step 2.

Make ahead

The chive cream can be refrigerated for up to 2 days. The salmon can be smoked early in the day and reheated in a toaster oven at 300 degrees just before serving.

FRESH MORELS WITH SHERRY AND SEMOLINA DUMPLINGS

Morcheln in Sherrysauce mit Griessnockerln

This is a really beautiful starter I like to serve as part of a decadent meal. The sherry adds sweetness to the creamy sauce and complements the earthy morels. And the dumplings soak up the fusion of flavors.

4 SERVINGS

1   pound fresh morels (see Tips, page 54)

6   tablespoons unsalted butter

3   shallots, minced

1   garlic clove, minced

½   cup dry sherry

2   cups heavy cream

1   cup water

1   large egg

One   2.8-ounce package farina dumpling mix (see Tips)

Salt and freshly ground pepper

Finely chopped chives, for sprinkling (optional)

1 Cut off the morel stems and reserve. Cut the caps lengthwise in half. Swish the morel stems and caps separately in a large bowl of water, draining them and adding fresh water as necessary until the water remains clear. Lift out, leaving any grit behind, and pat dry with paper towels.

2 In a medium saucepan, melt 3 tablespoons of the butter. Add two-thirds of the shallots, the garlic, and mushroom stems and cook over high heat, stirring frequently, until the water the mushroom stems release has evaporated, about 10 minutes. Add ¼ cup of the sherry and simmer, scraping up any browned bits stuck to the bottom, for 1 to 2 minutes. Add the cream and water and bring to a boil, then simmer over medium-low heat until reduced by half, 10 to 15 minutes. Remove the pan from the heat and, using an immersion blender or a regular blender, puree the sauce until smooth.

3 Bring a large pot of water to a boil.

4 Meanwhile, in a small saucepan, melt 1 tablespoon of the butter; remove from the heat and let cool slightly. Whisk in the egg until smooth. Add the dumpling mix and ⅛ teaspoon of salt and whisk well; let rest for 5 minutes.

5 Using 2 wet soupspoons, form the dough into 8 egg-shaped dumplings and add them to the boiling water. Cook the dumplings until they have set and floated to the top, about 10 minutes. Remove the pot from the heat and leave the dumplings in the water for 10 minutes; drain.

6 Meanwhile, in a large sauté pan, melt the remaining 2 tablespoons of butter over medium-high heat. Add the morel caps and remaining shallot, season with salt, and cook for 2 to 3 minutes. Add the remaining ¼ cup of sherry and the mushroom sauce and cook, stirring frequently, until the morels are tender, about 5 minutes. Season with salt and pepper.

7 Transfer the dumplings to warmed plates. Spoon the morels and sauce around them. Sprinkle with the chives, if desired, and serve.

Tips

In Step 4, letting the butter cool slightly prevents the egg from curdling.

Farina dumpling mix is available at specialty markets.

Serve with

I like to serve this dish before something with similar earthy undertones such as Blood Sausage Strudel (page 118) or Pheasant Roasted in Salt Dough à la Heinz Winkler (page 114).

Variation

Morels are really the standout ingredient in this dish, but other woodsy mushrooms such as chanterelles or black trumpets could be substituted.

Make ahead

The dumplings can be refrigerated for up to 2 days. Warm them in a little butter before serving.

CHILLED SMOKED TROUT CREPES WITH HORSERADISH CRÈME FRAÎCHE

Palatschinken mit Räucherforelle und Oberskren

6 APPETIZER OR 4 ENTRÉE SERVINGS

⅔ cup all-purpose flour

Kosher salt

⅛ teaspoon sugar

1 cup milk

2 large eggs

¾ cup crème fraîche

3 tablespoons drained prepared horseradish

2 tablespoons chopped dill, plus 12 dill sprigs, for garnishing

Freshly ground pepper

½ teaspoon unsalted butter

1 small red onion, thinly sliced

1 small Golden Delicious apple, halved lengthwise, cored, and thinly sliced

1 smoked trout fillet (7 ounces), skinned, flesh flaked into ½-inch pieces

Edible flowers, for garnishing (optional)

2 tablespoons American sturgeon caviar (optional)

In Austria, *Palatschinken*, or crepes, are usually eaten for breakfast with a sweet fruit compote or jam. Here I've created a savory appetizer by filling the delicate pancakes with a blend of smoky trout, crisp apples, red onions, and crème fraîche. It's creamy, crunchy, refined—and fun.

1 In a medium bowl, whisk the flour with ¼ teaspoon of salt and the sugar. Whisk in the milk and eggs until the batter is smooth. Let rest for 15 minutes.

2 In a small bowl, mix the crème fraîche with the horseradish and chopped dill. Season with salt and pepper.

3 Strain the crepe batter through a fine sieve set over a small bowl. Heat a 6-inch crepe pan or nonstick skillet over medium-high heat. Add the butter. When the butter stops foaming, add 2 tablespoons of batter, tilting the pan to coat the bottom evenly, and cook until the edges of the crepes are lightly browned, about 1 minute. Using a spatula, flip the crepe and cook until lightly colored on the second side, about 30 seconds. Transfer to a plate. Repeat with the remaining batter, adjusting the heat as necessary so that the crepes don't burn and stacking the crepes as they're done. You should have 12 crepes.

4 Spread each crepe with 1 tablespoon of the horseradish cream and top with 3 red onion slices, 2 or 3 apple slices, and 1 heaping tablespoon of trout. Roll up the crepes and transfer to plates or a platter. Garnish each crepe with edible flowers and ½ teaspoon of caviar, if desired, and a dill sprig, and serve.

Tips

I get a lot of my fresh produce from Berried Treasures farm in Roscoe, New York, which also happens to be a major trout fishing area. My smoked trout also comes from them.

I use the American sturgeon caviar sold at Caviar Russe in Manhattan (caviarrusse.com).

Serve with

Try this dish for brunch or as a light lunch, with a big green salad.

Variations

The stuffed crepes can be sliced crosswise and served as finger food.

For traditional sweet crepes, fill the pancakes with sliced fresh fruit, jam, honey, or Nutella.

Make ahead

The plain crepes can be covered with plastic wrap and refrigerated for up to 3 days.

Slices of Chilled Smoked Trout Crepes with Horseradish Crème Fraîche are garnished with a mound of caviar and served on a black stoneware plate against a hand-loomed tablemat inspired by the Wiener Werkstätte, from Neue Galerie Design Shop. Edible flowers add bold color to the black-and-white composition.

POTATO RÖSTI WITH LOBSTER AND FENNEL SALAD

Erdäpfelrösti mit mariniertem Hummer und Fenchelsalat

4 SERVINGS

Kosher salt

2 live lobsters (about 1 ¼ pounds each)

4 radishes, thinly sliced on a mandoline

Sea salt

1 orange

2 fennel bulbs, trimmed, halved
        lengthwise, and thinly sliced on
        a mandoline

¼ cup extra-virgin olive oil

2 teaspoons white wine vinegar

Freshly ground pepper

Chive Cream

½ cup sour cream

1 tablespoon chopped chives

1 teaspoon fresh lemon juice

Salt and freshly ground pepper

Small herb sprigs and edible flowers,
        for garnishing (optional)

Rösti

Salt

2 pounds russet (baking) potatoes,
        scrubbed

½ teaspoon freshly ground pepper

Pinch of freshly grated nutmeg

Canola oil, for frying

I introduced this dish a long time ago, in the early years of Wallsé. The actress Connie Nielson used to come in all the time and order it. I always say how I like to start with something classic and throw in a contemporary twist, and this dish is just that. I toss freshly cooked lobster in a fennel and orange vinaigrette and pile it on a traditional fried potato rösti. Sometimes the weirdest things just come together and you're like, "Wow, this is really good!" I was just playing around with some ingredients I had, and somehow it ended being one of my most popular menu items.

1 Bring a large pot of salted water to a boil. Fill a large bowl with ice water.

2 Twist the lobster tails and claws off the bodies. Add to the boiling water and cook until bright red, 4 to 6 minutes. Using tongs, transfer to the ice water to cool down as quickly as possible, 1 to 2 minutes. Drain.

3 Using scissors, slit open the tail shells, both top and bottom, down the center and remove the meat. Cut the tails lengthwise in half and discard the dark intestinal veins. Crack the knuckles and claws and remove the meat. Transfer the lobster meat to a bowl.

4 Make the chive cream: In a small bowl, combine the sour cream with the chives and lemon juice. Season with salt and pepper and refrigerate.

5 In a medium bowl, season the radishes with sea salt. Using a sharp knife, peel the orange, removing all the white pith. Working over a medium bowl, cut between the membranes to release the segments, letting them drop into the bowl; squeeze in the juice from the membranes. Stir in the fennel, radishes, olive oil, and vinegar. Season with salt and pepper.

6 Make the rösti: Bring a large pot of salted

water to a boil. Fill a large bowl with ice water. Add the potatoes to the boiling water and cook until they are beginning to soften but still almost raw in the middle, about 10 minutes. Drain and add to the ice water to cool as quickly as possible, 1 to 2 minutes.

7 Drain the potatoes and peel them. Using the large holes of a box grater, shred them into a large bowl. Season with 1 teaspoon of salt, the pepper, and nutmeg and toss well to mix.

8 Film a 5-inch cast-iron skillet with oil. For each rösti, press 1 to 1 ½ cups of the potatoes into the skillet, spreading them to the edges. Fry over medium heat, turning once, until crispy and golden brown on both sides, 3 to 4 minutes per side. Transfer to a baking sheet and keep warm in a low oven.

9 In a medium bowl, toss the lobster with 2 tablespoons of the orange and fennel vinaigrette.

10 Dollop 2 to 3 tablespoons of the chive cream onto each plate. Top with a rösti and some lobster and fennel salad. Drizzle any remaining vinaigrette over the top. Garnish with the herbs and flowers, if desired, and serve.

Tips

The rösti recipe yields 4 to 6 small potato cakes; for this recipe you need only 4. Leftovers can be refrigerated for up to 1 day. Reheat them in the microwave or under the broiler for a couple of minutes.

The lobster should be at room temperature for serving. Before adding it to the vinaigrette though, you could

warm the pieces in a little melted butter. This gives the lobster a glaze, plus extra richness and flavor.

Serve with

Serve as a first course before Rib-Eye Steaks with Crispy Onion Rings (page 128) or Cod Strudel with Sauerkraut in Riesling Sauce (page 109).

Variation

Turn this first-course recipe into a main course by doubling it and serving the meat from 1 lobster per person on top of 2 rösti.

Make ahead

The chive cream can be refrigerated for up to 1 day.

BLOOD SAUSAGE AND
FINGERLING POTATO HASH WITH SAUERKRAUT

Blutwurst Gröst'l

4 APPETIZER OR 2 ENTRÉE SERVINGS

¾ *pound fingerling potatoes*

 Salt

1 *tablespoon canola oil*

¾ *pound blood sausage,*
 sliced ½ inch thick (see Tips)

4 *scallions, white part only, thinly sliced*

1 *teaspoon caraway seeds*

1 *teaspoon dried marjoram*

 Freshly ground pepper

½ *cup sauerkraut, drained and*
 squeezed dry

2 *tablespoons beef stock*

 Dijon mustard, for serving

 Freshly grated horseradish, for serving

2 *tablespoons chervil leaves*
 or snipped chives

A *Gröst'l* is a kind of hash made with potatoes, onions, and some sort of meat, typically bacon or sausage. When I think of eating blood sausage, I imagine having it alongside sautéed potatoes, sauerkraut, fresh horseradish, and mustard. In this dish it's possible to have it all—in one rich and pungent bite.

1 Add the potatoes to a medium saucepan of salted water and bring to a boil. Cook until the potatoes are tender but still firm in the middle, about 10 minutes. Drain and let cool slightly, then slice ½ inch thick.

2 In a medium skillet, heat the oil. Add the blood sausage, potatoes, scallions, caraway seeds, and marjoram and cook over medium-high heat, stirring often, until the potatoes are golden brown, 3 to 4 minutes. Season lightly with salt and with pepper.

3 Meanwhile, in a medium saucepan, combine the sauerkraut and stock and warm through over medium heat.

4 Mound the sauerkraut on a warmed platter or plates. Spoon the hash onto the sauerkraut. Top with a little mustard and horseradish, sprinkle with the herbs, and serve. Pass additional mustard and horseradish.

Tips

Blood sausage is available from German and Irish butchers and at some specialty supermarkets.

Blood sausage is often loosely packed, so slicing can be messy. Tearing it into ½-inch-thick pieces is fine.

Serve with

A light green salad adds brightness to the rich sausage and makes the dish a simple weekday lunch or dinner.

Variations

If blood sausage isn't your thing, this dish is just as delicious with many other types of meat. Try using bratwurst or thick slabs of pancetta or bacon in its place.

Feel free to play around and add any number of other ingredients here. Sautéed mushrooms, diced ham, and grated Emmentaler or other sharp white cheese on top all work well.

Albert Oehlen's work is a brawny platform for earthy blood sausage.

SAVORY SAUSAGES

Sausages play a big role in Austrian cooking. Their quality can vary, so it's essential to find a great butcher shop. In New York City my go-to place is Schaller & Weber on the Upper East Side (schallerandweber.com), a family business that's been around since 1937.

I like to prepare them in many different ways. At the Beer Garden at the Standard Hotel in New York, I grill all kinds and serve them with large, doughy pretzels and frothy steins of beer. At Café Sabarsky, they come roasted with sauerkraut and sautéed with potato salad. I love blood sausage in strudel (page 118) and in hearty potato hash with fingerling potatoes and sauerkraut (page 62). I know many people avoid blood sausage because of its major ingredient, but I think it's delicious and versatile.

Sausages come in a wide range of styles, including beef, pork, veal, coarse, smooth, spicy, and cheese-filled. Here's a primer of the most common ones along with their traditional condiments, Dijon mustard, sweet mustard, and horseradish.

OPPOSITE, CLOCKWISE FROM TOP RIGHT The slightly spicy pork-based Nürnbergerwurst is similar to American breakfast sausage but is flavored with marjoram. The familiar frankfurter is eaten on a roll with mustard. Cheddar cheese-filled Käsekreiner is pan-seared or grilled and served with bread, sauerkraut, or potato puree. Typically pan-seared or grilled, pork-and-beef bratwurst is enjoyed with fiery mustard and horseradish. Weisswurst is a white veal sausage; it's usually boiled, peeled, and served for breakfast with sweet mustard and bread.

RIGHT Wiener Werkstätte Postcard Number 91 by Moriz Jung, Variety Act 7: Sepp and Kathi Steidler, Popular House Comedians, 1907. Leonard A. Lauder Collection, Neue Galerie New York.

SPÄTZLE WITH WHITE CORN, BRUSSELS SPROUTS, MUSHROOMS, AND TARRAGON

Spätzle mit Schwammerln, Erbsen, Mais und Estragon

When people come to my restaurants looking for a meatless option, I always steer them to this dish. While it makes a great starter or accompaniment, the spätzle is also substantial enough (lots of vegetables) to serve as a main dish.

6 APPETIZER OR 4 ENTRÉE SERVINGS

Salt

2 cups all-purpose flour

Freshly ground pepper

⅛ teaspoon freshly grated nutmeg

2 large eggs, lightly beaten

1 cup quark cheese (see Tips, page 162)

⅔ cup heavy cream

½ ear of white corn

2 tablespoons unsalted butter

½ pound mushrooms, such as cremini, sliced or quartered

Fresh lemon juice

½ pound brussels sprouts, leaves separated (see Tips)

½ cup diced carrots

½ cup peas

Tarragon leaves, for garnishing

1 Bring a large saucepan of salted water to a boil. In a large bowl, whisk the flour with ½ teaspoon of salt, ¼ teaspoon of pepper, and the nutmeg. Add the eggs, cheese, and ⅓ cup of the cream and beat until smooth.

2 Fill a large bowl with ice water. Working in batches, press the dough through a spätzle maker into the boiling water; or use a colander with large holes and a rubber spatula. Cook until the spätzle float to the surface, 2 to 3 minutes. Using a fine sieve, transfer to the ice water for 1 to 2 minutes, then remove to a colander to drain.

3 Bring a small saucepan of salted water to a boil. Fill a small bowl with ice water. Add the corn to the boiling water and cook until tender, about 5 minutes. Transfer to the ice water to cool as quickly as possible, 1 to 2 minutes, then drain. Cut the corn kernels off the cob.

4 In a medium saucepan, melt 1 tablespoon of the butter. Add the mushrooms and cook, stirring occasionally, until the water they release has evaporated, about 7 minutes. Season with salt, pepper, and lemon juice.

5 In a large saucepan, melt the remaining 1 tablespoon of butter over medium-high heat. Add the brussels sprouts and carrots and cook for 30 seconds. Add the spätzle, corn, peas, mushrooms, and the remaining ⅓ cup of cream and cook until warmed through, about 2 minutes. Season with salt and pepper.

6 Spoon the spätzle into a warmed serving bowl or onto plates, garnish with the tarragon, and serve.

Tips

The holes of the colander should be no bigger than an eraser tip. Also, see page 162.

The most common way to cook brussels sprouts is, of course, to boil or steam them whole or halved until fully tender, but separating the leaves allows you to cook them until crisp-tender.

Serve with

When serving this dish as a vegetarian main course, start with a light salad or soup such as Marinated Heirloom Tomato Salad (page 86) or Spring Pea Soup with Pineapple Mint (page 72).

Make ahead

The spätzle recipe can be prepared through Step 2 and refrigerated for up to 2 days. Toss with a little olive oil before chilling.

Wiener Werkstätte Postcard Number 489 by Gustav Kalhammer, Hütteldorf Brewery, A. Brussati, 1911.
Leonard A. Lauder Collection, Neue Galerie New York.

QUARK CHEESE RAVIOLI
WITH MINT AND BROWNED BUTTER

Topfenravioli mit Minze und Nussbutter

4 APPETIZER OR 2 ENTRÉE SERVINGS

1 large russet (baking) potato, scrubbed
    Salt

½ cup quark cheese (see Tips, page 162)

2 mint sprigs, leaves thinly sliced (see Tips)

¼ teaspoon freshly ground pepper

⅛ teaspoon freshly grated nutmeg

1 large egg

1 tablespoon water

Forty-eight 3-inch round wonton wrappers
    (from one 16-ounce package)
    All-purpose flour

6 tablespoons unsalted butter

1 tablespoon fresh lemon juice

½ cup peas

This is a lovely spring dish that I serve a lot of at Blaue Gans. Using wonton wrappers makes the ravioli simple to prepare, and the creamy flavor of the quark cheese is enlivened by the fresh mint and nutty butter sauce.

1 Add the potato to a medium saucepan of salted water, bring to a boil, and cook until tender, about 20 minutes. Drain the potato and let cool slightly.

2 Peel the warm potato and pass it through a ricer or a food mill into a medium bowl. Beat in the cheese, mint, ½ teaspoon of salt, the pepper, and nutmeg.

3 In a small bowl, beat the egg with the water. Spread 24 of the wonton wrappers on a work surface and brush with the beaten egg. Using a pastry bag fitted with a ½-inch round tip or a tablespoon, mound about 1 tablespoon of the filling on each brushed wonton wrapper, then cover with a plain wonton wrapper. Press the edges of the wrappers together, forming a tight seal. Transfer the ravioli to a lightly floured sheet of parchment paper.

4 Bring a large pot of salted water to a boil. Add the ravioli and cook until tender, about 3 minutes; drain.

5 Meanwhile, in a large skillet, melt the butter over medium heat and cook, swirling the pan occasionally, until the butter is golden brown and has a nutty aroma, 3 to 5 minutes. Add the lemon juice and peas and cook until the peas are tender but still bright green, 2 to 3 minutes.

6 Add the ravioli to the skillet and gently stir to coat with the butter. Spoon the ravioli onto warmed plates, drizzle with the browned butter, and serve immediately.

Tips
To slice the mint leaves easily, stack them, roll up, and cut crosswise into thin strips, called chiffonade.
If using frozen wonton wrappers, note that they need to thaw overnight in the refrigerator, so plan accordingly.
I use a ricer to mash the potatoes to get a filling with an especially light, fluffy texture.

Serve with
When turning the ravioli into an entrée, I like to stay meat-free and sauté fresh snap peas or prepare Creamed Spinach (page 153) as the side dish.

Variation
For extra flavor, add ½ cup chopped cooked bacon or ham in Step 5 with the peas.

Make ahead
The ravioli can be frozen on baking sheets until firm, then transferred to a sturdy plastic bag for up to 2 weeks before cooking. Add them, still frozen, to the boiling water in Step 4.

BUTTERFLY PASTA WITH BAVARIAN HAM, CREAM, AND EMMENTALER CHEESE

Schinkenfleckerl

4 SERVINGS

2 tablespoons unsalted butter,
    plus more for brushing
Salt
1 pound butterfly pasta
1 large yellow onion, finely chopped
¾ pound Bavarian ham, cut into ½-inch
    dice (see Tip)
2 garlic cloves, chopped
½ cup heavy cream
½ cup sour cream
2 tablespoons chopped parsley
Freshly ground pepper
Freshly grated nutmeg
¼ pound Emmentaler cheese, shredded
    (about 1 cup)

Who doesn't love noodles? Rich, cheesy, and studded with salty ham, this baked pasta is a favorite of mine. It's easy to make, and you won't have a hard time getting your kids to eat it; in fact, you'll be lucky if you get your share!

1 Preheat the oven to 400 degrees. Brush an 8-inch gratin dish (or 4 individual gratin dishes) lightly with butter. Bring a large pot of salted water to a boil. Add the pasta and cook, stirring occasionally, until al dente. Drain.

2 Meanwhile, in a medium saucepan, melt the butter. Add the onion and cook over medium-high heat, stirring occasionally, until lightly browned, 8 to 10 minutes.

3 Add the ham, garlic, heavy cream, and sour cream to the onion and warm over low heat. Stir in the pasta and parsley and season with salt, pepper, and nutmeg. Remove the pan from the heat.

4 Spread the pasta in the prepared gratin dish and sprinkle with the cheese. Bake until the top is lightly browned, 10 to 15 minutes. Remove from the oven and let stand for 2 minutes before serving.

Tip
Bavarian ham is cured with salt and spices, then pressed into small metal boxes and boiled. It is fairly lean. Black Forest ham can be substituted.

Serve with
At lunch, try this with simple tossed greens such as Boston Lettuce Salad with Spicy Radishes, Pumpkin Seed Oil, and Lemon Vinaigrette (page 88).

Variations
Add some peas, chopped tomatoes, or sliced zucchini. Or, for a vegetarian version, omit the ham and toss the pasta with caramelized cabbage and onions instead.

Make ahead
The recipe can be assembled ahead and refrigerated for up to 3 hours. Bake it at 350 degrees until heated through and browned, 20 to 30 minutes.

SOUPS

AND

SALADS

SPRING PEA SOUP WITH PINEAPPLE MINT

Grüne Erbsensuppe mit Minze

8 SERVINGS

8 cups vegetable stock
3 cups shelled peas (1 pound)
1 bunch of mint (about 1 ½ ounces),
    preferably pineapple mint, stems
    discarded (see Tip)
  Salt and freshly ground pepper
  Fresh lemon juice

As soon as March comes around, I start getting anxious to see the first spring produce at the Union Square Greenmarket. Enough with the apples and pears already—bring on the peas! My brother and I always ate a lot of peas as kids. In fact, my mother used to scold us for depleting the backyard garden supply. I love them raw, cooked, even straight from the pod. This vibrant vegetarian pea soup is incredibly light and fresh tasting.

1 In a large pot fitted with a colander, bring the boiling stock to a boil. Fill a large bowl with ice water. Add half the peas to the stock and cook until tender, 5 minutes. Add the mint leaves and cook briefly, about 1 minute. Remove the colander from the stock, letting the stock drain back into the pot, and immediately pour the peas and mint into the ice water to cool as quickly as possible, 1 to 2 minutes; drain. Let the stock cool slightly.

2 Working in batches, use a blender to puree the cooked peas and mint with the remaining peas and stock. Season with salt, pepper, and lemon juice. Transfer to a large saucepan and warm over high heat until hot. Serve immediately.

Tip
Pineapple mint is a variety of mint with a slight pineapple aroma. It is available at some specialty food stores and farmers' markets.

Serve with
For a light main course, try a fish like Lake Perch with Julienne Vegetables and Riesling Butter Sauce (page 100) or Halibut with Cucumber-Dill Sauce and Chanterelles (page 104).

Make ahead
Before it's heated, the pureed soup can be transferred to a medium bowl set in a second bowl of ice water and refrigerated for up to 3 hours.

Variation
I like to cook large lobster ravioli and add one to each bowl, then ladle the soup over it.

Spring Pea Soup with Pineapple Mint is served in crystal tumblers by Adolf Loos, set on a 1905 nickel-plated wine coaster by Josef Hoffmann, from Neue Galerie Design Shop.

RAMP SOUP WITH SCALLOP RAVIOLI

Bärlauchsuppe mit Jakobsmuschelravioli

6 SERVINGS

Soup base

4 tablespoons unsalted butter

½ large onion, chopped

1 shallot, sliced

1 garlic clove, sliced

Salt and freshly ground pepper

1 quart chicken stock

2 cups heavy cream

1 bay leaf

Ramp puree

Salt

½ pound ramps (see Tips)

½ cup packed parsley leaves

¼ cup heavy cream

¼ cup milk

2 tablespoons sour cream

2 ice cubes

Freshly ground pepper

Scallop ravioli

1 large egg

1 tablespoon water

Twenty-four 3-inch round wonton wrappers

4 large scallops, sliced horizontally into 3 pieces

Salt and freshly ground pepper

All-purpose flour, for dusting

Ramps are another great spring vegetable I love. The best are the fresh ones usually available in March. They give this soup a pungent, garlicky flavor and beautiful green color. If you think the scallop ravioli are too chef-y, add the thinly sliced raw scallops to each bowl instead and ladle the steaming soup on top. The heat of the soup will lightly cook the seafood.

1 Make the soup base: In a large saucepan, melt the butter over medium heat. Add the onion, shallot, and garlic, season with salt and pepper, and cook, stirring occasionally, until softened, about 5 minutes. Add the stock, cream, and bay leaf and bring to a boil, then reduce the heat to medium-low and simmer for 15 minutes. Puree using an immersion blender, or in batches using a regular blender.

2 Make the ramp puree: Bring a large saucepan of water to a boil. Fill a large bowl with ice water. Add 2 tablespoons of salt and the ramps to the boiling water and cook until the ramps are tender but the leaves are still green, about 1 minute. Drain and transfer to the ice water to cool as quickly as possible, 1 to 2 minutes. Drain again and gently squeeze out the water.

3 In a blender, combine the ramps with the parsley, heavy cream, milk, sour cream, 1 teaspoon of salt, and the ice cubes and puree until smooth.

4 Make the scallop ravioli: In a small bowl, beat the egg with the water. Spread 12 wonton wrappers on a work surface and brush with the beaten egg. Set 1 slice of scallop on each brushed wrapper, season with salt and pepper, and cover with a plain wonton wrapper. Press the edges of the wrappers together, forming a tight seal. Transfer the ravioli to a lightly floured sheet of parchment paper.

5 Just before serving, bring a large pot of salted water to a boil. Add the ravioli and cook until tender, about 3 minutes; drain.

6 Meanwhile, reheat the soup base and stir in the ramp puree.

7 Arrange 2 ravioli in each warmed soup plate. Ladle the soup over the ravioli, and serve.

Tips

Ramps need to be cleaned well to remove any dirt between the tight layers.

The ramp puree is stirred into the soup base right before serving to keep the color green and fresh looking.

Serve with

Because of the strong taste of the ramps, I like to follow this soup with something hearty and seasonal, like Roasted Leg of Lamb (page 133).

Variation

Instead of the scallop ravioli or sliced raw scallops, you can add fresh or smoked salmon to the bowls before ladling in the soup. If using fresh salmon, cut it into bite-size pieces.

Make ahead

The soup base can be refrigerated overnight, but the ramp puree should be prepared as close to serving time as possible.

TOMATO CONSOMMÉ WITH SALMON

Paradeiserconsommé mit Lachs

4 SERVINGS

12 pounds very ripe tomatoes, chopped
    Salt
¾ teaspoon cayenne pepper
1 tablespoon sugar
1 ½ ounces (3 tablespoons) gin
3 tablespoons white wine vinegar
    Squeeze of fresh lemon juice
4 skinless salmon fillets
    (about 4 ounces each)
    Freshly ground pepper
8 cherry tomatoes, quartered
    Small basil leaves, for garnishing
    (optional)

I learned the technique for making tomato water while I was cooking at Tantris in Munich. During my time at David Bouley's original restaurant in New York City, I created this dish, heating the tomato water to make a hot consommé with a garnish of diced fresh salmon and cherry tomatoes. Save it for late summer, when vine-ripened tomatoes are plentiful at farmers' markets and roadside stands. It's a beautiful and elegant starter that is flavorful yet light.

1 Working in batches, using a blender, puree the chopped tomatoes until smooth. Transfer the tomatoes to a large bowl as they're pureed. Stir in 1 tablespoon of the salt, the cayenne, sugar, gin, vinegar, and lemon juice.
2 Line a large colander with a large piece of cheesecloth and set the colander over another large bowl. Pour the tomato puree into the colander. Using kitchen string, tie the cheesecloth into a loose bundle. Transfer to the refrigerator and let the tomato water drip into the bowl overnight. Discard or reserve the pulp and pour the tomato water into a medium saucepan.
3 Just before serving, cut the salmon into ¼-inch dice. Season lightly with salt and pepper.
4 Bring the tomato water to a simmer over medium heat.
5 Add some of the salmon dice to each bowl and pour the hot tomato water on top. Garnish with the cherry tomatoes and, if desired, basil leaves, and serve.

Tip
Juicy, ripe tomatoes work best here. I like the beefsteak variety. For more tips, see Tomato Water (page 45).

Serve with
I love this dish with a glass of crisp Grüner Veltliner.

Variation
Thinly sliced sea scallops can be substituted for the diced salmon.

Make ahead
The tomato water can be refrigerated for up to 2 weeks.

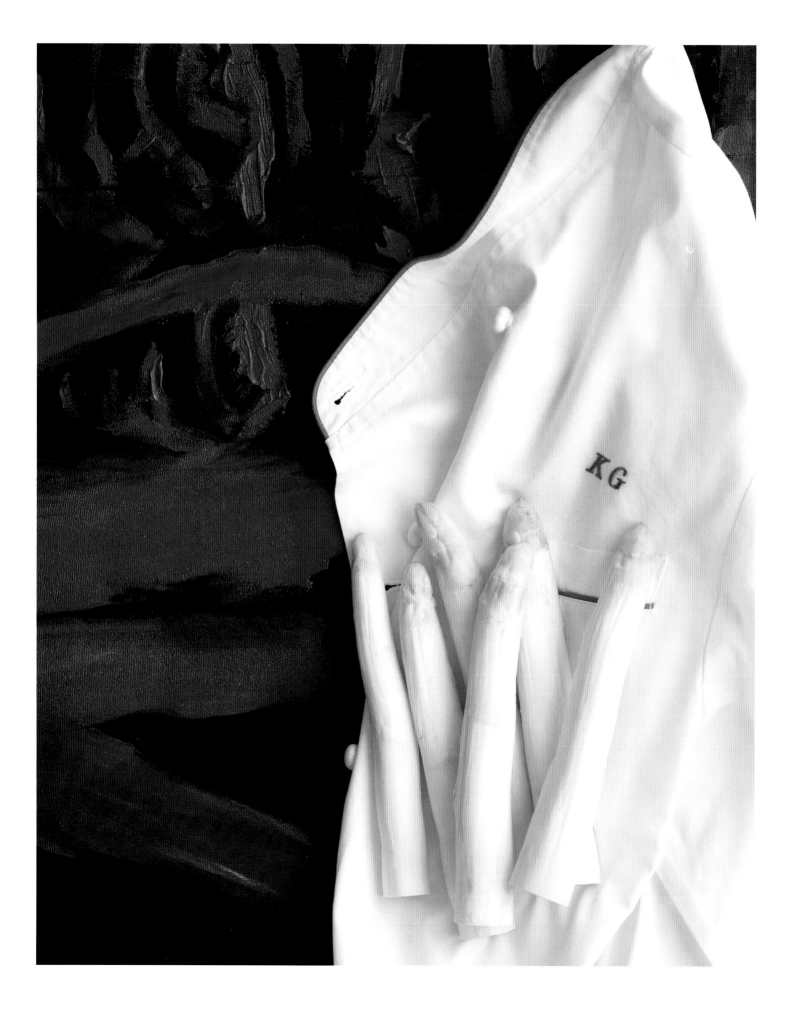

ALL ABOUT WHITE ASPARAGUS

White asparagus differs from green asparagus in that it's etiolated; that is, dirt is kept mounded around the stalk as it grows, depriving it of sun. The plant cannot produce chlorophyll without light, so it stays ivory white. Also, the spears are usually thicker and sweeter than the green variety. White asparagus is adored in northern Europe, especially in Austria, Germany, and France. However, the season is short—usually from April to the end of June. Here are a few pointers for taking advantage of it while it's available.

White asparagus should not be stored for too long. Store it in the refrigerator, wrapped in a damp kitchen towel.

Unlike its green counterpart, white asparagus has a tough, bitter peel that must be removed before cooking. This is my method for peeling the brittle spears, which can snap easily: Turn a soup bowl upside down. Lean each asparagus spear, tip up, against the bowl and hold it in place near the top 2 inches with three fingers. Using a sharp paring knife, peel off the skin, turning the spear as you go. Slice off 1 inch of the woody ends.

White asparagus should be cooked, typically in plenty of boiling water, immediately after it's peeled. Traditionally the water is seasoned with salt, sugar, and butter. I often add a piece of white bread or baguette to the pot to help remove any bitterness from the asparagus. The asparagus are done when the spears are easily pierced with the tip of a knife. They should still be firm to the bite.

Using tongs, transfer the asparagus to a kitchen towel. Pat the asparagus dry; there's nothing worse than soggy white asparagus. You are now ready to serve the asparagus. A simple herb vinaigrette or hollandaise sauce is all you need to accompany it.

Julian Schnabel's painting of Oskar Kokoschka (detail) contrasts with my chef's jacket and delicate white asparagus.

WHITE ASPARAGUS SOUP

Weisse Spargelsuppe

8 SERVINGS

8 cups water

1/3 cup sugar

2 tablespoons kosher salt

1/2 pound (2 sticks) unsalted butter

2 pounds white asparagus, peeled and trimmed (see All About White Asparagus, page 77)

2 large onions, finely diced

2 cups heavy cream

Fine sea salt and freshly ground white pepper

Creamy white asparagus soup is a quintessential Austrian spring dish. Now that white asparagus is more readily available here, you can make it yourself. It's not hard and can be prepared in advance—just the thing for a luxe dinner party.

1 In a large saucepan, combine the water with the sugar, kosher salt, and half of the butter and bring to a boil over high heat. Add the asparagus and cook until just tender, about 6 minutes. Using tongs, transfer the asparagus to a cutting board. Cut off the tips and transfer to a bowl. Reserve the asparagus stalks and broth.

2 In another large saucepan, melt the remaining butter over medium-high heat. Add the onions and cook, stirring, until soft and lightly browned, about 4 minutes. Add the reserved asparagus stems and broth and the cream and bring to a boil. Reduce the heat to medium and simmer until tender, 10 to 15 minutes. Remove the pan from the heat.

3 Using a blender, puree the soup in batches. Strain through a medium sieve. Season with sea salt and pepper.

4 Add a few of the reserved asparagus tips to each warmed soup plate, ladle in the soup, and serve.

Tip

Take care not to cook the asparagus for too long, or it will turn bitter.

Make ahead

The soup can be refrigerated for up to 5 days or frozen for up to 3 months.

CHILLED CRAYFISH SOUP WITH MELON

Kalte Flusskrebssuppe mit Melone

8 SERVINGS

2 ½ quarts water

25 live crayfish (about 4 ounces each)

¾ cup canola oil

1 medium carrot, coarsely chopped

4 celery ribs, coarsely chopped

1 small onion, coarsely chopped

6 tablespoons unsalted butter

1 medium leek, white and light green
    parts only, coarsely chopped

¼ cup tomato paste
    Salt

⅓ cup Cognac or other brandy

¼ cup dry white wine

20 black peppercorns

2 bay leaves

1 teaspoon caraway seeds
    Juice of ½ lime

¼ cantaloupe, scooped into small balls

¼ cup mixed herbs, such as basil, dill,
    and tarragon (optional)

Similar to lobster bisque, this summer soup gets its intense flavor from browning and flambéing crayfish shells and aromatic vegetables, then adding the crayfish cooking liquid and simmering it until tasty. An impressive make-ahead dish for a dinner party, it requires only a few minutes to assemble before serving.

1 In a large pot, bring the water to a boil over high heat. Fill a large bowl with ice water. Working in batches, add the crayfish to the boiling water and cook until they are bright red, 1 to 2 minutes. Using a slotted spoon, transfer them to the ice water as they are done to cool as quickly as possible, 1 to 2 minutes; drain. Reserve the crayfish cooking liquid.

2 Gently twist off the crayfish heads and transfer to a bowl. Using scissors, slit the tail shells open down the center and remove the meat. Add the crayfish shells to the heads. Discard the dark intestinal veins from the tails. In a bowl, cover the crayfish meat with water, and refrigerate.

3 In a large pot, heat the oil over high heat until shimmering. Crush the crayfish heads and shells and add to the pot. Cook, stirring frequently, until they are well browned, 5 to 7 minutes. Add the carrot, celery, and onion and cook, stirring from time to time, until nicely browned, 3 to 4 minutes. Stir in the butter, leek, tomato paste, and 1 tablespoon of salt and cook for 1 minute.

4 Add the Cognac to the pot and bring to a boil, then tilt the pot and, using a long match, carefully ignite it (see Tips). When the flames subside, add the wine, peppercorns, bay leaves, caraway seeds, and reserved crayfish cooking liquid and bring to a boil. Reduce the heat to medium and simmer until well flavored, about 45 minutes.

5 Fill a large bowl with ice water. Set a large fine sieve over another bowl. Strain the broth through the sieve, and set the bowl of broth in the ice water, cover, and refrigerate overnight.

6 The next day, using a large spoon, skim as much fat as possible from the broth. Remove any remaining fat with a paper towel. Add the lime juice and taste for seasoning.

7 Drain the crayfish meat and pat dry. Cut into ¼- to ½-inch pieces.

8 Divide the crayfish and melon among chilled soup plates. Ladle the crayfish broth into the plates, garnish with the herbs, if desired, and serve.

Tip

It is not essential to flame the Cognac in Step 4. You can simply add it to the pot and proceed with the recipe.

Serve with

I like this fragrant soup with a piece of crusty baguette and a glass of rosé. Lake Perch with Melted Leeks, Tomatoes, Capers, and Kalamata Olives (page 96) is an ideal main dish to follow it.

Variation

The soup can also be served hot. Omit the melon and after skimming the broth, reheat it. Serve with the crayfish warmed slightly.

Make ahead

The strained crayfish broth must be refrigerated overnight, so plan accordingly.

ROASTED SQUASH SOUP

Geröstete Kürbissuppe

8 SERVINGS

3 medium butternut squash
   (1 ½ pounds each)

¼ cup honey

1 teaspoon ground cinnamon

1 teaspoon freshly grated nutmeg
   Sea salt and freshly ground pepper

6 tablespoons unsalted butter

2 medium carrots, peeled and chopped

1 onion, chopped

7 cups water

1 tablespoon pumpkin seed oil

Austria isn't really known for squash although the pumpkin seed oil is a specialty. I learned about hard-shelled butternut squash by talking to other chefs and the farmers at the Union Square Greenmarket. My soup has a beautiful color and an incredibly opulent, buttery taste. Because fall brings to mind cozy things, I had the idea of including warm spices, like cinnamon and nutmeg, as well as honey. When you walk into the kitchen and smell this soup, you instantly feel comforted and at home. Just before serving, I drizzle pumpkin seed oil over the top and, voilà, an instant mix of the classic and the contemporary. I just love that.

1 Heat the oven to 450 degrees. Cut 2 of the squash lengthwise in half and scoop out the seeds. Drizzle the honey over the cut surface of the squash halves and sprinkle with the cinnamon and nutmeg. Season with salt and pepper.

2 Set the squash on a baking sheet and roast until soft, about 1 hour. Remove and let cool slightly.

3 Meanwhile, peel the remaining squash, halve it, and scoop out the seeds. Cut the flesh into 1-inch pieces.

4 When the roasted squash is cool enough to handle, scoop out the flesh. Reserve the pan juices.

5 In a large flameproof casserole, melt the butter. Add the raw squash, carrots, and onion and season with salt and pepper. Cook over medium heat, stirring occasionally, until soft, 15 to 20 minutes. Add the roasted squash, any pan juices, and the water. Bring to a simmer and cook, uncovered, stirring occasionally, for 15 to 20 minutes.

6 Puree the soup using an immersion blender, or in batches using a regular blender. Work the soup through a fine sieve; if it's too thick, thin it with water. Taste for seasoning. Reheat if necessary. Ladle into bowls, drizzle with the pumpkin seed oil, and serve.

Serve with
Pass a basket of crusty rye bread at the table.

Variation
To make this soup into a vegetable puree, reduce the amount of water, and serve as a side dish with grilled fish, like monkfish or sea bass, and a tossed salad.

Make ahead
The soup can be refrigerated for up to 2 days.

CHESTNUT SOUP WITH VIENNESE MÉLANGE

Maronensuppe mit Wiener Mélange

8 SERVINGS

Prunes

8 pitted prunes

½ cup Armagnac or Cognac

½ cup water

Mushroom broth

¾ pound mixed mushrooms,
 such as hen-of-the-woods,
 shiitake, and oyster mushrooms

2 ½ cups water

2 dried porcini or other mushrooms

Soup

1 pound chestnuts in the shell

4 tablespoons unsalted butter

1 medium celery root (about 12
 ounces), thickly peeled and cut into
 ½-inch dice

Salt and freshly ground pepper

1 tablespoon sugar

5 cups chicken stock

1 cup heavy cream

2 cups skim milk

⅛ teaspoon freshly grated nutmeg

1 black truffle, cut into shavings
 (optional)

8 flat-leaf parsley leaves

We cook a lot of celery root in Austria, and I had the idea of creating a soup with it, plus wild mushrooms and roasted chestnuts. The sweetness of the Armagnac-soaked prunes and the earthy, foamy porcini mushroom mélange on top really make this a terrific holiday dish. It's festive and beautiful, but even I couldn't have predicted the results. It became such a huge success that we receive requests for the soup even on the hottest summer days, when it's not on the menu. What's more, I know if I want to make my daughters happy, I just make this soup.

1 Make the prunes: In a small saucepan, combine the prunes with the Armagnac and water. Bring to a simmer, then remove from the heat, cover, and let soak for at least 6 hours. Drain.

2 Make the mushroom broth: In a small saucepan, cover the mixed mushrooms with the water, and bring to a simmer, then cook over low heat for 1 hour. Strain the liquid and reserve the mushrooms for another use. You should have at least 1 cup of mushroom broth. If you have less than 1 cup, add chicken stock.

3 In a spice or coffee grinder, whir the porcini mushrooms to a powder.

4 Make the soup: Heat the oven to 375 degrees. Using a small sharp knife, score the flat side of each chestnut with an X. Spread the chestnuts on a baking sheet and roast in the center of the oven until the skin curls, 10 to 12 minutes. Let cool slightly, and peel.

5 In a large saucepan, melt the butter. Add the celery root and cook over low heat, stirring occasionally, for 5 minutes, without browning. Add the chestnuts and season with salt and pepper, then add the sugar and cook over medium heat, stirring, until the mixture caramelizes. Add the mushroom broth and chicken stock and bring to a boil, then reduce the heat to low and cook for 15 minutes. Add the cream and cook for 5 minutes. Remove the pan from the heat and let cool slightly.

6 Puree the soup using an immersion blender, or in batches using a regular blender. Work the soup through a fine sieve.

7 Return the soup to the pan and reheat. Taste for seasoning.

8 Add a prune to each warmed soup plate. Using an espresso machine or a frother, foam the milk with ¼ teaspoon of the porcini powder and the nutmeg. Ladle the soup into the plates, top each with a spoonful of the foam, some truffle shavings, if using, and a parsley leaf, and serve.

Tip

Wiener Mélange is the name of an Austrian coffee drink, composed of strong espresso topped with fluffy steamed milk. It's similar to cappuccino. In this recipe, the "mélange" is the porcini mushroom foam dolloped on the soup.

Serve with

This soup really stands alone. Not even bread is necessary. To follow, serve a light entrée like pan-seared fish—Brook Trout with Cauliflower, Raisins, and Almonds (page 98), for instance. Or try something that shares the soup's smoky richness, such as Blood Sausage Strudel (page 118). It would also make a delicious weekday meal served with a large green salad.

Variations

While this soup is typically served as a first course, we often send it out to special customers in tiny glass teacups as an amuse bouche.

For a simpler version, omit the prunes and porcini mushroom mélange. The mushroom broth could be replaced with chicken or beef stock, though you'll lose some of the earthy flavor.

Make ahead

The soup can be prepared through Step 6 and refrigerated overnight. The mushroom powder can be stored indefinitely in an airtight container. The prunes in Armagnac can be refrigerated indefinitely in a jar.

OXTAIL CONSOMMÉ WITH BONE MARROW DUMPLINGS

Ochsenschwanz Consommé mit Markknödeln

8 SERVINGS

8 cups Oxtail Consommé (opposite)
   or broth from Boiled Beef Shoulder
   with Vegetables and Fresh
   Horseradish (page 138)
1 tablespoon finely chopped chives

Dumplings

2 ounces beef bone marrow (see Tips)
1 tablespoon unsalted butter, softened
1 large egg
1 ½ cups cubed crustless white bread
¼ cup whole milk
½ cup dry bread crumbs
1 teaspoon finely chopped lovage
   (see Tips; optional)
   Freshly grated nutmeg
   Salt and freshly ground pepper

Boiled beef dishes like *Kavalierspitz* (page 138) are common in Austria. Traditionally a soup or consommé is prepared with the extra broth. I like to make a rich beef broth using oxtails and then clarify it to get a limpid consommé. You can prepare this recipe either way. In any case, we vary the consommé by adding different garnishes—for instance, these rich and buttery marrow dumplings.

1 Make the dumplings: Using a spoon, work the bone marrow through a fine sieve into a medium bowl. Add the butter and beat until creamy and light pink. Add the egg and beat until smooth.

2 In a bowl, soak the bread cubes in the milk. Squeeze out as much of the milk as possible and discard it. Work the bread through a medium sieve into the marrow mixture. Beat in the bread crumbs and lovage. Season with nutmeg, salt, and pepper. Let the dough rest for 10 minutes.

3 Bring a large wide pot of salted water to a boil. Using 2 wet soupspoons, form the dough into 8 egg-shaped dumplings and transfer to a plate.

4 Add the dumplings to the boiling water, without crowding, and cook at a gentle boil for 5 minutes. Remove the pan from the heat and leave the dumplings in the water for 5 minutes.

5 Fill a large bowl with ice water. Using a slotted spoon, transfer the dumplings to the ice water to cool, 1 to 2 minutes, then transfer to paper towels to drain.

6 Meanwhile, heat the consommé.

7 Ladle the consommé into soup plates and add the dumplings. Sprinkle with the chives, and serve.

Tips

Beef bone marrow can be special-ordered from butchers. Lovage is a leafy vegetable that has a mildly spicy flavor similar to that of celery. Its leaves are often used as an aromatic flavoring and for color, in particular for soups. You can usually find it at farmers' markets.

Serve with

Follow this light consommé with a poultry entrée such as Pheasant Roasted in Salt Dough à la Heinz Winkler (page 114).

Variations

Instead of the marrow dumplings, you could make small semolina dumplings (see Fresh Morels with Sherry and Semolina Dumplings, page 57), or chicken quenelles, using the chicken mousse filling in Cabbage-Wrapped Chicken Strudel (page 116), which you poach in the same way as the semolina dumplings.

Make ahead

The consommé (without the dumplings) can be refrigerated for up to 2 days or frozen for up to 1 month.

OXTAIL CONSOMMÉ

Ochsenschwanz Consommé

This deeply flavored consommé can be used in soups and sauces as well as in the dish opposite, or simply reheat it with the reserved oxtail meat and serve.

2 tablespoons canola oil

4 pounds oxtails cut into
      1- to 2-inch lengths

   Salt and freshly ground white
      pepper

3 tablespoons unsalted butter

2 large carrots, coarsely chopped

2 medium onions, coarsely
      chopped (see Tips)

2 medium celery roots
      (about 12 ounces each),
      coarsely chopped

1 tablespoon tomato paste

2 medium tomatoes, coarsely
      chopped

5 cups ice cubes

2 cups ruby port

1 ½ cups dry red wine

1 garlic clove, crushed

15 black peppercorns

3 rosemary sprigs

6 thyme sprigs

1 pound ground beef

4 large egg whites, lightly beaten

1 cup dry Madeira

1 In a large stockpot, heat the oil until smoking. Add the oxtails, season with salt and white pepper, and cook over high heat, stirring occasionally, until nicely browned all over, 5 to 10 minutes. Add the butter and half of the carrots, onions, and celery root and cook, stirring occasionally, until browned, about 5 minutes. Add the tomato paste and tomatoes and cook for a few more minutes.
2 Remove the pot from the heat and add 2 cups of the ice cubes; stir gently until melted. Return the pot to high heat, add ½ cup of the port and ½ cup of the red wine, and bring to a boil, then cook until the liquid has almost evaporated. Repeat 2 more times.
3 Add the garlic, 10 peppercorns, 2 rosemary sprigs, 4 thyme sprigs, and enough water to cover the oxtails by 3 inches. Bring to a boil, then reduce the heat to medium-low and simmer until the meat is very tender, about 2 ½ hours. Remove the oxtails from the pot and let cool.
4 Fill a large bowl with ice water. Line a fine sieve with cheesecloth and set over a large bowl. Strain the broth through the sieve; discard everything in the sieve. Set the bowl of broth in the ice water to speed the cooling.
5 When the oxtails are cool enough to handle, remove the meat from the bones and reserve for another use; discard the bones. Skim the fat from the broth.
6 In a stockpot, season the ground beef with 2 teaspoons of salt and 1 teaspoon of white pepper. Using a large wooden spoon, stir in the egg whites, the remaining 3 cups of ice cubes, the Madeira, and the remaining ½ cup of port. Add the remaining carrots, onions, and celery root, 5 peppercorns, 1 rosemary sprig, 2 thyme sprigs, and the broth, and bring to a boil, stirring. Reduce the heat to medium-low and simmer for at least 45 minutes.
7 Line a fine sieve with cheesecloth and set it over a bowl. Remove the pot from the heat and ladle the broth into the sieve to strain.

Tips

Stirring ice cubes into the mixture in Step 2 helps deglaze the browned bits from the bottom of the pot without the need to scrape.

Egg whites act like a natural trap, catching any scum, so the finished consommé is perfectly clear. This is called clarifying. Ground beef boosts the meaty flavor and rich brown color.

You can leave the skin on the onions, carrots, and celery root, since they're removed at the end. In fact, the onion skin especially adds extra color to the consommé.

The more you cook and reduce the consommé, the darker it will become and the stronger the flavor will get.

Serve with

Traditionally consommé is served before a hearty fish like sea bass or swordfish, but on a cold day, try it with a salad for lunch.

Variations

You can always play around with the consommé add-ins. For instance, make the basic crepe recipe for Chilled Smoked Trout Crepes with Horseradish Crème Fraîche (page 58), roll them up, and cut crosswise into ribbons for a garnish.

Make ahead

The consommé can be refrigerated for up to 3 days or frozen for up to 1 month.

GOULASH SOUP

Gulaschsuppe

6 SERVINGS

3 tablespoons duck fat or canola oil

2 small onions, finely chopped

3 large garlic cloves, finely chopped

¼ cup Hungarian sweet paprika (see Tips)

1 tablespoon tomato paste

1 tablespoon ground caraway

1 teaspoon dried marjoram

½ teaspoon dried thyme

1 bay leaf

3 pounds beef shin, bones removed, meat cut into ½-inch pieces (see Tips)

6 cups water

1 tablespoon red wine vinegar

1 large German Butterball potato (see Tips), peeled and cut into ½-inch dice

2 teaspoons fresh lemon juice

Fine sea salt and freshly ground pepper

There is nothing better than a bowl of soup and a piece of good bread. When I was a boy, I'd come home and smell meat and spices cooking—goulash!—and want some right away. The main difference between the goulash you serve for dinner and goulash soup is that for the soup, you cut everything smaller. Most of the ingredients are the same, and once you know how to make the soup, you will know how to make a good goulash too.

This is one of the dishes Austrians incorporated into their cuisine because of a long history with Hungary. But the addition of potatoes and the fact that everything is cut into small pieces makes it distinctly Austrian. This is a coffeehouse favorite, often eaten at any time of the day along with a hunk of baguette or sour rye bread.

1 In a large skillet, heat the fat. Add the onions and garlic and cook over medium heat, stirring frequently, until browned, about 10 minutes.

2 Add the paprika and cook, stirring frequently, for 2 minutes. Stir in the tomato paste and cook for 1 minute. Stir in the caraway, marjoram, thyme, and bay leaf and cook until fragrant. Add the meat, water, and vinegar and bring to a simmer. Cover and cook over low heat until the meat is very tender, about 40 minutes.

3 Add the potato and cook, uncovered, until tender, about 15 minutes.

4 Add the lemon juice, season with salt and pepper, and serve.

Tips

I cook the onions in duck fat because I like the flavor, but you can use oil.

I love beef shin, because when it's braised for a long time, the texture becomes gelatin-like and the tender meat almost melts in your mouth.

German Butterball potatoes are a late-season heirloom variety that is often available at farmers' markets. They have the advantage of keeping extremely well. If you can't find them, another type can be substituted, such as Yukon Gold, fingerling, or creamer.

Where I come from, paprika is used so often in home cooking it doesn't have a chance to get stale. But, unless you use paprika all the time, you should buy it fresh for the soup. Cooking with paprika can be tricky. You want to cook it long enough so it loses its raw taste. At the same time, you need to be careful not to burn it. I add some tomato paste, which has water in it, so I can cook the paprika a little longer. Do not confuse Hungarian sweet paprika with smoky Spanish pimenton.

Serve with

This dish is a meal in a bowl. As with all goulash recipes, it's often served with some sort of starch. You really need only a hefty slice of rye bread, but both Fresh Herbed Quark Spätzle (page 162) and Bread Dumplings in a Napkin (page 160) are satisfying accompaniments. At Wallsé, the dish comes with a small bowl of spätzle, which customers add to the thick soup to taste.

Variations

You can play around, adding some cooked shell beans, such as cranberry beans or pale green flageolets. Sauerkraut or shredded cabbage would also be a terrific addition. Or use pork instead of beef.

Make ahead

Goulash soup is even better the next day. The flavors really deepen, and the consistency of the soup improves too. It can be refrigerated for up to 3 days. If the soup becomes too thick, add a little water when reheating.

For a bowl of Goulash Soup, I'd toot my horn any day.

MARINATED HEIRLOOM TOMATO SALAD

"Heirloom" Paradeisersalat

4 SERVINGS

4 or 5 large ripe heirloom tomatoes (about 2 pounds), cut into ¾-inch wedges

1 ½ teaspoons kosher salt

1 teaspoon sugar

1 teaspoon freshly ground pepper

¾ cup finely chopped scallions

¼ cup balsamic vinegar (see Tips)

½ cup extra-virgin olive oil

Small basil sprigs and edible flowers, for garnishing (optional)

Like any good dish, a well-made salad has layers of flavor and texture. The first thing you're looking for is acid, for a taste that's refreshing. At the same time, I like to make salad a little bit sweet, for balance. The sugar, as here, or, sometimes, fruit acts like a bridge between the vinegar and the greens or vegetables and herbs. As soon as heirloom tomatoes hit the market, I round up as many as I can find to make this simple salad with an extra dimension.

1 In a large bowl, combine the tomatoes with the salt, sugar, and pepper. Let stand for 5 minutes.

2 Add the scallions, vinegar, and olive oil and let marinate for 10 minutes.

3 Pour off most of the juice that has accumulated. Arrange the tomatoes on plates, garnish with the basil and flowers, if using, and serve.

Tips

A mix of red, yellow, and green (such as Evergreen or Green Zebra) tomatoes is especially nice here.

Marinating the tomatoes in a blend of salt and sugar makes them super juicy. You want to pour off most of the liquid, but a little makes a delicious broth for dipping chunks of bread.

I like to use white balsamic vinegar in this salad because it's a touch sweeter than the regular red balsamic.

Serve with

Pass a crusty country bread for mopping up the juice. Or serve the salad as a side dish with seafood dishes such as seared scallops or a piece of grilled Arctic char. The salad's juices become the sauce for the fish.

Josef Hoffmann's 1908 silver cruet stand contains olive oil and balsamic vinegar for Marinated Heirloom Tomato Salad. The silver salt and pepper cellar with a long handle reminiscent of rivets, also by Hoffmann, is one of his early designs. Behind the salad is a work by gothic fantasy artist Gerald Brom. Salt and pepper cellar and cruet stand, both First Edition for Neue Galerie Design Shop.

BOSTON LETTUCE SALAD WITH SPICY RADISHES, PUMPKIN SEED OIL, AND LEMON VINAIGRETTE

Kopfsalat mit Radischen, Kürbiskernöl und Zitronenvinaigrette

4 SERVINGS

4 radishes, thinly sliced

½ cup raw pumpkin seeds

¼ cup fresh lemon juice

1 teaspoon Dijon mustard
   Salt and freshly ground pepper

½ cup extra-virgin olive oil

4 small heads Boston lettuce,
   preferably hydroponic (see Tips),
   leaves separated

¼ cup plus 2 tablespoons pumpkin
   seed oil (see Tips)

Simple Boston lettuce is my favorite green for salads. I think the reason this recipe is so popular at my restaurants is that it's uncomplicated and entirely classic. The delicate lettuce is lightly dressed with slightly bitter pumpkin seed oil. Lemon juice and radishes add tang and a little spice, while toasted pumpkin seeds lend crunch.

1 Add the radish slices to a bowl of cold water to crisp.

2 Line a plate with a paper towel. In a dry medium skillet, toast the pumpkin seeds over medium heat, stirring occasionally, until fragrant. Transfer to the paper-towel-lined plate and let cool.

3 In a small bowl, whisk the lemon juice with the mustard. Season with salt and pepper. Gradually whisk in the olive oil.

4 In a large bowl, lightly toss the lettuce with some of the lemon vinaigrette; you may not need all of it. Drain the radishes and pat dry; sprinkle lightly with salt.

5 Stack the lettuce leaves on plates, scattering the radishes between the leaves and around the plates. Sprinkle the pumpkin seeds over the salad, drizzle with the pumpkin seed oil, and serve.

Tips

The Italians have their olive oil, and we Austrians have our pumpkin seed oil. My favorite is Wolf Naturprodukte, which I import, but the brands offered at most specialty food shops are good. The oil comes from the *Ölkurbis* (roughly translated as "oil pumpkin") and is indigenous to Styria, the southeastern part of Austria. The rich, nutty oil turns bitter when heated. But raw, in small doses, it works very nicely in salad dressings and sauces.

There is no need to add oil or butter to the skillet while toasting pumpkin seeds, because their natural oil is released when they are heated.

The advantage of hydroponic lettuce is that it's available at most supermarkets year-round.

Serve with

I enjoy this light salad by itself as an appetizer. Or take away the toasted pumpkin seeds, and serve it as a side dish with a main course like Veal Schnitzel (page 122) or roast chicken.

Make ahead

The pumpkin seeds can be toasted ahead and stored in an airtight container for 1 week.

Dagobert Peche, Box in the shape of a Pumpkin, ca. 1920, Executed by the Wiener Werkstätte, silver. Neue Galerie New York.

MIXED BEAN SALAD WITH TOASTED PISTACHIOS

Gemischter Bohnensalat mit gerösteten Pistazienkernen

Both shell and string beans were common where I grew up, and bean salads were often on the menu. This is one of those simple, traditional dishes that have stuck with me throughout my career. I think it's very important to keep these kinds of salads alive. Also, I love vegetarian salads.

4 SERVINGS

Salt

1 cup fava beans (about 1 pound
    in the shell)

6 ounces haricots verts, cut into
    1 $1/2$-inch pieces

6 ounces wax beans, cut into
    1 $1/2$-inch pieces

1 cup raw shelled pistachios (5 ounces),
    toasted (see Tips), skinned,
    and chopped

1 shallot, finely chopped
    Opal or other basil leaves,
    for garnishing (optional)

Marinade

$1/4$ cup unseasoned rice vinegar

2 tablespoons sherry vinegar

$1/4$ cup water

$1/4$ cup plus 2 tablespoons olive oil

1 tablespoon fresh lemon juice

1 teaspoon salt
    Freshly ground pepper
    Sugar

Dressing

$1/4$ cup plain yogurt

$1/4$ cup sour cream

3 tablespoons pistachio oil or extra-virgin
    olive oil
    Dash of unseasoned rice vinegar
    Squeeze of fresh lemon juice
    Salt and freshly ground pepper
    Cayenne pepper
    Opal or other basil leaves,
    for garnishing (optional)

1 Bring a large saucepan of salted water to a boil. Fill a large bowl with ice water. Add the fava beans to the boiling water, and blanch for 1 minute. Using a slotted spoon, transfer the fava beans to the ice water to cool for 1 to 2 minutes. Lift out with a slotted spoon and peel them. (Keep the water boiling.)

2 Add the haricot verts, wax beans, and peeled fava beans to the boiling water and cook until crisp-tender, 3 to 4 minutes. Drain and add to the ice water to cool quickly, 1 to 2 minutes. Drain well and pat dry.

3 Make the marinade: In a large bowl, whisk the rice and sherry vinegars with the water, olive oil, and lemon juice. Season with the salt, pepper, and sugar and whisk to blend.

4 Make the dressing: In a small bowl, combine the yogurt with the sour cream and pistachio oil. Season with the vinegar, lemon juice, salt, black pepper, and cayenne and whisk to blend.

5 Add the beans to the marinade and toss to coat. Let stand for 10 minutes.

6 Drain the beans and transfer them to a large serving bowl or platter. Sprinkle with the pistachios and shallot. Drizzle the dressing over the top, garnish with the basil, if using, and serve.

Tips

To toast pistachios, heat the oven to 350 degrees. Spread the pistachios in a pie plate and toast until golden and fragrant, 8 to 10 minutes. Let cool, then rub off the skins. To make the salad a little lighter, omit the sour cream in the dressing and increase the yogurt to $1/2$ cup.

Serve with

This salad is usually eaten by itself, but it's so light and crunchy that it goes beautifully with smoked pork ribs. It also makes a nice lunch served with Chilled Smoked Trout Crepes with Horseradish Crème Fraîche (page 58).

Variation

Tailor your beans to the season. For instance, in the fall/winter, try canned chickpeas or thawed frozen shelled soybeans in place of the fresh fava beans, which are typically only available in the spring and summer.

Make ahead

The bean salad can be prepared through Step 4 up to 3 days ahead; refrigerate the beans, marinade, and dressing separately.

RED CABBAGE SALAD WITH APPLES AND TOASTED WALNUTS

Rotkraut mit Äpfeln und Walnüssen

¼ cup plus 2 tablespoons lingonberry
    or cranberry preserves

¼ cup walnut oil

2 tablespoons sherry vinegar

1 very small head red cabbage
    (about 1 pound), quartered, cored,
    and thinly sliced

¼ cup walnut halves, toasted (see Tip)
    and very coarsely chopped
    Salt and freshly ground pepper

½ Granny Smith or Golden Delicious
    apple, cored and sliced lengthwise
    into very thin rounds on a mandoline
    or cut into julienne strips
    Edible flowers and small herb sprigs,
    for garnishing (optional)

Red cabbage is often underrated or overlooked. But sometimes you can take a cheap product and make something beautiful out of it. We usually serve braised red cabbage as a side for hearty dishes like roasted duck, or pheasant, but I really liked the idea of creating a raw cabbage salad. So I took the traditional side dish—cabbage braised in red wine, lingonberries, salt, and spices—and transformed it into a fresh salad of shredded cabbage and toasted walnuts.

This salad especially evokes autumn for me. The cabbage, slicked with dressing, is ruby red and the apples are pale yellow or white-green, depending on the variety. Every ingredient is crunchy. Still, it's the sweet-and-sour lingonberries that make the salad distinctive. They make it play.

1 In a medium bowl, mix the preserves with the walnut oil and vinegar. Add the cabbage and walnuts and toss to coat. Season with salt and pepper and toss again.

2 Mound the salad on plates. Garnish with the apple and, if desired, the flowers and herbs, and serve.

Tip
To toast walnuts, heat the oven to 350 degrees. Spread the walnuts in a pie plate and toast until golden and fragrant, about 8 minutes. Let cool completely.

Serve with
I like this dish as a midafternoon meal with a sour brown bread, like rye, plus a Cheddar or soft blue cheese and a small cold beer.
For a totally indulgent meal, I love this salad with some foie gras, either seared or sliced from a cold terrine.

Variations
Substitute a crisp Bosc or Bartlett pear for the apple.
Diced cooked beets could be added to the cabbage with

a pinch of caraway seeds for a salad to serve with marinated herring.
Sometimes I scatter country bacon on top and then I garnish it for color and freshness with mâche dressed in the tossed cabbage juices. I love the sweet freshness of mâche against the rich saltiness of bacon, all on a bed of marinated cabbage.
If you are allergic to nuts, you can use sunflower oil or avocado oil instead of the walnut oil. Substitute croutons for the nuts, so you have a similar crunchy texture.

Make ahead
Unlike coleslaw, this is a salad that you definitely want to eat right away. Its beauty is in its inherent freshness.

A light Red Cabbage Salad with Apples and Toasted Walnuts in an *Urania* bowl by Trude Petri for KPM, from Neue Galerie Design Shop, rests on a wispy drawing by Martin Kippenberger.

FENNEL AND BLOOD ORANGE SALAD

Fenchelsalat mit Blutorangen

4 SERVINGS

¼ cup very coarsely chopped walnuts

1 teaspoon walnut oil

2 medium fennel bulbs, stalks trimmed,
   fronds reserved, for garnishing
   Salt and freshly ground pepper
   Juice of 1 lemon

1 tablespoon Pernod, Ricard,
   or other anise-flavored liqueur

2 large blood oranges

1 tablespoon paper-thin shallot slices

10 small mint leaves

2 tablespoons extra-virgin olive oil

1 teaspoon grated lime zest

I think of my fennel salad as a sort of Power Vitamin C Pill, because both the blood orange and the fennel are packed with vitamin C. It's definitely one of my more contemporary recipes. I start with the fennel sliced very thin. I can't stop nibbling the fennel as I prepare it—the taste is so fresh, and the licorice quality keeps your appetite going. The fennel, blood orange segments, walnuts, and a dressing made of olive oil with orange juice and lemon are all you need—no vinegar is necessary. A splash of Pernod enhances the fennel, and a touch of mint also helps make the flavor pop.

1 In a dry skillet, toast the walnuts over medium heat until fragrant and lightly browned, 4 to 5 minutes. Remove from the heat and stir in the walnut oil.

2 Slice about ½ inch from the bottom of the fennel bulb and discard. Starting with the flat bottom side, slice the fennel very fine on a mandoline. Transfer to a bowl. Season with salt and pepper and add the lemon juice and Pernod.

3 Using a sharp knife, peel the oranges, re-moving all the white pith. Holding the fruit over the bowl containing the fennel, cut be-tween the membranes to release the sec-tions letting them drop into the bowl; discard the seeds. Squeeze the juice from the mem-branes into the bowl.

4 Add the shallots, mint, olive oil, and wal-nuts, and toss gently.

5 Mound the salad on a platter or plates. Sprinkle with the lime zest, garnish with the reserved fennel fronds, and serve.

Tip

When slicing the fennel, it is best to use a mandoline. You get much thinner slices than by using a knife, closer to shavings than slices. Fennel can be a pretty intense flavor, but this way you keep it light and fresh.

Serve with

I love scallops and blood oranges together. I often serve this salad as a starter or a side with grilled or pan-seared scallops. I mound the salad on a plate and top it with the scallops. A lot of other fish could work with this as well; for instance, salmon or sea bass fillets grilled with the skin, sautéed skate, or lightly breaded soft-shell crabs. You could turn this salad into a light meal by serving it with smoked mackerel or slices of smoked salmon and brown bread.

Variations

If blood oranges are not available, substitute regular or-anges, clementines, or tangerines.

Make ahead

This dish is really best when eaten right away, because otherwise it loses its crunch.

CELERY ROOT AND APPLE SALAD

Apfel-Selleriesalat

6 SERVINGS

1 large celery root (about 2 pounds),
    thickly peeled and cut into julienne
    strips
    Juice of 1 lemon

1 *teaspoon sugar*
    Salt

2 *Granny Smith apples, peeled, cored,*
    and cut into julienne strips

⅓ *cup cider vinegar*

¼ *cup plus 2 tablespoons grapeseed*
    or sunflower oil

10 *parsley leaves*

I don't like a meal without salad. When I was growing up, we had a root cellar with a sandy floor where we kept celery and apples all winter, and one of my favorite salads begins with celery root and apples, cut into julienne strips and dressed with a good cider vinegar. The combination may go back to my childhood, but the recipe is my creation. It reminds me of Waldorf salad, but it's a lot lighter (no mayonnaise) and has a really great crunch. A few parsley leaves, which heighten the celery flavor, are all the garnish it needs.

1 In a medium saucepan, cover the celery root with water. Add the lemon juice and sugar and season with salt. Bring to a simmer and cook until the celery is crisp-tender, about 3 minutes. Let cool to room temperature in the cooking liquid, about 20 minutes. Drain and pat dry.

2 Transfer the celery root to a large bowl. Add the apples, vinegar, and oil and toss to coat. Taste for seasoning, and add salt if needed. Garnish with the parsley, and serve.

Tip

Celery root is common in Austrian dishes, but it is almost always served cooked. While I love it that way, I really, really enjoy the crunch of a piece of raw celery root. With a little bit of sea salt sprinkled on top, it's just awesome.

Serve with

I like the way the whiteness of this celery root salad contrasts with slices of dark meat, like Braised Venison Shoulder with Red Wine and Root Vegetables (page 140), or with game birds. But it's also good with grilled duck breasts, or chicken.

Variations

For a more Waldorf-like salad, add ½ cup of mayonnaise along with the oil in Step 2. Gently toss other fruit, such as halved, seedless grapes or sliced pears, into the mixture.

Make ahead

This salad should be eaten right away so it doesn't lose its crisp texture and fresh flavor.

MAIN DISHES

LAKE PERCH WITH MELTED LEEKS, TOMATOES, CAPERS, AND KALAMATA OLIVES

Zander mit geschmolzenem Porree, Paradeiser, Kapern und Kalamata Oliven

4 SERVINGS

5 tablespoons unsalted butter

8 large leeks, white and light green parts
only, cut into julienne strips

¼ cup vegetable stock
Salt and freshly ground pepper

2 shallots, finely chopped

½ cup dry white wine

1 cup kalamata olives, pitted and halved
lengthwise

¼ cup heavy cream

2 tablespoons canola oil

4 lake perch fillets with skin
(about 6 ounces each)

1 tablespoon fresh lemon juice

¾ cup grape tomatoes, halved lengthwise

2 tablespoons drained capers

2 tablespoons chopped parsley
Marjoram, lemon thyme, or opal basil
sprigs, for garnishing (optional)

This is one of my Blaue Gans creations, pan-roasted freshwater fish with Mediterranean flavors. The buttery richness of softened leeks gets a jolt from the acidity of the white wine and kalamata olives—which turn the sauce a stunning purple. The crispy skin on the perch fillets gives the dish some crunch.

1 Heat the oven to 375 degrees. In a large saucepan, melt 2 tablespoons of the butter over medium heat. Add the leeks and cook, stirring, until coated with the butter. Add the stock and season with salt and pepper. Reduce the heat to low, cover, and cook for 10 minutes.

2 Remove the cover and cook until all the moisture has evaporated and the leeks are very soft, about 5 minutes. Take care not to color the leeks; if they start to brown, reduce the heat.

3 In a small saucepan, melt 1 tablespoon of the butter over high heat. Add half the shallots and cook until translucent, about 2 minutes. Add the wine and bring to a boil. Reduce to a simmer, add ¼ cup of the olives, and cook, stirring frequently, until the liquid reduces by half, about 5 minutes.

4 Stir in the cream and bring to a boil. Reduce to a simmer and cook until the liquid reduces by half, about 5 minutes. Remove the pan from the heat. Using an immersion blender or a regular blender, puree the sauce until smooth.

5 In a large ovenproof skillet, heat the oil over high heat until shimmering. Add the fish fillets, skin side down, and cook, pressing down with a spatula from time to time so that the skin gets brown and crisp, for 3 to 4 minutes. Transfer the skillet to the oven and bake until the fish is just opaque throughout, 3 to 4 minutes.

6 Remove the skillet from the oven and set it over medium-high heat. Add the remaining shallots, the remaining 2 tablespoons of butter, and the lemon juice and when the butter melts, using a large spoon, quickly baste the fillets for a minute. Using a fish slice or a spatula, transfer the fish, skin side up, to a warmed platter. Cover loosely with foil and keep warm.

7 Add the remaining ¾ cup of olives, the tomatoes, and capers to the skillet and cook over medium-high heat until heated through, about 3 minutes. Add the parsley and stir briefly, then remove from the heat.

8 Mound the leeks on warmed plates. Set a fish fillet, skin side up, on each plate, and spoon some of the olive-tomato mixture on top. Drizzle the sauce around the plates, garnish with the marjoram, if desired, and serve.

Tip
Kalamata olives pack a lot of flavor, so the sauce here is pretty intense. A little on each plate will suffice.

Serve with
I like to serve this with steamed rice, potato puree, or Fresh Herbed Quark Spätzle (page 162).

Variation
I like to use perch because of its firm consistency and mild flavor, but striped bass can be substituted.

Make ahead
The leeks can be prepared ahead and refrigerated for up to 1 day.

BROOK TROUT WITH CAULIFLOWER, RAISINS, AND ALMONDS

Forelle mit gebratenem Karfiol, Rosinen und Mandeln

I grew up by the Danube, and freshwater fish, including trout, carp, and perch, was often on the menu. At the same time, we were served bland, boiled cauliflower—and I didn't really care for it. I wanted to find a way to make these ingredients work together in a dish, so I decided to toast some almonds, sauté the cauliflower until golden and crispy, and mix them both with a syrupy golden raisin reduction as an accompaniment to sautéed trout. The result is a bit crunchy and a bit sweet, with a touch of acidity. And it's simple to prepare.

4 SERVINGS

2 ounces sliced almonds (about ⅔ cup)
1 cup golden raisins
2 cups water
1 cup red wine vinegar
¼ cup plus 2 tablespoons canola oil
1 cauliflower (about 2 pounds), cut into
    small florets
    Salt and freshly ground pepper
2 tablespoons unsalted butter
1 cup sugar
4 brook trout fillets with skin
    (about 6 ounces each)
2 tablespoons all-purpose flour
    Baby sprouts, for garnishing (optional)

1 Heat the oven to 375 degrees. Spread the almonds in a pie plate and toast in the oven until lightly browned and fragrant, about 5 minutes. Let cool.

2 In a medium saucepan, combine the raisins with the water, vinegar, and sugar and cook over medium-high heat until the raisins are plump and the liquid is syrupy, 25 to 30 minutes. Remove from the heat.

3 In a large skillet, heat ¼ cup of the oil until shimmering. Add the cauliflower, season with salt and pepper, and cook over medium-high heat, stirring occasionally, until lightly browned and crisp-tender, about 5 minutes. Stir in the butter and toasted almonds.

4 Season the trout fillets with salt and pepper. Lightly dust with the flour, patting off the excess. In a large skillet, heat the remaining 2 tablespoons of oil until shimmering. Add the fish, skin side down, and cook over high heat until lightly browned, about 2 minutes. Turn the fish, reduce the heat to medium, and cook until the flesh is opaque through, about 3 minutes.

5 Meanwhile, add the raisins to the cauliflower, leaving the syrup in the pan, and warm over medium-high heat for 3 to 4 minutes.

6 Set the fillets, skin side up, on warmed plates. Spoon the cauliflower-raisin mixture around the fish and drizzle the raisin syrup over the top. Garnish with the sprouts, if desired, and serve.

Tip
Make sure the cauliflower is just golden, because it can burn quickly. If it begins to color before it's sufficiently tender, reduce the heat and add another tablespoon of butter.

Serve with
I like the trout with a side of braised greens or Creamed Spinach (page 153)

Variation
The sautéed cauliflower with toasted almonds is also terrific on its own as a side dish. I serve it alongside grilled swordfish or halibut or as part of a summer antipasto buffet.

Make ahead
The raisins and cauliflower can be prepared ahead and refrigerated, separately, for up to 3 days.

Gustav Klimt, *The Park of Schloss Kammer*, ca. 1910, oil on canvas. Private Collection, Courtesy Neue Galerie New York.

LAKE PERCH WITH JULIENNE VEGETABLES AND RIESLING BUTTER SAUCE

Zander "Esterhazy" mit Rieslingsauce

---

4 SERVINGS

4 lake perch fillets with skin
    (about 6 ounces each)
    Salt and freshly ground pepper
2 tablespoons all-purpose flour
$1/4$ cup canola oil
1 garlic clove, crushed
1 thyme sprig
6 tablespoons unsalted butter,
    4 tablespoons diced and chilled
1 medium carrot, cut into julienne strips
1 large leek, white and light green parts
    only, cut into julienne strips
$1/2$ medium celery root, thickly peeled and
    cut into julienne strips
1 cup dry Riesling
1 tablespoon chopped parsley
$1/4$ cup freshly grated horseradish

An Esterhazy garnish—julienned carrot, leek, and celery root—usually accompanies steaks or sautéed beef dishes. My variation uses the classic components, but I serve them alongside crispy lake perch fillets and drizzle the fish with a luscious Riesling butter sauce.

1 Heat the oven to 300 degrees. Pat the fish dry and season generously with salt and pepper. Lightly dust the skin side of the fillets with the flour, patting off the excess. In a large ovenproof skillet, heat the oil over high heat until shimmering. Add the fish, skin side down, and cook until the bottom is golden brown, 1 to 2 minutes.

2 Add the garlic and thyme, then transfer the skillet to the oven and bake until the fish is opaque throughout, 6 to 8 minutes. Remove the skillet from the oven and transfer the fish, skin side up, to a warmed platter. Cover loosely with foil and keep warm.

3 In the same skillet, melt 2 tablespoons of the butter (not the diced butter) over medium-high heat. Add the carrot, leek, and celery root and cook, stirring occasionally, until lightly browned, about 3 minutes. Season with salt. Add the wine and bring to a simmer, scraping up any browned bits stuck to the bottom. Remove the skillet from the heat and add the diced butter, swirling to coat the vegetables with the sauce. Stir in the parsley.

4 Using a slotted spoon, spread the vegetables on warmed plates, leaving the sauce in the pan. Set a fillet, skin side up, on each plate, and generously spoon the butter sauce over the top. Garnish with the horseradish, and serve.

Tips

Dusting the fish skin before sautéing it ensures that it is dry (it can hold a lot of moisture), so it won't splatter when added to the hot oil.

When removing the skillet from the oven and making the butter sauce, keep in mind that the handle will be very hot.

Serve with

I love this fish with something plain—steamed rice or a potato puree.

Variation

The delicious rich sauce is great with other types of fish or seafood. Try sautéed striped bass, skate, or sea scallops.

TUNA WITH WHITE ASPARAGUS, CITRUS MARINADE, AND PICKLED RAMPS

Thunfisch mit Spargel, Zitrusfrüchten und eingelegtem Bärlauch

2 tablespoons unsalted butter
  Salt
1 tablespoon sugar
4 pounds white asparagus,
    peeled and trimmed (see All About
    White Asparagus, page 77)
1 pound skinless sushi-grade tuna steaks
  Freshly ground pepper
3 tablespoons coriander seeds
1 cup dry white wine
½ cup extra-virgin olive oil
½ cup low-sodium soy sauce
½ cup fresh lemon juice
1 garlic clove, finely chopped
3 oranges, cut into segments (see Tips)
3 lemons, cut into segments (see Tips)
3 limes, cut into segments (see Tips)

Pickled Ramps

2 ½ cups white balsamic vinegar
1 tablespoon mustard seeds
2 ½ teaspoons freshly ground white pepper
5 bay leaves
1 ½ tablespoons sugar
4 cups water
½ pound ramps (see Tips, page 161)

Sweet and tart, citrus marinade is delicious with raw sushi-grade tuna. What gives the dish its Austrian accent are the white asparagus and the ramps. Ramps are available only in early spring, so I serve them as much as possible when I can get them—and extend the season by pickling them, as I do here.

1 Make the pickled ramps: In a medium saucepan, combine the vinegar with the mustard seeds, pepper, bay leaves, sugar, and water and bring to a boil over high heat. Remove the pan from the heat and pour the pickling mixture into a 2-quart jar. Add the ramps, close the jar, and refrigerate overnight.

2 The next day, in a large pot, melt the butter with 2 tablespoons of salt and the sugar over high heat. Add 3 cups of water and bring to a boil. Add the asparagus and cook until crisp-tender, 8 to 10 minutes. Drain and let cool. If needed, season with salt.

3 Slice the tuna crosswise about ½ inch thick. Lay each slice between 2 sheets of plastic wrap and flatten with a rolling pin or the bottom of a heavy pan. Season lightly with salt and pepper.

4 In a medium saucepan, combine the coriander seeds and wine and boil over medium heat until the seeds have softened and the wine has nearly evaporated, about 15 minutes. Remove the pan from the heat and stir in the olive oil, soy sauce, lemon juice, garlic, and orange, lemon, and lime segments.

5 Line up the asparagus on a chilled platter or plates. Arrange the tuna slices, slightly overlapping, on top. Drizzle with the citrus marinade and top with the pickled ramps.

Tips

Pickling is a common way of preserving vegetables in Austria, especially in the countryside. My mother and grandmother used to pickle a wide variety of vegetables and then serve them throughout the winter.

The white and light green parts of scallions can be used instead of the ramps.

To cut citrus fruit into segments, use a sharp knife to peel the fruit, removing all the white pith. Cut between the membranes to release the sections. Discard the seeds. If you have any citrus marinade left over, pass it at the table. Or cover and refrigerate to use later as a sauce for grilled fish.

Serve with

For an exquisite spring dinner, serve the Spring Pea Soup with Pineapple Mint (page 72) as a first course.

Variations

Any type of sushi-grade fish is delicious in this dish. Try it with salmon or large sea scallops, very thinly sliced. The pickled ramps can also be served as a pungent condiment with hearty meat dishes, such as Beef Goulash (page 134) or Boiled Beef Shoulder with Vegetables and Fresh Horseradish (page 140). Or add them to a salad of lightly cooked Swiss chard, fava beans, and haricot verts.

Make ahead

The pickled ramps need to marinate overnight, so plan accordingly. They can be refrigerated for up to 2 months; their taste will intensify.

MONKFISH WITH CHANTERELLES AND JERUSALEM ARTICHOKES

Seeteufel mit Eierschwammerln und Topinambur

You don't often see monkfish on menus, but I think it's a great fish to cook—so similar in texture and flavor to lobster, yet about half the price. In this recipe, I panfry the fish, then baste it in a buttery lemon-thyme sauce and serve it with an earthy ragout of Jerusalem artichokes and chanterelles.

4 SERVINGS

¼ cup canola oil

¾ pound Jerusalem artichokes, sliced
⅛ inch thick on a mandoline

6 tablespoons unsalted butter

6 ounces chanterelle mushrooms,
halved lengthwise if large

3 tablespoons fresh lemon juice
Salt and freshly ground white pepper

1 ½ pounds skinless monkfish fillets,
cut into 2-inch pieces

4 thyme sprigs

1 shallot, minced
Mixed herbs, such as small marjoram
sprigs, snipped chives, and sage
leaves, for garnishing (optional)

1 In a large skillet, heat 2 tablespoons of the oil until smoking. Add the Jerusalem artichokes and cook over medium-high heat until browned, 3 to 4 minutes. Add 2 tablespoons of the butter and the chanterelles and cook, stirring constantly, until the water they release has evaporated and the mixture is lightly browned, about 5 minutes. Add 1 tablespoon of the lemon juice and season with salt and pepper.

2 Set 2 large skillets over high heat. Season the monkfish with salt and pepper. In each skillet, heat 1 tablespoon of the oil until shim-mering. Add half the fish to each pan and cook over medium-high heat until lightly browned, 3 to 4 minutes per side. Add half the thyme and shallots, 1 tablespoon of the lemon juice, and 2 tablespoons of the butter to each skillet. Cook the fish, basting with the sauce, over medium heat until opaque throughout, 2 to 3 minutes. Discard the thyme.

3 Transfer the fish to warmed plates and spoon the vegetable ragout around it. Drizzle the pan sauce over the fish, garnish with the mixed herbs, if desired, and serve.

Tips

Jerusalem artichokes, also called sunchokes, are knobby little tubers that resemble fresh ginger but have a potato-like texture and a sweet, nutty taste.

I season the fish with white pepper because it has a sharper flavor than black, and it also looks better on white or light foods.

Serve with

Because I can never have enough vegetables, I make Roasted Summer Vegetables with Herbs (page 148) or sautéed brussels sprouts to go with this fish.

Variations

I like to serve monkfish tail a lot of different ways, starting with simply changing the vegetables here, according to what's in season. In the warm weather, for instance, I re-place the Jerusalem artichokes and mushrooms with a light ratatouille of cherry tomatoes, zucchini, and eggplant. If you find a whole monkfish that is on the smaller side (1 ½ to 2 pounds), it can be great to roast. Have your fishmonger remove the skin, and any really dark parts and membranes, but leave in the bone. In a large oven-proof skillet, heat ¼ cup of canola oil until smoking. Season the fish with salt and pepper and sear until nicely browned, about 2 minutes per side. Transfer the skillet to a 350-degree oven and cook until the fish is opaque throughout, 8 to 10 minutes.

Make ahead

The Jerusalem artichoke and chanterelle ragout can be refrigerated for up to 3 days. Reheat on the stovetop with a little butter.

HALIBUT WITH CUCUMBER-DILL SAUCE AND CHANTERELLES

Heilbutt mit Gartengurken, Dill und Eierschwammerln

My customers won't let me take this off the menu. The sauce, with cucumber juice and dill oil, tastes rich even though there's no butter. It's an incredibly clean, fresh, and healthy recipe. Try to find East Coast halibut.

4 SERVINGS

- 2 large cucumbers, peeled
- ½ teaspoon sugar
- Salt
- 2 onions, coarsely chopped
- 1 cup canola oil
- ¾ cup dill fronds, plus more for garnishing
- 1 cup extra-virgin olive oil
- 1 tablespoon sunflower oil
- ½ pound chanterelle mushrooms, halved lengthwise if large
- 1 tablespoon finely chopped shallots
- 1 tablespoon finely chopped thyme
- Freshly ground pepper
- 4 skinless halibut fillets (about 6 ounces each)
- About 3 tablespoons fresh lemon juice
- Edible flowers, for garnishing (optional)

1 Cut 1 of the cucumbers lengthwise in half. Using a small spoon, scrape out the seeds and add to a medium bowl. Cut the cucumber into ¼-inch dice.

2 Coarsely chop the second cucumber and add it to the seeds. Sprinkle with the sugar and ½ teaspoon of salt and mix gently. Let stand for 10 minutes.

3 In the blender, puree the chopped cucumber mixture until smooth. Line a fine sieve with cheesecloth and set it over a bowl. Add the cucumber puree, transfer it to the refrigerator, and let drip for 2 hours.

4 Heat the oven to 375 degrees. In a shallow baking dish, stir the onions with the canola oil. Spread evenly over the bottom and cover with foil. Bake until the onions are soft and translucent, about 30 minutes. Remove from the oven and let cool slightly.

5 Transfer the onions to the blender, and puree, then scrape into a bowl.

6 Fill a medium bowl with ice water. In the blender, puree the dill with the olive oil at high speed until smooth. Scrape the dill oil into a small bowl, set in the ice water, and refrigerate.

7 In a large sauté pan, warm the sunflower oil over high heat. Add the mushrooms and cook, stirring frequently, until the water they release has evaporated, 3 to 4 minutes. Add the shallots and thyme, season with salt and pepper, and cook until the shallots are lightly browned, 1 to 2 minutes.

8 Bring 4 cups of water to a simmer in the bottom of a steamer. Season the halibut with salt and pepper and arrange on the steaming rack. Set the rack over the simmering water, cover, and steam just until the fish is opaque throughout, 4 to 5 minutes. Transfer the halibut to a warmed platter and drizzle with some of the lemon juice.

9 Meanwhile, in a small saucepan, combine the diced cucumbers, 1 ½ cups of the drained cucumber water, and 1 ½ cups of the onion puree. Season with salt and pepper and bring to a simmer, then remove the pan from the heat. Whisk in ¼ cup of the dill oil and season with lemon juice, salt, and pepper. Briefly reheat the mushrooms.

10 Spread the cucumber sauce on warmed plates. Set a fillet on each plate and spoon the mushrooms on top. Garnish with dill fronds and, if desired, flowers, and serve.

Tips

Chilling the dill oil and leaving it in the ice water, refrigerated, until ready to use ensures that it keeps its vibrant green color.

Any leftover dill oil can be used to make dill vinaigrette.

Serve with

I like to serve this dish with a side of Celery Root Puree (page 152) or creamy potato puree.

Variations

Honshimeji and hen-of-the-woods also work well.

To make basil oil, substitute basil leaves for the dill in Step 6.

Make ahead

The onion puree and dill oil can be refrigerated, separately, overnight. Store the oil in a tightly sealed dark container covered with foil, so the oil keeps its bright green color. The dill oil can also be frozen in an ice cube tray and used as needed.

LOBSTER WITH CHERRIES, FAVA BEANS, AND BÉARNAISE SAUCE

Hummer mit Kirschen, Saubohnen und Sauce Béarnaise

4 ENTRÉE OR 8 APPETIZER SERVINGS

3 pounds fava beans in the pod,
    shelled (about 2 ¹/₂ cups)

2 tablespoons extra-virgin olive oil

1 tablespoon minced shallots

2 tablespoons fresh lemon juice
    Salt and freshly ground pepper

4 live lobsters (about 1 ¹/₄ pounds each)

¹/₂ cup sugar

2 cups ruby port

1 cup dry red wine

2 pounds Bing cherries, pitted

1 vanilla bean, split, seeds scraped out and
    reserved for another use (see Tips)

2 tablespoons unsalted butter
    Sage leaves and edible flowers,
    for garnishing (optional)

Béarnaise sauce

1 tablespoon minced shallots

¹/₂ cup dry white wine

2 tablespoons Champagne vinegar

¹/₂ teaspoon cracked black peppercorns

2 thyme sprigs

¹/₂ pound (2 sticks) unsalted butter, diced

3 large egg yolks
    Salt and freshly ground white pepper
    Juice of ¹/₂ lemon

1 tablespoon chopped tarragon

Josef Hoffmann's avant-garde 1906–1907 *Rundes Modell* spoon and fork seem as modern as my Lobster with Cherries, Fava Beans, and Béarnaise Sauce. Cutlery from Neue Galerie Design Shop.

Like a beautiful Tom Waits song, this is a dish you just can't get enough of. I came up with the recipe almost by accident. We were making another lobster dish and got in a crate of gorgeous fresh cherries for a chocolate dessert. I experimented, adding the cherries to a port-red wine reduction, and realized that that the two paired great together.

The most important part of this dish, however, is the béarnaise sauce. It's one of those classic sauces you can never underestimate: it's buttery and rich and ties all the elements together. Have no doubt that this recipe is worth the extra time in the kitchen. It's a showstopper, and you won't regret the effort, not for one bite.

1 Bring a large saucepan of water to a boil. Fill a large bowl with ice water. Add the fava beans to the boiling water and blanch for 1 minute; drain. Transfer to the ice water to cool as quickly as possible, 1 to 2 minutes. Drain and peel them.

2 In a large saucepan, warm the olive oil over medium-high heat. Add the shallots and cook for 1 minute. Add the favas and cook over medium heat, stirring occasionally, until the shallots are slightly golden and the favas are just warmed but still have a bite to them, about 5 minutes. Remove the pan from the heat, add the lemon juice, and season with salt and pepper.

3 Bring a large stockpot of water to a boil. Fill a very large bowl or pot with ice water. Add the lobsters to the stock pot, headfirst, and cook until bright red, about 5 minutes. Using tongs, transfer them to the ice water. Keep the water boiling.

4 When the lobsters are cool enough to handle, twist the claws off the bodies. Return the claws to the boiling water and cook for 3 minutes, then transfer them to the ice water.

5 Twist off the lobster tails. Discard the lobster bodies. Using scissors, slit the tail shells down the center, both top and bottom, and remove the meat; cut lengthwise in half.

Discard the dark intestinal veins. Crack the claws and knuckles and remove the meat.

6 In a large sauté pan, cook the sugar over high heat, swirling the pan, until it caramelizes, 2 to 3 minutes. Remove the pan from the heat and carefully add the port and red wine. Return to the heat and bring to a boil, stirring to dissolve the hardened caramel. Cook over medium-high heat until reduced by half, about 10 minutes. Add the cherries and vanilla bean and cook, stirring constantly, until the sauce is reduced and syrupy, about 5 minutes. Remove the vanilla bean, rinse, and reserve for another use, if desired. Remove the pan from the heat and let cool, then season with salt and pepper.

7 Make the béarnaise sauce: In a small saucepan, combine the shallots with the white wine, Champagne vinegar, cracked peppercorns, and thyme and bring to a boil over high heat. Cook until the liquid is reduced to 2 tablespoons, about 10 minutes. Strain through a fine sieve and reserve.

8 Bring a large saucepan of water to a boil. Set a large bowl over, but not touching, the boiling water and add the butter. Whisk until the butter melts but is still creamy, then remove the bowl from the heat.

Continues on page 108

MAIN DISHES

Continued from page 106 **LOBSTER WITH CHERRIES, FAVA BEANS, AND BÉARNAISE SAUCE**

9 In another large bowl, combine the egg yolks and shallot reduction. Set over the boiling water and whisk constantly until the mixture turns pale yellow and a thick ribbon falls from the whisk. Take care not to let the mixture get too hot, or the egg yolks will curdle. Remove the bowl from the heat and slowly drizzle in the warm butter, whisking constantly. Season with salt, white pepper, the lemon juice, and tarragon. Keep warm.

10 In a large saucepan, melt the 2 tablespoons of butter over medium-high heat. Add the lobster meat and warm through, about 3 minutes. Transfer the lobster to a warmed platter.

11 Mound the favas in warmed soup plates, reserving a few for garnish. Reheat the cherry mixture briefly and spoon over the favas. Set the lobster meat on top. Spoon the béarnaise sauce over the lobster. Garnish with the reserved favas and, if using, the sage and flowers, and serve.

Tips

To remove the claw and knuckle meat easily from the shells, first separate the claws and knuckles by twisting them in opposite directions. Using the back of a heavy knife, pound the claw shell in a circular pattern so it cracks all over, and pop out the meat in one piece.

Take care when caramelizing the sugar in Step 6. Caramel is superhot and can splatter when you add cool liquids, like the port and red wine. Also, it can go from deep amber to black and burned in an instant, especially if you're cooking it over high heat.

The reserved vanilla seeds can be used in the same way as you'd use vanilla extract—to flavor whipped cream, custard, pastry cream, or syrup for poaching pears or peaches. The used vanilla bean can be rinsed, dried, and added to the sugar jar to make vanilla sugar.

Serve with

A light salad is a nice starter for this. Try the Fennel and Blood Orange Salad (page 92).

For a side dish, cook fresh green or white asparagus.

Variations

In place of lobster, feel free to substitute monkfish fillet or shrimp—shell-on shrimp tastes the best.

If the dish seems too rich as an entrée, scale back the ingredients and serve it as an appetizer instead.

Make ahead

The cherry mixture can be refrigerated for up to 1 day.

COD STRUDEL WITH SAUERKRAUT IN RIESLING SAUCE

Kabeljau Strudel mit Sauerkraut und Rieslingsauce

4 SERVINGS

1 tablespoon duck fat or unsalted butter

1 medium onion, finely chopped

10 ounces sauerkraut, drained and squeezed dry

One 2-inch-square slab bacon

2 bay leaves, 12 black peppercorns, and 6 juniper berries, all tied in a cheesecloth bundle

½ cup chicken stock

1 ¼ pounds skinless cod fillet, cut into 4 equal portions (see Tip)

Salt and freshly ground white pepper

Leaves from 4 tarragon sprigs

8 chervil sprigs or 16 opal basil leaves

12 frozen phyllo sheets, thawed

6 tablespoons clarified unsalted butter (see Strudel Secrets, page 175)

½ medium russet (baking) potato, peeled and shredded on a box grater

1 cup dry Riesling

⅓ cup dry vermouth

Juice of ½ lemon

½ cup heavy cream

I created this contemporary take on a classic strudel recipe because I really wanted to have a fish strudel on the menu and I wanted another way to prepare cod. This delicate, rich fish can be tricky, though, because if you overcook it, its silky texture can become stringy. Baking it inside strudel dough keeps it moist.

I serve the strudel on a bed of sauerkraut with a Riesling sauce. I like sauerkraut to be a little creamy, so I make the sauce with shredded potato. I prefer using potato as a thickener to flour; the result seems lighter and not so starchy. So you have moist fish, crisp strudel, a sauce that is a bit creamy, and the sauerkraut, which is a little sharp, in contrast to the richness of the rest of the ingredients. It keeps the dish in balance. The lightness of the dish may come as a surprise.

1 In a medium saucepan, melt the fat. Add the onion and cook over medium heat until lightly browned, 5 to 7 minutes. Add the sauerkraut, bacon, spice bundle, and stock and bring to a simmer, then cover and cook over very low heat for 45 minutes.

2 Meanwhile, season the cod with salt and pepper. Pat the tarragon and chervil onto both sides of the fish.

3 Line a large baking sheet with parchment paper. Cut the phyllo sheets crosswise in half to make 24. Stack them and cover with a damp cloth. For each strudel, spread 1 phyllo sheet on the work surface. Brush it lightly with clarified butter. Top with 5 more sheets, brushing each with butter.

4 Set a portion of cod at one end of the phyllo stack, leaving about ½ inch on the bottom and 1 inch on each side, and roll up tightly, tucking in the ends. Brush the strudel with clarified butter and transfer to the prepared baking sheet, seam side down.

5 Heat the oven to 450 degrees. After the sauerkraut has cooked for 45 minutes; stir it and add the potato, Riesling, and vermouth. Simmer, uncovered, for 10 minutes. Add the lemon juice and simmer for a few minutes longer, then stir in the cream. Bring to a simmer, then remove from the heat and taste for seasoning. Keep warm.

6 Bake the strudels in the center of the oven until golden brown, 12 to 15 minutes. Remove from the oven and let the strudels rest on the baking sheet for 2 to 3 minutes.

7 Meanwhile, using a slotted spoon, lift the sauerkraut out of the pan, draining it well and letting the sauce drip back into the pan, and mound in warmed soup plates. Cut each strudel in half and set on top of the sauerkraut.

8 Bring the sauce to a simmer and strain into a blender. Process briefly at high speed until frothy. Pour the sauce around the sauerkraut in each plate, and serve.

Tip

The pieces of cod should measure about 2 by 5 inches and 1 ½ inches thick. If the fillet is flatter and the pieces are larger, cut them in half and stack two of them for each portion.

Serve with

Any kind of sauerkraut or tangy braised cabbage side goes well, as you want acid to balance the rich and flavorful fish.

Variation

The cod can be replaced with another flaky, rich fish, like salmon. Or consider halibut.

Make ahead

Once the sauerkraut and sauce have been mixed together in Step 5, they can be set aside and then reheated. The assembled strudels can be refrigerated for up to 5 hours before baking.

CHRISTMAS GOOSE

Weihnachtsgans

6 SERVINGS

1 goose (10 to 12 pounds), giblets,
     neck, and wing tips reserved
3 carrots, cut into 1-inch dice
6 celery ribs, cut into 1-inch dice
3 onions, 1 quartered,
     2 cut into 1-inch dice
   Salt and freshly ground pepper
1 apple, quartered
1 orange, quartered (with skin)
12 thyme sprigs

Sauce

3 tablespoons canola oil
   Reserved giblets, neck, and wing tips
     from the goose
1 cup chopped onions
½ cup chopped carrots
½ cup chopped celery
1 garlic clove, crushed
2 tablespoons tomato paste
1 cup dry red wine
½ cup ice cubes
2 thyme sprigs
2 rosemary sprigs

Christmas Goose and all the fixings stand against
a background of Albert Oehlen's 1987 *Object (Dinge)*.

Everybody likes a roast turkey for the holidays, and in Austria, we also enjoy a fat goose. Usually we serve it roasted on Christmas Day and also on November 11th, St. Martin's Day, which is why it's sometimes called *Martini Gans*. It really is a festive dish to serve friends and family.

1 Using paper towels, pat the goose dry inside and out. Set it in a roasting pan and refrigerate, uncovered, overnight.

2 The next day, remove the goose from the refrigerator and bring to room temperature, about 1 hour. If the bird is still moist, pat it dry inside and out with paper towels.

3 Heat the oven to 350 degrees. In a large roasting pan, scatter the carrots, celery, and onions.

4 Generously season the inside of the goose with salt and pepper and stuff it with the apple, orange, quartered onion, and thyme. Prick the skin of the goose all over. Season the outside of the bird with salt and pepper. Truss it (see Tips) and set it directly on top of the vegetables. Add ½ inch of hot water to the pan.

5 Transfer the roasting pan to the oven and roast the goose until an instant-read thermometer inserted in the thigh reads 165 to 180 degrees and the juices run clear, 2 ½ to 3 hours. Remove the fat from the pan with a bulb baster as necessary, and reserve the fat for the braised cabbage, if making it. If the skin is not crisp, increase the oven temperature to 375 degrees and roast for 10 minutes more. Transfer the goose to a cutting board, cover loosely with foil, and let rest for 30 minutes.

6 Meanwhile, make the sauce: In a large casserole, heat the oil until smoking. Add the giblets, neck, and wing tips and cook over medium-high heat, stirring occasionally, until browned all over, 8 to 10 minutes. Using a slotted spoon, transfer the giblets, neck, and wing tips to a bowl. Pour off most of the fat in the pot.

7 Add the onions, carrots, celery, and garlic to the pot and cook, stirring frequently, until browned, about 8 minutes. Stir in the tomato paste. Add the wine and ice cubes and cook, scraping up the browned bits stuck to the bottom, until almost all the liquid has evaporated, about 5 minutes. Return the giblets, neck, and wing tips to the pot and add enough water to cover the ingredients by 2 inches. Add the thyme and rosemary and bring to a boil, then reduce the heat to medium-low and cook for 1 hour.

8 Strain the stock into a large bowl; discard the solids. Return the stock to the pot and boil over high heat until it's flavorful and coats the back of a spoon, about 10 minutes.

9 Discard the apple, orange, onion, and thyme in the goose's cavity. Carve the goose and serve with the sauce.

Tips

Goose is typically very fatty; air-drying it and pricking the skin before roasting helps release the fat and ensures delicious golden skin. You can use the trussing needle to poke the skin, or a paring knife or skewer.
To truss the goose, thread a trussing needle with kitchen string. Turn the goose breast side down on a work surface. Push the needle through 1 wing, the shoulders, and the skin of the neck, and then through the other wing. Turn the goose over and push the needle though 1 leg, the body, and the other leg. Pull the string tight and tie the ends over the wings into a tight knot.

Serve with

Braised Red Cabbage (page 151) and Baked Marzipan-Stuffed Apples (page 149) are the perfect accompaniments. Other traditional side dishes include roasted chestnuts or apples, Bread Dumplings in a Napkin (page 160), and Celery Root Puree (page 152).

Make ahead

The goose is refrigerated overnight before roasting to dry it slightly and produce crisp skin when roasted, so plan accordingly.

SILVERWARE AND CUTLERY

One of the first designs executed by architect Josef Hoffmann for the Wiener Werkstätte after its founding in 1903 was a radical new vision for cutlery. Known as the *Flaches Modell*, or "Flat Model," it sparked a heated controversy. The service made its public debut at the *Der gedeckte Tisch* (The Laid Table) exhibition in 1906. Critic Ludwig Hevesi could hardly contain his praise; he found it practical to use and logical in its construction. Not everyone shared his enthusiasm. A German writer found it closer to medical instruments used for dissection. Offered in silver, plated-silver, or gilded-silver, its only adornment was a row of balls that punctuated the end of each handle.

Hoffmann's *Rundes Modell* or "Round Model" flatware series from 1906 was also shown at The Laid Table exhibition. The service represented a subtle but important adaptation of the "Flat Model" series. The handles are smooth and rounded—Hoffmann dispensed with the ornamental beads—but otherwise the two are practically identical. The curved forms of the round version are both more traditional and more comfortable in the hand. Produced in silver and in silver-plated alpacca (alpacca, also known as German silver, is an alloy of copper, nickel, and zinc), it found a wider audience. The "Round Model" was used in the Cabaret Fledermaus and subsequently acquired by important patrons of the Wiener Werkstätte. Alessi produces the service today, a sign of its continuing popularity.

One of Josef Hoffmann's students from Vienna's Kunstgewerbeschule (School of Applied Arts) demonstrated the same range of talent as Hoffmann himself. Otto Prutscher joined the Wiener Werkstätte and soon was working in all media. Prutscher's cutlery patterns for various firms, including Klinkosch and Wiener Silber, show particular restraint; he is most appreciated for his work in glass. Hoffmann's "Flat Model" and "Round Model," however, remain icons of early twentieth-century design.

Josef Hoffmann, Six pieces from *Rundes Modell* (Round Model)
flatware set, designed 1906–1907, silver-plated stainless steel (left to right):
tablespoon, knife, fork, dessert knife, dessert fork, dessert spoon.
Neue Galerie Design Shop.

PHEASANT ROASTED
IN SALT DOUGH À LA HEINZ WINKLER

Fasanbrust im Salzteig "Heinz Winkler"

4 SERVINGS

8 strips thick-sliced bacon,
        halved crosswise
2 pheasants, breasts sliced off the
        carcass and skinned; carcasses
        coarsely chopped
    Freshly ground white pepper
12 juniper berries
3 tablespoons extra-virgin olive oil
1 carrot, finely chopped
1 celery rib, finely chopped
1 leek, white and light green parts only,
        finely chopped
1 medium onion, finely chopped
2 bay leaves
2 tablespoons plus ½ teaspoon white
        peppercorns, cracked (see Tips)
½ cup chicken or veal stock
¼ cup brandy
1 cup heavy cream
    Salt

Dough

2 ½ cups all-purpose flour
2 ½ cups kosher salt
4 large eggs
⅔ cup plus 1 ½ teaspoons cold water

I learned this dish in Munich while working at the restaurant Tantris under chef Heinz Winkler. Individual pheasant breasts are wrapped in bacon and then in a simple dough of flour, salt, eggs, and water. The dough is very pliable, almost like one for sugar cookies, but because it has a lot of salt in it, you don't eat it. Essentially, it's just a cooking vessel. I thought this was an interesting technique for roasting a bird, and I've continued to use it over the years. I still believe it's one of the best methods for cooking pheasant, which can easily dry out and taste like straw. The result is amazing: beautifully tender and juicy meat. It's not a difficult or time-consuming thing to do. In fact, you set the whole thing up in advance, and the roasting takes only about 15 minutes.

1 Make the dough: In a large bowl, whisk the flour with the salt. Make a well in the center. Add 3 of the eggs and lightly whisk to blend. Using your fingertips, mix the eggs into the flour-salt mixture until absorbed. Add the ⅔ cup of water and knead to form a firm but pliable dough.

2 Divide the dough into 4 equal pieces, and roll into balls. Cover each with plastic wrap. Beat the remaining egg with the 1 ½ teaspoons of water, and reserve.

3 Place 4 half-strips of bacon side by side on the work surface. Set 1 pheasant breast crosswise on the bacon, season with pepper, and top with 3 juniper berries. Fold the ends of the bacon strips over the pheasant breast to enclose it completely, with no overlap. (If the bacon is not long enough, it can be stretched by rolling it with a rolling pin.) Repeat with the remaining bacon and pheasant breasts.

4 Roll 1 dough ball into an 8-inch round. Set a bacon-wrapped pheasant breast in the center and brush the dough with some of the reserved beaten egg. Wrap the breast completely in the dough to make a package about 3 by 6 inches. Pinch the seams to seal. Turn seam side down and brush the top with egg. Transfer to a baking sheet. Repeat with the remaining breasts and dough.

5 In a large, deep, heavy skillet, heat 2 tablespoons of the oil. Add the pheasant carcasses and cook over medium-high heat until lightly browned, about 7 minutes. Add the carrot, celery, leek, onion, and bay leaves and cook until the vegetables are softened, about 5 minutes.

6 In a small skillet, heat the remaining 1 tablespoon of oil. Add 2 tablespoons of the cracked peppercorns and cook until fragrant and sizzling, about 2 minutes. Transfer to the skillet with the carcasses, add the stock and brandy, and boil for 2 minutes. Add the cream, bring to a simmer, cook for 20 minutes. Strain the sauce into a medium saucepan, and season with salt.

7 Meanwhile, heat the oven to 425 degrees. Bake the pheasant packages for 10 minutes. Turn the packages over and bake until an instant-read thermometer inserted in the center registers 125 degrees, about 5 minutes. Remove the packages from the oven and let rest for 5 minutes.

8 Slice through the sides of each package and lift off the tops. Remove the breasts and discard the dough. Peel off the bacon and discard. Slice the pheasant on the diagonal ½ inch thick, and arrange on warmed plates. Spoon the sauce over and around the breast, scatter with the remaining ½ teaspoon cracked peppercorns, and serve.

Tips

The salt dough can also be made in a stand mixer using the hook attachment.

Fatback, the unsmoked, unsalted layer of fat that runs down the back of a pig, can be substituted for the bacon. Encasing the pheasant breasts in either adds flavor even though it isn't served.

To crack peppercorns, put them in a sturdy resealable plastic bag so they don't go flying, then pound them with the bottom of a small heavy pot or a rolling pin.

Serve with

This is an impressive entrée, so I like to serve it with simple side dishes, such as green cabbage salad, Fresh Herbed Quark Spätzle (page 162), or sauerkraut and onions sautéed with a little bacon.

Variation

The recipe can also be made with skinless, boneless chicken breasts. Top each with a rosemary sprig instead of the juniper berries and bake the chicken packages, turning once, until an instant-read thermometer inserted in the center registers 145 degrees, about 20 minutes. Let rest for 10 minutes before opening the packages and serving. Use chicken necks, backs, and wings to make the sauce.

Make ahead

The dough can be covered with plastic wrap and kept at room temperature for up to 2 hours. Putting it in the fridge makes it soggy.

The assembled packages can be covered with plastic wrap and kept at room temperature for up to 30 minutes before baking.

Wiener Werkstätte Postcard Number 486 by Moriz Jung, Café Heinrichhof, 1911. Leonard A. Lauder Collection, Neue Galerie New York.

CABBAGE-WRAPPED-CHICKEN STRUDEL

Hendlbrust Strudel

4 SERVINGS

Salt

8 large Savoy cabbage leaves

5 skinless, boneless chicken breasts
(about 6 ounces each)

Freshly ground pepper

2 ice cubes

2 cups heavy cream

12 frozen phyllo sheets, thawed

6 tablespoons clarified unsalted butter
(see Strudel Secrets, page 175)

In this recipe, chicken breasts are spread with a creamy chicken mousse, then swaddled in Savoy cabbage leaves and sheets of buttery phyllo and baked until golden. It's comfort food for my customers, because even though the strudel is prepared in a nontraditional way, it is still familiar. It's like a song they know most of the words to.

1 Bring a large pot of salted water to a boil. Fill 2 large bowls with ice water.

2 Add the cabbage leaves to the boiling water and cook until slightly tender, 2 to 3 minutes. Using tongs, transfer the cabbage to one bowl of ice water to cool as quickly as possible, 1 to 2 minutes. Drain and pat dry with paper towels. If the center rib of any of the leaves is very thick, cut out part of it.

3 Set a medium bowl in the second bowl of ice water. Cut 1 chicken breast into 1-inch pieces. Add the pieces to the bowl in the ice water and season with salt and pepper. Working quickly, transfer the chicken to a food processor, add the ice cubes, and grind until well chopped, 30 seconds to 1 minute. Gradually add the cream and process until the mixture turns light pink and has thickened to a mousse, 3 to 4 minutes. Set the food processor bowl in the ice water and keep the mousse cold.

4 Heat the oven to 450 degrees. Line a large baking sheet with parchment paper. Set 1 chicken breast in the center of a cabbage leaf. Spread the breast with 3 table-spoons of the chicken mousse. Top with another cabbage leaf and tuck the cabbage around the chicken, making a neat bundle. Repeat with the remaining cabbage, chicken breasts, and mousse.

5 Cut the phyllo sheets crosswise in half to make 24. Stack them and cover with a damp cloth. For each strudel, spread 1 phyllo sheet on the work surface. Brush it lightly with clarified butter. Top with 5 more sheets, brushing each with butter.

6 Set a bundle at one end of the phyllo stack, leaving about $\frac{1}{2}$ inch on the bottom and 1 inch on each side, and roll up tightly, tucking in the ends. Brush the strudel with clarified butter and transfer to the prepared baking sheet, seam side down.

7 Bake the strudels in the center of the oven until golden brown, 15 to 20 minutes. Remove from the oven and cut into a strudel to make sure the chicken is cooked through; if necessary, return it to the oven for a few minutes. Let the strudels rest on the baking sheet for 2 to 3 minutes before serving warm.

Tip

The chicken mousse is extremely heat-sensitive: If it gets too warm, it will separate. Chilling the chicken and adding some ice cubes to the food processor while you grind the chicken helps prevent this, as does keeping the mousse in the ice water while you prepare the strudel.

Serve with

When serving a savory strudel like this as the entrée in a multicourse meal, I like to accompany it with a starchy puree such as Celery Root Puree (page 152). But the strudel is pretty easy to prepare, you can also eat it as a weekday dinner with just a tossed green salad. Or cut it crosswise into thin slices to make a fun starter.

Variations

Pheasant breast can be used in place of the chicken. The chicken mousse can be shaped into small quenelles (dumplings) to use as a soup garnish. Poach rounded tablespoons of the mixture in consommé or stock until they are cooked through and float, about 10 minutes.

Make ahead

The assembled strudels can be refrigerated for up to 5 hours before baking.

POTATO-AND-CABBAGE STRUDEL WITH HERBED SOUR CREAM

Erdäpfel-Krautstrudel mit Sauerrahm-Kräutersauce

This fantastic dish proves that vegetables can be just as satisfying as meat. The potato-and-cabbage filling is flavored with garlic and caraway seeds, and the accompanying sour cream and chive sauce makes a tart and cooling garnish. We serve it with a side of tangy sauerkraut, and suddenly meat becomes an afterthought.

4 SERVINGS

- 2 pounds russet (baking) potatoes, peeled and quartered
- Salt
- ½ cup sour cream
- 3 tablespoons crème fraîche
- 3 tablespoons finely chopped chives
- Juice of 1 lemon
- Freshly ground pepper
- 2 tablespoons unsalted butter
- ½ pound white onions, diced
- 1 large white or green cabbage (about 3 pounds), quartered, cored, and thinly sliced
- 1 garlic clove, chopped
- 1 tablespoon caraway seeds
- Freshly grated nutmeg
- 12 frozen phyllo sheets, thawed
- 6 tablespoons clarified unsalted butter (see Strudel Secrets, page 175)

1 Add the potatoes to a large pot of salted water and bring to a boil. Cook until tender, about 20 minutes; drain. Using a potato ricer or food mill, mash the potatoes.

2 Meanwhile, in a medium bowl, whisk the sour cream with the crème fraîche, chives, and lemon juice. Season with salt and pepper. Refrigerate.

3 Heat the oven to 450 degrees. Line a large baking sheet with parchment paper. In a large casserole, melt the 2 tablespoons of butter. Add the onions and cook over medium-high heat until lightly browned, 5 to 7 minutes. Add the cabbage, garlic, and caraway seeds, season with salt, pepper, and nutmeg, and cook until the cabbage has softened, about 10 minutes. Remove from the heat and let cool slightly, then add the mashed potatoes and stir to mix.

4 Cut the phyllo sheets crosswise in half to make 24. Stack them and cover with a damp cloth. For each strudel, spread 1 phyllo sheet on the work surface. Brush it lightly with clarified butter. Top with 5 more sheets, brushing each with butter.

5 Dollop about 2 cups of the potato mixture at one end of the phyllo stack, leaving about ½ inch on the bottom and 1 inch on each side, and roll up tightly, tucking in the ends. Brush the strudel with clarified butter and transfer to the prepared baking sheet, seam side down.

6 Bake the strudels in the center of the oven until golden brown, 12 to 15 minutes. Remove from the oven and let the strudels rest on the baking sheet for 2 to 3 minutes.

7 Serve, passing the herbed sour cream separately.

Serve with

This strudel can swing as either an appetizer or entrée. Eaten with a salad, it makes a meatless meal. Or serve a half strudel per serving as an appetizer before Roasted Leg of Lamb (page 133) or Roast Pork Loin with Armagnac-Prune Sauce (page 132). You can stay vegetarian and serve the strudel with a sautéed mushroom stew and a side of Creamed Spinach (page 153).

Variations

The great thing about phyllo pastry is that you can fill it with just about anything and it will be delicious. Experiment with sautéed vegetables such as chanterelles, broccoli, or spinach instead of the cabbage. Or, for a nonvegetarian variation, add ½ cup of diced smoked ham or bacon.

Make ahead

The assembled strudels can be refrigerated for up to 5 hours before baking.

BLOOD SAUSAGE STRUDEL

Blutwurststrudel

4 SERVINGS

One ½-pound russet (baking) potato,
    peeled and quartered
    Salt
  2 tablespoons unsalted butter
  1 medium onion, finely chopped
  2 teaspoons dried marjoram
  2 garlic cloves, chopped
  ½ teaspoon freshly ground pepper
 10 ounces blood sausage,
    casing removed (see Tip)
  1 cup sauerkraut,
    drained and squeezed dry
  2 teaspoons Dijon mustard
  2 teaspoons chopped parsley
 12 frozen phyllo sheets, thawed
  6 tablespoons clarified unsalted butter
    (see Strudel Secrets, page 175)

Earthy, rich blood sausage, also called blood pudding or, in French, boudin noir, is extremely popular in Austria. In this recipe, I use phyllo sheets to make a flaky, buttery sausage strudel. It's delicious as an entrée but can easily be cut into bite-size portions and served as an hors d'oeuvre.

1 Add the potato to a medium saucepan of salted water and bring to a boil. Cook until tender, about 20 minutes; drain.

2 Meanwhile, heat the oven to 450 degrees. Line a large baking sheet with parchment paper. In a medium saucepan, melt the 2 tablespoons of butter over high heat. Add the onion, marjoram, garlic, 1 teaspoon of salt, and the pepper and cook, stirring occasionally, until the onion is lightly browned, about 5 minutes. Remove from the heat.

3 In a large bowl, combine the sausage with the potato, onion mixture, sauerkraut, mustard, and parsley and stir to mix, breaking up the sausage and potato.

4 Cut the phyllo sheets crosswise in half to make 24. Stack them and cover with a damp cloth. For each strudel, spread 1 phyllo sheet on the work surface. Brush it lightly with clarified butter. Top with 5 more sheets, brushing each with butter.

5 Mound about 2 cups of the sausage mixture at one end of the phyllo stack, leaving about ½ inch on the bottom and 1 inch on each side, and roll up tightly, tucking in the ends. Brush the strudel with clarified butter and transfer to the prepared baking sheet, seam side down.

6 Bake the strudels in the center of the oven until golden brown, 12 to 15 minutes. Remove from the oven and let the strudels rest on the baking sheet for 2 to 3 minutes before serving.

Tip

Making blood sausage involves poaching pork and/or beef blood, fat, and skin in casing until it congeals. Obviously, it is much easier for the home cook to buy it. For me, the secret to a good blood sausage is simple: find yourself a good butcher. Mine is Schaller & Weber (schallerandweber.com).

Serve with

I like a simple side dish with this, either sautéed brussels sprouts or a salad.

Variation

You can use spicy breakfast or Italian sausage. We often substitute beef-and-pork bratwurst.

Make ahead

The assembled strudels can be refrigerated for up to 5 hours before baking.

WIENER WERKSTÄTTE № 409

Wiener Werkstätte Postcard Number 409 by Gustav Kalhammer, National Railway Station Restaurant, Vienna X, Josef Pohl, 1911. Leonard A. Lauder Collection, Neue Galerie New York.

SCHNITZEL SECRETS

Perfect golden schnitzel can be a work of art. Or it can be the worst dish of your life, more like a piece of lead. When I showed my chef de cuisine how to make Wiener Schnitzel, he thought it was a mistake. The thin slices of veal were coated with a breading so delicate it almost floated on the surface of the veal. Here are the tricks I teach all my cooks.

The classic meat in a Wiener Schnitzel is veal, usually top round or loin. I prefer the top round cut, because it is a little juicier. The very white milk-fed veal doesn't have enough flavor. You don't have to worry so much about tenderness, because the veal is pounded. To pound cutlets for schnitzel, make sure all the membrane, or silver skin, is removed. Lay 1 cutlet at a time between 2 sheets of plastic wrap, or put in a heavy 1-quart plastic bag, and whack with a mallet, rolling pin, or the bottom of a heavy skillet to an even thickness. You can trim away any ragged edges.

To save a little time, the cutlets can be pounded ahead, covered with plastic wrap, and refrigerated for up to 2 days.

Take care when beating the eggs: Adding a tablespoon or two of heavy cream makes them fluffier. Using a fork, beat only until they are slightly loosened but still somewhat thick. The less you beat, the better they will envelop the veal cutlets and then create a puckery crust with more volume when fried.

Be sure to have enough bread crumbs to dip the cutlets into, and turn each cutlet so it comes away coated, without having to shovel or pat the crumbs on. Everything is put on very gently, at the last minute. The Turks used to put gold leaf on their meat; in Austria, we use bread crumbs and turn them into gold.

Your skillet should be 2 inches deep. I like cooking schnitzel in both oil and butter. When the butter melts and browns, you get a delicious nutty flavor.

The fried schnitzels can be kept warm in a 250-degree oven for up to 10 minutes.

VEAL SCHNITZEL

Wiener Schnitzel

4 SERVINGS

*4 veal top round cutlets (about 6 ounces
    each), pounded 1/8 inch thick
    (see Schnitzel Secrets, page 121)
    Salt and freshly ground white pepper*
1 cup all-purpose flour
2 cups fine dry bread crumbs
2 large eggs
2 tablespoons heavy cream
2 cups canola oil
*1/2 cup flat-leaf parsley leaves,
    coarsely chopped*
3 tablespoons unsalted butter
1 lemon, cut into slices, seeds removed
1/4 cup lingonberry or cranberry preserves

**This dish goes back to my childhood, when it was a typical Sunday lunch entrée.
Now, at my family of restaurants in New York, it is hands down the most popular
item on the menu. My version is crisp, light, and tender, and the veal is gently
pounded until it practically covers the plate. Served with lingonberry preserves,
lemon slices, and fried parsley, this is an indisputable classic.**

1 Season the veal cutlets with salt and pepper. In two separate baking pans, spread the flour and bread crumbs. In a third baking pan, using a fork, lightly beat the eggs with the cream. Line a large baking sheet with paper towels.

2 In a large skillet, the deeper the better, heat the oil until quite hot. Put the parsley in a strainer, dip it into the oil, and fry for 10 seconds. Remove the strainer, draining well, and transfer the parsley to a small plate.

3 Dredge 1 cutlet in the flour, patting off the excess. Dip in the egg mixture, letting the excess drip back into the pan. Coat lightly with the bread crumbs. Do not press the crumbs onto the veal.

4 Add the butter to the skillet. Add the cutlet to the skillet and fry over high heat, gently moving the skillet in a circular motion to cover the cutlet with fat, until the breading looks bubbly and is starting to brown, about 1 minute. Turn and cook for another minute, swirling the skillet. Using a slotted spatula, transfer the schnitzel to the baking sheet. Repeat with the remaining cutlets, adjusting the heat as necessary so the coating cooks gradually and evenly, without burning.

5 Transfer the schnitzels to a warmed platter or plates. Top each with a lemon slice and some fried parsley. Serve with the preserves.

Serve with

A slightly tangy salad like Potato and Cucumber Salad (page 156) cuts the richness of the fried meat. Sautéed potatoes sprinkled with a little chopped parsley are also a good pairing.

VEAL SCHNITZEL WITH PAPRIKA SAUCE

Paprika Schnitzel

During the summer I get all my peppers from my friend Tim Stark at the Union Square Greenmarket. He owns Eckerton Hill Farm in Pennsylvania, and his peppers are the absolute best.

4 SERVINGS

2 tablespoons canola oil

2 onions, 1 finely chopped, 1 thinly sliced

4 red bell peppers, cored and seeded, 2 cut into large squares, 2 cut into julienne strips

2 garlic cloves, finely chopped

2 tablespoons Hungarian sweet paprika

1 tablespoon thyme leaves

1 tablespoon tomato paste

$\frac{1}{2}$ cup dry white wine

1 $\frac{1}{2}$ cups beef stock

Salt and freshly ground white pepper

$\frac{1}{2}$ cup sour cream

2 tablespoons unsalted butter

4 veal top round cutlets (about 6 ounces each), pounded $\frac{1}{8}$ inch thick (see Schnitzel Secrets, page 121)

$\frac{1}{4}$ cup all-purpose flour

2 tablespoons canola oil

$\frac{1}{4}$ cup chopped parsley

1 In a medium saucepan, heat the oil over medium heat. Add the chopped onion and cook until translucent, 2 to 3 minutes. Add the diced bell peppers and half the garlic and cook until the onions are golden brown, 2 to 3 minutes. Add the paprika and 1 $\frac{1}{2}$ teaspoons of the thyme and cook for 2 minutes, taking care not to brown the paprika. Stir in the tomato paste and cook until lightly browned, about 2 minutes.

2 Add the wine to the pan and bring to a simmer, scraping up any brown bits stuck to the bottom. Cook over medium heat, stirring occasionally, until the wine has reduced by half, about 5 minutes. Stir in the stock and simmer over medium-low heat until the sauce coats the back of a spoon, about 10 minutes. Season with salt and pepper, and let the sauce cool slightly.

3 In a blender, puree the sauce until smooth. Scrape into another saucepan. Heat to a bare simmer and whisk in the sour cream.

4 In a medium saucepan, melt the butter over medium heat. Add the julienned peppers, the remaining garlic, and the sliced onion and cook until the onion is lightly browned and the peppers are softened, about 10 minutes. Stir in the remaining 1 $\frac{1}{2}$ teaspoons of thyme and season with salt and pepper.

5 Season the veal cutlets with salt and pepper. Lightly dust with the flour, patting off the excess. In a large skillet, heat the oil over high heat. Add 2 of the cutlets and cook until they begin to brown around the edges. Turn and cook until the other side browns, about 4 minutes total. Remove to a warmed platter or plates. Repeat with the remaining 2 cutlets.

6 Pour the sauce over the schnitzels and spoon the julienned peppers over the top. Sprinkle with the parsley, and serve.

Tip

Be careful not to brown the paprika, or it will get bitter.

Serve with

This dish is often accompanied by simple boiled rice, boiled potatoes with butter and chopped parsley, or Fresh Herbed Quark Spätzle (page 162). I also like to roast tiny sweet red peppers in a 350-degree oven for 10 minutes, sprinkle them with a little sea salt, and serve as a colorful garnish.

Variation

Another similar Austrian dish is paprika chicken, which is essentially sautéed chicken breasts served with the same sauce.

Make ahead

The paprika sauce can be refrigerated for up to 3 days.

PORK SCHNITZEL WITH BACON, CHANTERELLES, AND CREAM SAUCE

Jäger Schnitzel

4 SERVINGS

¹/₄ pound thick-sliced bacon, cut crosswise
   into ¹/₄-inch-thick strips

¹/₂ pound chanterelle mushrooms,
   quartered lengthwise (see Tips)

1 cup heavy cream

¹/₂ cup beef or chicken stock

8 tablespoons (1 stick) cold unsalted
   butter, diced, plus additional
   2 tablespoons
   Salt and freshly ground white pepper

4 pork loin cutlets (about 6 ounces each),
   pounded ¹/₈ inch thick
   (see Schnitzel Secrets, page 121)

¹/₄ cup all-purpose flour

2 tablespoons canola oil

¹/₄ cup chopped parsley

This creamy, rich, and filling dish is a staple at *Gasthaus* restaurants—casual countryside taverns found all over Austria. I ate a lot of it as a boy, and it's still a favorite of mine. I like this schnitzel best with pork, but other types of meat can be substituted.

1 Heat a medium saucepan over medium heat. Add the bacon and cook, stirring occasionally, until nicely browned, about 4 minutes. Using a slotted spoon, remove to a plate.

2 Add the mushrooms to the pan and cook, stirring occasionally, until their water is released and then evaporates, about 7 minutes. Using a slotted spoon, add the mushrooms to the bacon.

3 Add the heavy cream to the pan and cook until reduced by half, about 7 minutes. Return the bacon and mushrooms to the pan, add the stock, and simmer the sauce until it thickens slightly, 3 to 4 minutes. Remove the pan from the heat and gradually whisk in the diced butter until it melts but stays creamy. Season lightly with salt and pepper.

4 Season the pork cutlets with salt and pepper. Lightly dust with the flour, patting off the excess. Heat a large skillet over high heat. Add the oil, then add 1 tablespoon of the remaining butter. Add 2 of the cutlets and cook until they begin to brown around the edges about 2 minutes, then turn and cook until the other side browns, about 2 minutes. Remove to a warmed platter or plates. Repeat with the remaining 2 cutlets, adding the remaining 1 tablespoon of butter.

5 Pour the sauce over the schnitzels, dividing the bacon and mushrooms evenly. Sprinkle with the parsley, and serve.

Tips

Any kind of mushroom can be used here. I like chanterelles, but the sliced mixed wild mushrooms available at many markets are also good.

The bacon can be smoked—i.e., regular bacon—or unsmoked, like pancetta.

Serve with

Fresh Herbed Quark Spätzle (page 162) is the classic accompaniment to schnitzel, but a side of sautéed green beans would work nicely too.

Variations

With both cream and bacon, this dish is delicious but rich. Add a splash of lemon juice (roughly 1 tablespoon) to the sauce at the very end for some zing.

Stirring in some sautéed chopped onions and/or shallots will give the sauce extra crunch and flavor.

VEAL SCHNITZEL STUFFED WITH HAM AND CHEESE

Cordon Bleu

4 veal top round cutlets (about 6 ounces
    each), pounded ⅛ inch thick
    (see Schnitzel Secrets, page 121)
    Salt and freshly ground white pepper
4 slices Black Forest ham
4 slices Gruyère or Emmentaler cheese
1 cup all-purpose flour
2 cups fine dry bread crumbs
2 large eggs, at room temperature
2 tablespoons heavy cream
2 cups canola oil
2 tablespoons unsalted butter, diced
1 lemon, cut into slices, seeds removed
    Fried parsley, for garnishing
        (see Veal Schnitzel, page 122)
¼ cup lingonberry or cranberry preserves

This is another *Gasthaus* staple that I like to serve. People love the ham and the melted cheese that oozes out of the schnitzel when it's cut. A common French variation uses chicken instead of veal, and you could also substitute pork.

1 Season the veal cutlets with salt and pepper. Arrange them on a work surface. Lay a slice of ham and cheese on each. Fold the cutlets crosswise in half, making sure that no ham or cheese is peeking out.

2 In two separate baking pans, spread the flour and bread crumbs. In a third baking pan, lightly beat the eggs with the heavy cream, using a fork. Line a baking sheet with paper towels.

3 Making sure to hold it together, dredge 1 stuffed cutlet in the flour and pat off the excess, dip in the egg mixture, letting the excess drip back into the pan. Coat lightly with bread crumbs. Do not press the crumbs onto the cutlet. Repeat with the remaining cutlets.

4 In a large skillet, the deeper the better, heat the oil over medium heat. Add 1 tablespoon of the butter, and when it melts, carefully add 2 breaded cutlets. Fry, gently moving the skillet in a circular motion to cover the top of the cutlets with fat, until the bottom is golden brown, about 4 minutes. Turn and cook on the second side, swirling the skillet, until golden brown, about 4 minutes. Using a slotted spatula, transfer the schnitzels to a warmed platter or plates. Add the remaining 1 tablespoon of butter to the pan and repeat with the remaining cutlets, adjusting the heat as necessary so the coating cooks gradually and evenly, without burning.

5 Top each schnitzel with a lemon slice and some fried parsley. Serve with the preserves.

Tips

When you add the stuffed breaded cutlets to the skillet, make sure to let them fall away from yourself so you don't get splattered with hot oil.
If the oil darkens too much after cooking the first batch of cutlets, you may need to replace it with fresh oil.

Serve with

Classically, you would serve this with panfried potatoes sprinkled with chopped parsley. If it's summer, I would also add a tomato salad, such as the Marinated Heirloom Tomato Salad (page 86). Potato and Cucumber Salad (page 156) and American-style potato salad are also good accompaniments.

PORK SCHNITZEL STUFFED WITH MUSHROOMS

Gefülltes Pariser Schnitzel

4 SERVINGS

¼ cup canola oil

½ pound shiitake mushrooms, stems
removed, caps cut into julienne strips

2 shallots, finely chopped

1 garlic clove, finely chopped

3 tablespoons chopped parsley

3 tablespoons chopped thyme
Salt and freshly ground white pepper

4 pork loin cutlets (about 6 ounces each),
pounded ⅛ inch thick
(see Schnitzel Secrets, page 121)

2 cups all-purpose flour

2 large eggs

¼ cup heavy cream

1 lemon, cut into slices, seeds removed
Fried parsley, for garnishing
(see Veal Schnitzel, page 122)

Like the Veal Schnitzel Stuffed with Ham and Cheese (opposite), this schnitzel is stuffed, but here pork cutlets are filled with sautéed mushrooms instead of ham and cheese. It's a very classic schnitzel, part of my taste memory.

1 In a large skillet, heat 2 tablespoons of the oil over medium heat. Add the mushrooms and cook, stirring occasionally, until their water is released and then evaporates. Add the shallots, garlic, parsley, and thyme and cook until the shallots and garlic are nicely browned, about 2 minutes. Season with salt and pepper. Remove the skillet from the heat and let cool.

2 Season the pork cutlets with salt and pepper. Arrange the cutlets on a work surface. Spoon one-quarter of the mushrooms onto the center of each, leaving a ½-inch border. Fold the cutlets crosswise in half.

3 In one baking pan, spread the flour. In another baking pan, lightly beat the eggs with the heavy cream, using a fork. Making sure to hold it together, dredge 1 stuffed cutlet at a time in the flour, patting off the excess. Dip in the egg mixture, letting the excess drip back into the pan. Repeat, dredging the cutlet in the flour and then the eggs. Repeat with the remaining cutlets.

4 In a large skillet, heat the remaining 2 tablespoons of oil over medium-high heat. Add 2 cutlets and cook until the bottom is golden brown, about 4 minutes. Turn and cook on the second side until browned, about 4 minutes. Transfer to a warmed platter or plates and repeat with the remaining cutlets.

5 Top each schnitzel with a lemon slice and some fried parsley, and serve.

Tips

Any kind of mushroom can be used here. The mixed, sliced wild mushrooms available at many specialty markets are great.

It may seem odd to dredge the stuffed cutlets in the flour and egg and then repeat, ending with the egg coating, but it's the traditional way to make this schnitzel and gives them a more substantial coating.

Serve with

I like to serve this with white asparagus and zucchini linguine. For the linguine, buy any type of fresh linguine. (Raffetto's on Houston Street in Greenwich Village makes good pasta.) Using a vegetable peeler or paring knife, cut green and yellow zucchini into long thin ribbons. Toss these with a little bit of olive oil and the just-coated linguine and heat briefly in a skillet.

Variations

The schnitzel can be stuffed with other vegetables such as chopped spinach, if desired. Add a little chopped bacon to the mushroom mixture, if you like.

RIB-EYE STEAKS WITH CRISPY ONION RINGS

"Rib-Eye Steak" mit gebackenen Zwiebelringen

4 SERVINGS

2 tablespoons canola oil
4 boneless rib-eye steaks
    (about 10 ounces each)
    Salt and freshly ground pepper
1 tablespoon all-purpose flour
1 cup beef or veal stock

Onion Rings

1 large onion, sliced crosswise $1/4$ inch
    thick and separated into rings
    Table salt and freshly ground pepper
$1/4$ teaspoon Hungarian sweet paprika
2 $1/4$ cups all-purpose flour
1 tablespoon sugar
1 teaspoon baking powder
One 12-ounce bottle of pilsner
    or lager beer
    Canola oil, for deep-frying
    Fine sea salt

In Austria, steak is usually thinly sliced and seared until medium. However, here in America, "the land of steaks," customers are more accustomed to hefty cuts and to choosing the degree of doneness. So at Wallsé, I adapt my cooking a bit—the steak is thick and cooked to my guests' desired doneness—while keeping the traditional onion rings and pan sauce. These onion rings, by the way, are lighter than the typical American version and absolutely outrageous. Customers looking for the familiar *Zwiebelrostbraten* are happy, and so are the Americans.

1 Make the onion rings: In a large bowl, season the onion rings with table salt, pepper, and the paprika, and toss to coat.

2 In a medium bowl, whisk the flour with 1 teaspoon of table salt, the sugar, baking powder, and beer until smooth, about 1 minute. Let the batter stand until slightly thickened, at least 10 minutes.

3 Fill a large deep saucepan with 3 inches of oil and heat to 320 degrees. Line a baking sheet with paper towels. Working in batches, dip the onion rings in the batter, letting the excess batter drip back into the bowl, carefully add to the hot oil, without crowding, and cook, turning once, until golden on both sides, about 3 minutes. Using tongs or a slotted spoon, transfer the rings as they are done to the prepared baking sheet to drain. Sprinkle with sea salt.

4 In a large skillet, heat the oil until shimmering. Season the steaks with salt and pepper and sear them over high heat for about 2 minutes per side. Reduce the heat to medium-low and cook, turning once, for about 5 minutes for medium-rare. Remove the steaks to a warmed platter or plates.

5 Add the flour to the same skillet and stir over medium-high heat until lightly browned. Add the stock and simmer over high heat, scraping up any brown bits stuck to the bottom, until slightly thickened, about 2 minutes.

6 Pour the sauce over the steaks. Top with the onion rings, and serve.

Tip
Make sure to let the batter rest for at least 10 minutes so it thickens and coats the onion rings well.

Serve with
I typically serve this dish with a side of Creamed Spinach (page 153) or a light potato puree. Other great accompaniments include roasted brussels sprouts, sautéed green beans, and potato croquettes.

Make ahead
The fried onion rings can be stored at room temperature in an airtight container overnight.

STEAK WITH CRISPY POTATO CAKES

"Rib-Eye Steak" mit Erdäpfelrösti

4 SERVINGS

Salt

½ *pound haricots verts, trimmed*

¼ *cup fresh lemon juice*

1 *teaspoon Dijon mustard*
  Freshly ground pepper

½ *cup extra-virgin olive oil*

2 *tablespoons canola oil*

4 *boneless rib-eye or sirloin steaks*
   (about 6 ounces each)

1 *tablespoon unsalted butter*

4 *large eggs*

4 *Classic Potato Rösti (page 158)*

Steak rösti is one of Wallsé's most-ordered brunch items, but it is quite simple to make at home. It's sort of my own version of steak and eggs. I set a fried potato rösti on the plate and layer haricots verts and strips of steak on top, then finish it off with an egg cooked sunny-side up.

1 Bring a medium saucepan of salted water to a boil. Add the haricots verts and cook until crisp-tender, about 5 minutes. Drain in a colander and cool under cold running water. Pat dry thoroughly.

2 In a medium bowl, whisk the lemon juice with the mustard. Season with salt and pepper. Gradually whisk in the olive oil.

3 Add the haricots verts to the vinaigrette and toss to coat.

4 In a large skillet, heat the canola oil until shimmering. Season the steaks with salt and pepper and sear them over high heat for about 2 minutes per side. Reduce the heat to medium-low and cook, turning once, for about 3 minutes for medium-rare. Remove the steaks to a cutting board, cover loosely with foil, and let rest while you cook the eggs.

5 In a large skillet, melt the butter. Add the eggs and fry sunny-side up over medium-high heat until the whites are set and the yolks are slightly runny, 2 to 3 minutes. Remove from the heat.

6 Thinly slice the steaks on the diagonal. Arrange 1 rösti in the center of each warmed plate. Spread some haricot verts on top, cover with slices of steak, and finish with a fried egg. Season with salt and pepper, and serve.

Tip

All the elements of this dish—except the haricots verts—should be hot when served.

Serve with

I like this hearty brunch dish with a light salad, such as radicchio or frisée with herbs.

Variation

During different seasons, I substitute other types of beans. In the spring, for instance, I'll use marinated fresh fava beans in place of the haricots verts.

Make ahead

The rösti are best served hot and crispy right off the stove, but they can be prepared up to 2 hours ahead and reheated in a low oven. The steaks can be kept warm for a few minutes in a low oven until serving.

ROASTED PORK SHANKS WITH SAUERKRAUT

Schweinshax'n mit Sauerkraut

8 SERVINGS

2 tablespoons caraway seeds

4 garlic cloves, finely chopped

2 tablespoons kosher salt

$1/4$ cup plus 2 tablespoons canola oil

4 pork shanks with skin (1 $1/2$ to
    2 pounds each), fat trimmed
    (see Tips)

Two $1/2$-liter bottles Bavarian wheat beer
    (see Tips)

One 24-ounce jar sauerkraut (see Tips)

2 ounces bacon, cut into $1/2$-inch dice

1 onion, chopped

$1/2$ cup dry white wine

1 cup beef stock

1 bay leaf, 1 tablespoon caraway
    seeds, 2 thyme sprigs, and
    1 tablespoon white peppercorns,
    all tied in a cheesecloth bundle

1 russet (baking) potato, peeled and
    shredded on a box grater
    Table salt and freshly ground pepper

One of my favorite pork recipes is this beer-basted roast. It's a traditional Sunday lunch dish and a real crowd pleaser. I serve it with peppery fresh horseradish and some sauerkraut flavored with rich, salty bacon. Add a platter of root vegetables to the table, and you've got yourself a great family meal.

1 In a large bowl, combine the caraway seeds with the garlic, kosher salt, and $1/4$ cup of the oil. Add the pork shanks and rub all over with the caraway mixture. Cover and refrigerate overnight.

2 The next day, heat the oven to 350 degrees. Arrange the shanks, skin side up, on a rack in a roasting pan. Roast for 2 $1/2$ to 3 hours, pouring 2 cups of the beer over the pork after 1 hour and the rest over it after 2 hours. Then continue basting with the hot beer every 20 minutes until the shanks are crispy, deep golden brown, and very tender. Remove from the oven and cover loosely with foil.

3 Meanwhile, drain the sauerkraut in a strainer and run it under cold water; let drain thoroughly.

4 In a casserole, warm the remaining 2 tablespoons of oil over medium heat. Add the bacon and cook, stirring occasionally, until the fat is rendered, about 5 minutes. Add the onion and cook until lightly browned, 3 to 4 minutes. Add the sauerkraut and cook, stirring occasionally, for 5 minutes.

5 Add the wine to the casserole and bring to a simmer, stirring up any browned bits stuck to the bottom. Add the stock and bring to a boil, then reduce to a simmer. Add the spice bundle and stir in the shredded potato. Cover and cook over medium-low heat until most of the liquid has evaporated, about 25 minutes.

6 Remove the lid and cook until the mixture is just moist, about 5 minutes. Discard the spice bundle and season with salt, if needed, and pepper.

7 Mound the sauerkraut on warmed plates. Cut the shanks in half, set one half on each plate, and serve.

On the sidewalk in front of Wallsé, I recreated a classic Austrian Sunday lunch with Roasted Pork Shanks with Sauerkraut (this page), Bread Dumplings in a Napkin (page 160), and a refreshing Boston Lettuce Salad with Spicy Radishes, Pumpkin Seed Oil, and Lemon Vinaigrette (page 88). My long linen apron, made from Josef Hoffmann's 1909 *Rectangles* patterned fabric, complements another of Hoffmann's designs: the 1907 *Beehive* patterned napkins. For the table I selected stoneware edged with a blue check, designed in 1901–1902 by the School of Koloman Moser. A bouquet of glorious sunflowers in a 1915 Hoffmann bell-shaped vase completes the table scheme. All items provided by Neue Galerie Design Shop. The 1898 Adolf Loos bentwood chairs are a turn-of-the-century Viennese icon.

Tips

Pork shanks can be special-ordered from any butcher. Wheat beers are fizzy, thirst-quenching, tangy ales with a white head from the addition of malted wheat to a malted barley base. Basting the shanks with beer makes the skin crispier and the meat more tender. It also gives the pork a lot more flavor.

For sauerkraut, I like the German brand Mildessa, available at hengstenberg.de.

Sauerkraut is usually well seasoned to begin with, so it may not need more salt in Step 6.

The starch from the shredded potato helps thicken the sauerkraut mixture.

Serve with

With this rustic entree, pass a homey side dish like boiled potatoes or any kind of dumpling, such as Bread Dumplings in a Napkin (page 160).

A light salad like the Boston Lettuce Salad with Spicy Radishes, Pumpkin Seed Oil, and Lemon Vinaigrette (page 88) adds a refreshing taste.

Variation

We help celebrate Germany's famous Oktoberfest by offering a similar dish called *Bauernschmaus* (literally "feast of the farmers"). It's the Austrian cousin to Alsatian choucroute garnie. We serve the pork shank with bratwurst, smoked pork shoulder, Bread Dumplings in a Napkin (page 160), and sauerkraut. People adore it!

Make ahead

The pork shanks need to marinate in the caraway mixture overnight, so plan accordingly.

ROAST PORK LOIN WITH ARMAGNAC-PRUNE SAUCE

Schweinebraten mit Armagnac-Pflaumen Sauce

6   garlic cloves, 3 peeled and left whole,
    3 minced

2   teaspoons caraway seeds, crushed
    Kosher salt

1   bone-in pork loin roast (about 6 ½
    pounds), rack of rib bones
    removed in one piece and reserved
    (have the butcher do this)

½   cup Armagnac or other brandy

18 large pitted prunes
    Freshly ground pepper

6   cups water

1   tablespoon unsalted butter, softened

3   tablespoons all-purpose flour

The roasted pork dishes typically served at Sunday lunch are some of my favorite childhood memories. In this recipe, I give the classic roast a different spin with the addition of Armagnac-prune sauce, which happens to go fantastically.

1 In a small bowl, combine the minced garlic, caraway seeds, and 1 teaspoon of salt. Rub the mixture all over the pork loin and let stand at room temperature for 1 hour.

2 Heat the oven to 375 degrees. In a medium saucepan, bring the Armagnac to a boil. Add the prunes and simmer over low heat for 3 minutes, then remove from the heat.

3 Set the rack of rib bones in a large roasting pan, meaty side up, and season with salt and pepper. Set the pork loin on the rack, fat side down. Add the 3 garlic cloves to the pan and pour in 2 cups of the water. Roast the pork for 30 minutes.

4 Add 1 cup of the water to the pan and roast the meat for 30 minutes longer. Then turn the pork loin fat side up and roast for about 30 minutes longer, or until an instant-read thermometer inserted in the thickest part of the meat registers 145 degrees. Transfer the pork to a cutting board and cover loosely with foil. Let rest for at least 10 minutes, or up to 20 minutes.

5 Meanwhile, turn the rib rack meaty side down. Set the pan over 2 burners on medium-high heat. Add the remaining 3 cups of water, and bring to a simmer, scraping up the browned bits from the bottom and sides of the pan. Reduce the heat to medium and simmer for 10 minutes, stirring often and mashing the garlic cloves.

6 In a small bowl, blend the butter with the flour to make a paste. Whisk ½ cup of the pan juices into the butter paste until smooth. Discard the rib rack from the roasting pan. Whisk the dissolved butter mixture into the pan juices and simmer, whisking often, for 5 minutes.

7 Strain the sauce into a medium saucepan. Add the prunes and their liquid and simmer over medium heat for 5 minutes. Season with salt and pepper.

8 Cut the pork loin into ¼-inch-thick slices, and serve with the sauce.

Tips

Caraway seeds are used in a variety of Austrian dishes. I really love their slight anise-flavor when cooked. Caraway is also often used to make tea and contains components that may aid digestion.

The rib bones make a natural rack for cooking the pork roast and they impart tremendous flavor to the sauce.

Serve with

Try the Green Cabbage with Granny Smith Apples (page 150) or roasted root vegetables.

I also like this pork roast with a side of Styrian-style cab-bage, which is basically a type of slaw. Savoy cabbage leaves are shredded and salted, then tossed with a little cooked bacon, bacon fat, sugar, and white balsamic vinegar.

Variation

You can substitute a 4-pound boneless pork loin or tied shoulder roast, which will cook in a fairly similar fashion. Set them on a rack in the roasting pan instead of the bones.

Make ahead The prunes can be soaked in the Armagnac for up to 1 week.

ROASTED LEG OF LAMB

Gebratene Lammkeule

8 SERVINGS

8 SERVINGS

$1/2$ cup extra-virgin olive oil

5 garlic cloves, finely chopped

5 thyme sprigs, leaves finely chopped

5 rosemary sprigs, leaves finely chopped

5 flat-leaf parsley sprigs, leaves
    finely chopped

5 marjoram sprigs, leaves finely chopped

1 semiboneless leg of lamb
    (about 7 pounds)
    Salt and freshly ground pepper

This traditional recipe is a perfect Easter dish. The beauty of it is that you stick the lamb in the oven and pretty much forget about it until it's ready to come out. In the meantime, you can make a side dish or spend time with the family. There is something exciting and very classic about carving a roast like this at the table in front of guests.

1 Heat the oven to 320 degrees. Heat a large roasting pan in the oven. In a large bowl, mix the oil with the garlic and herbs. Add the lamb and rub it all over with the mixture. Season with salt and pepper.

2 Carefully set the lamb, fat side down, in the hot roasting pan. Roast, turning the meat twice, until an instant-read thermometer inserted in the thickest part registers 130 degrees for medium-rare, 2 to 2 $1/2$ hours. Transfer the lamb to a cutting board, cover loosely with foil, and let rest for 10 to 15 minutes.

3 Carve the lamb into slices about $1/8$ inch thick. Arrange on a warmed platter, and serve.

Tip
The hot roasting pan makes the lamb slightly crispier and helps it cook faster.

Serve with
Golden Kohlrabi-Potato Gratin (page 157) is my favorite accompaniment here. I also like this lamb with fried potatoes sprinkled with chopped parsley, or Green Asparagus with Roasted Beets (page 146).

Variations
With such a traditional roast, I prefer to leave it just the way it is. There's nothing wrong with doing a classic the right way. But the garlicky rub, with all those fresh herbs, can be used as a flavor booster in many other lamb dishes, including sautéed lamb chops and grilled or roasted rack of lamb.

Make ahead
The herb-rubbed lamb can be refrigerated overnight before roasting.

BEEF GOULASH

Rinder Saftgulasch

10 SERVINGS

⅓ cup canola oil

6 onions, finely chopped

2 garlic cloves, chopped

3 tablespoons tomato paste

1 tablespoon crushed dried marjoram

1 teaspoon ground caraway

½ cup Hungarian sweet paprika
    (see Tips below, and page 84)

5 pounds boneless beef shin

4 ½ cups water

1 bay leaf
    Salt and freshly ground pepper
    Diced red and yellow bell pepper,
        for garnishing (optional)
    Small marjoram sprigs,
        for garnishing (optional)

This is one of the three most classic dishes of my childhood. (The other two are Veal Schnitzel, page 122, and Boiled Beef Shoulder with Vegetables and Fresh Horseradish, page 138.) When I was at cooking school in Austria, as well as during my apprenticeships, I learned how important it is to master these traditional recipes before experimenting with other more modern dishes.

Once all the ingredients for the goulash are combined, you can just let it simmer for a couple of hours and, in the meantime, prepare a starter and a side dish. Like Goulash Soup (page 84), this stew is eaten at lunchtime at coffeehouses as a *kleines Gulasch* (small goulash) as well as at dinner as a *grosses Gulasch* (big goulash).

The velvety texture of this simple cold-weather stew comes from the onions. As you cook them slowly, they become very soft and sweet. The ratio of onions to meat is important. You want a lot of onions. We always use beef shin meat. I absolutely love shin meat.

1 In a large casserole, heat the oil. Add the onions and cook over medium-high heat, stirring occasionally, until nicely browned, about 10 minutes.
2 Add the garlic, tomato paste, dried marjoram, caraway, and paprika and cook until fragrant, about 2 minutes. Add the beef, water, and bay leaf and season with 1 ½ teaspoons of salt and 1 teaspoon of pepper. Cover and bring to a boil, then reduce the heat to low and cook until the meat is very tender, 2 to 2 ½ hours.
3 Skim off the fat and taste the goulash for seasoning. Spoon onto warmed plates, garnish with the bell pepper dice and marjoram, if desired, and serve.

Tips

The beef should be so tender it cuts with a fork.
The paprika in this dish must be cooked so that it doesn't taste raw. I use a lot of it, which gives a big, rich flavor with a touch of spiciness and a beautiful color.
Once all the ingredients are in the pot and you bring it to a boil on top of the stove, you can transfer it to a 350-degree oven to finish cooking.

Serve with

The typical side dish for saucy goulash is some sort of starch. Both Fresh Herbed Quark Spätzle (page 162) and Bread Dumplings in a Napkin (page 160) are delicious. At my restaurants, customers happily spoon the spätzle right onto their plates.

Variation

I do love beef shin meat, but there's nothing wrong with beef chuck or cheeks.

Make ahead

The stew can be refrigerated for up to 2 days. The flavors develop over time.

PORK GOULASH WITH SAUERKRAUT AND CARAWAY

Szegediner Gulasch

4 SERVINGS

3 tablespoons canola oil

3 medium onions, finely chopped

$1/4$ cup Hungarian sweet paprika
(see Tips, page 84)

$1/4$ cup tomato paste

1 tablespoon thyme leaves (from about
5 large sprigs)

2 tablespoons dried marjoram

2 tablespoons ground caraway

2 pounds boneless pork butt,
cut into 1 $1/2$-inch pieces
Salt and freshly ground pepper

1 cup sauerkraut, drained
and squeezed dry

1 tablespoon coriander seeds,
2 teaspoons white peppercorns,
and 1 bay leaf, all tied in
a cheesecloth bundle

4 cups water
Chopped parsley, for sprinkling

This pork goulash with caraway and tangy-sweet sauerkraut is named after the Hungarian city of Szeged. Serve it with panfried potatoes and a nice cold lager, and you'll have a very traditional, very filling lunch.

1 In a large casserole, heat the oil. Add the onions and cook over medium-high heat, stirring often, until lightly browned, about 10 minutes. Reduce the heat to medium-low and cook, stirring occasionally, until the onions are golden brown, about 5 minutes. **2** Add the paprika and cook, stirring occasionally, until toasted and fragrant, 3 to 4 minutes. Add the tomato paste and cook until slightly browned, 3 to 4 minutes. Stir in the thyme, marjoram, and caraway.

3 Season the pork lightly with salt and pepper and add to the pot, along with the sauerkraut, spice bundle, and water. Bring to a simmer over medium-high heat, then cook over medium-low heat until the meat is tender, 45 minutes to 1 hour. **4** Remove the spice bundle and taste the stew for seasoning. Transfer the goulash to a warmed serving dish or bowls, sprinkle with parsley, and serve.

Tips
Browning the onions is essential for this dish. Even though it takes a little more time to cook them to the required golden brown over lower heat, don't rush it.
Season the goulash lightly with salt to begin, because the liquid reduces as the stew cooks, boosting the saltiness. Taste again for seasoning just before serving.

Serve with
The classic accompaniment is boiled or fried potatoes, like Salz Kartoffel (salt potatoes). To make them, boil peeled potatoes (russets work well) until just tender enough to slice. Cut crosswise into quarters or smaller slices and sauté in a large skillet with a couple of tablespoons of butter and salt and pepper until lightly browned. Sprinkle with chopped chives, and serve.

Variation
While the sauerkraut and caraway are what make this goulash special, the stew is still wonderful without them.

Make ahead
As for other braises, the flavors in this goulash develop over time. It can be refrigerated for up to 2 days.

VENISON GOULASH

Rehgulasch

Deer are common in Austria, and hunting is very popular. In autumn—deer-hunting season—the meat is often frozen, then added to hearty dishes like this through the winter months. The toasted traditional venison spices—allspice, juniper, coriander, peppercorns, and caraway—give this delicious stew a smoky, aromatic flavor.

4 SERVINGS

2 tablespoons allspice berries

2 tablespoons juniper berries

1 tablespoon black peppercorns

1 tablespoon coriander seeds

1 teaspoon caraway seeds

2 pounds boneless venison shoulder,
    cut into 1 ½-inch pieces

3 tablespoons canola oil

2 large onions, finely chopped
    Salt

3 large carrots, cut into ¼-inch dice

1 medium celery root (about 12 ounces),
    thickly peeled and cut into
    ¼-inch dice

2 garlic cloves, crushed

1 tablespoon white wine vinegar

¼ cup Hungarian sweet paprika
    (see Tips, page 84)

2 tablespoons tomato paste

1 teaspoon crushed dried marjoram
    Freshly ground pepper

2 cups water

1 cup dry red wine

1 Heat the oven to 400 degrees. Spread the allspice, juniper berries, peppercorns, coriander, and caraway in a pie plate and toast in the oven until fragrant, 5 to 7 minutes. Remove from the oven and let cool completely.

2 In a spice or coffee grinder, coarsely grind the spices. In a large bowl, stir the spice mixture into the venison, coating it evenly.

3 In a large casserole, heat the oil over medium-high heat. Add the onions, season lightly with salt, and cook until lightly browned, about 5 minutes. Add the venison and cook, stirring occasionally, until browned on all sides, 3 to 5 minutes. Transfer the meat to a bowl.

4 Add the carrots, celery root, and garlic to the pot and cook, stirring occasionally, until lightly browned, about 5 minutes. Stir in the vinegar, and return the meat to the pot. Add the paprika and cook, stirring, for 2 minutes. Add the tomato paste and marjoram and cook, stirring, for 2 minutes. Season with salt and pepper.

5 Add the water and wine, cover, and bring to a boil, then reduce the heat to low and cook, stirring occasionally, until the meat is tender, 2 to 3 hours. Add more water during cooking if the stew looks dry. The goulash should be saucy.

6 Taste for seasoning, and serve.

Tips

Farm-raised venison is the most readily available kind in the U.S. for both restaurateurs and home cooks and is sold at many butcher shops. Since the meat is so lean, the stew really doesn't need to be defatted, especially since a little fat adds a lot of flavor.

Once all the ingredients are in the pot and you bring them to a boil on top of the stove, you can transfer the stew to a 350-degree oven to finish cooking.

Serve with

You can play around with the side dishes and serve Braised Red Cabbage (page 151) or a fall vegetables like brussels sprouts or salsify.

For an appetizer, serve something light, such as Oxtail Consommé with Bone Marrow Dumplings (page 82) or Red Cabbage Salad with Apples and Toasted Walnuts (page 90).

Make ahead

The recipe can be made through Step 2, covered, and refrigerated overnight. The finished goulash can be refrigerated for up to 2 days.

BOILED BEEF SHOULDER
WITH VEGETABLES AND FRESH HORSERADISH

Kavalierspitz

My *Kavalierspitz* is a dish with a lot going on. It is essentially boiled beef, but it becomes something more because of the garnishes served with it. When this dish is prepared with a cut from the shoulder of a cow, it is called *Kavalierspitz*, and when it is prepared with the hindquarters (the rump), it's *Tafelspitz*. Here in America, I find more consistent success using beef shoulder. The two preparations are exactly the same otherwise, as are the traditional sides and garnishes—Classic Potato Rösti (page 158), Creamed Spinach (page 153), freshly grated horseradish, and sea salt.

1 In a large pot, combine the water with the kosher salt, peppercorns, bay leaves, juniper berries, onions, parsley stems, and mustard seeds and bring to a boil over medium-high heat. Add the beef, reduce the heat to medium-low, and simmer, skimming often during the first 10 to 15 minutes, until the meat is very tender, about 2 hours. A roasting fork should slip in easily and not stick.

2 Add the carrots and celery root and cook until just tender, 15 to 20 minutes.

3 Serve some of the broth as a first course, with a little of the carrots and celery root.

4 Then serve the meat: Transfer the meat to a cutting board and slice about ½ inch thick, across the grain. Arrange 2 or 3 slices in each warmed soup plate. Moisten with about 1 cup of the broth; the meat should not be completely submerged. Garnish with the remaining carrots and celery root, sprinkle with some of the horseradish, chives, and sea salt, and serve. Pass the remaining horseradish, chives, and sea salt separately.

Tips

I leave the onions unpeeled to intensify the color of the beef broth.

What makes this cut of meat so tender and juicy is the connective tissue. It is high in collagen, which turns gelatinous when cooked for a long time. In German, this is called the *Gallert*.

Don't trim the fat if you want extra flavor. Besides, the broth needs those little "eyes" of fat to give it some body. Horseradish is very common in Austrian cooking, and it is often grown at home since it's simple to cultivate. Its strong flavor punches up many dishes—including the weekend brunch Bloody Marys at Blaue Gans and Wallsé.

Serve with

Sometimes I serve this dish with a spicy-sweet apple horseradish sauce, which can easily be made at home. Simply stir 2 tablespoons (or 3, if you like it very spicy) of freshly grated horseradish into 1 cup of applesauce.

Variations

The flavorful leftover broth can be strained and used as the base of a sauce or a soup, such as Oxtail Consommé with Bone Marrow Dumplings (page 82).

Make ahead

Kavalierspitz can be refrigerated for up to 2 days.

A work by Albert Oehlen makes a graphic contrast to *Kavalierspitz*'s tender richness presented in a Trude Petri *Urbino* covered vegetable dish, designed for KPM, from Neue Galerie Design Shop.

BRAISED VENISON SHOULDER WITH RED WINE AND ROOT VEGETABLES

Rotwein geschmorte Rehschulter mit Wurzelgemüse

8 SERVINGS

2 tablespoons allspice berries

2 tablespoons juniper berries

1 tablespoon black peppercorns

1 tablespoon coriander seeds

1 tablespoon caraway seeds

2 boneless venison shoulder roasts
    (about 2 pounds each)

Salt

2 tablespoons canola oil

2 tablespoons unsalted butter

2 large onions, finely chopped

Freshly ground pepper

1 tablespoon tomato paste

One 14-ounce can diced tomatoes,
    with their liquid

1 garlic clove, finely chopped

4 cups dry red wine

2 cups ruby port

2 tablespoons lingonberry
    or cranberry preserves

About 6 cups beef stock,
    chicken stock, or water (see Tips)

2 large carrots, peeled and cut into
    $1/2$-inch dice

1 medium celery root (about
    12 ounces), thickly peeled and cut
    into $1/2$-inch dice

2 parsnips, peeled and cut into
    $1/2$-inch dice

Does using jam in a braise surprise you? But lingonberry preserves are tart. Their fruitiness keeps any gaminess from the venison from being overpowering. They also thicken the sauce and make the dish nice and glossy. The combination of fruit and spice flavors is a classic pairing with game meat—perfect as an entrée for company during the cold fall and winter months.

1 Heat the oven to 400 degrees. Spread the allspice, juniper berries, peppercorns, coriander, and caraway seeds in a pie plate and toast in the oven until fragrant, 5 to 7 minutes. Remove from the oven and let cool completely.

2 In a spice or coffee grinder, coarsely grind the spices. In a large bowl, rub the spice mixture all over the meat, and season with salt.

3 In a large casserole, heat the oil until shimmering. Add 1 shoulder at a time to the pot and cook over medium-high heat until lightly browned all over, about 2 minutes on each side. Remove the meat to a platter.

4 Add the butter and onions to the pot, season with salt and pepper, and cook over high heat until the onions are lightly browned, 5 to 7 minutes. Stir in the tomato paste, tomatoes, and garlic. Return the meat to the pot, add one-third of the red wine and port and cook until almost evaporated. Repeat 2 more times with the remaining port and wine.

5 Add the lingonberry preserves and enough stock to cover the meat by 1 inch. Cover and bring to a boil, then simmer over medium-low heat for 1 $1/2$ hours.

6 Add the carrots, celery root, and parsnips and simmer until the venison is tender, about 1 hour.

7 Transfer the meat to a cutting board and slice $1/4$ inch thick. Arrange on a large warmed platter, ladle the sauce and vegetables over the top, and serve.

Tips

By letting the wine and port slowly reduce three times, the sauce darkens significantly and the flavors become much more intense.

Do not let the spices darken too much in the oven, or they will become bitter.

If you don't have enough stock to cover the meat generously, you can add water to make up the difference.

Serve with

Traditional side dishes are Celery Root Puree (page 152), Fresh Herbed Quark Spätzle (page 162), and poached pears in vanilla-infused white wine syrup, topped with lingonberry preserves. Roasted brussels sprouts or cauliflower would also be a nice accompaniment.

Variation

You can use the venison spice blend for any kind of game. Or mix it with coarse sea salt (one-third spice blend to two-thirds salt) and pass it at the table for sprinkling over grilled steak.

Make ahead

The spice mixture can be stored in a sealed container indefinitely. The spice-rubbed venison can be refrigerated overnight.

BOILED VEAL TONGUE
WITH CREAMY HORSERADISH SAUCE

Gekochte Kalbszunge mit Krensauce

4 SERVINGS

8 cups water

¼ pound onions, chopped

8 black peppercorns

1 bay leaves

2 juniper berries

1 tablespoon kosher salt

A handful of parsley stems

1 ½ teaspoons mustard seeds

1 veal tongue (1 ½ to 2 pounds)

¼ pound carrots, peeled and cut into ½-inch dice

¼ pound celery root, thickly peeled and cut into ½-inch dice

½ cup heavy cream

Juice of ½ lemon

Salt and freshly ground pepper

¼ cup freshly grated horseradish

I was raised in a small village by the Danube. My family wasn't rich, and we knew the meaning of resourcefulness. Everything—including all parts of the animal—was used in some way, so that nothing was wasted. I love offal and this tongue recipe, with its rich, spicy sauce, in particular.

1 In a large pot, combine the water with the onions, peppercorns, bay leaves, juniper berries, kosher salt, parsley, and mustard seeds and bring to a boil over high heat. Add the tongue, reduce the heat to medium-low, and cook, skimming for the first 10 to 15 minutes, until the tip of the tongue is tender, 1 ½ to 2 hours.

2 Fill a large bowl with cold water. Transfer the tongue to the cold water to cool it slightly, about 1 minute. Working quickly, transfer the tongue to a cutting board and peel off the skin. Let the tongue cool completely.

3 Meanwhile, strain the broth through a fine sieve into a large saucepan; discard the contents of the sieve. Bring the broth to a boil over medium-high heat. Add the carrots and celery root and cook until just tender, about 10 minutes. Fill a medium bowl with ice water.

4 Using a slotted spoon, transfer the vegetables to the ice water to cool them quickly, 1 to 2 minutes, then drain.

5 In a medium saucepan, bring 2 cups of the broth to a simmer. Reserve the remaining broth for another use. Whisk in the cream and lemon juice and season with salt and pepper. Cook the sauce over medium-high heat until it lightly coats the back of a spoon, 7 to 10 minutes. Whisk in the horseradish and remove from the heat.

6 Thinly slice the tongue. Using a slotted spoon, spread the vegetables on a warmed platter or plates and arrange the tongue slices on top. Spoon some of the horseradish sauce on the tongue and serve, passing the remaining sauce at the table.

Tips

In Step 3, don't press down on the contents of the sieve. You want only the free-flowing juices.

To thicken the sauce in Step 5, you may want to add 1 to 2 teaspoons of cornstarch. Just before adding the horseradish, blend a little of the broth into the cornstarch, then whisk this slurry into the simmering broth.

Serve with

Bread Dumplings in a Napkin (page 160), Fresh Herbed Quark Spätzle (page 162), or boiled or mashed potatoes make a nice accompaniment.

Variations

I like to serve thin slices of the veal tongue alongside braised veal cheeks.

For a mid-afternoon snack, make a sandwich with rye bread and thinly sliced tongue, spread with a little spicy mustard and freshly grated horseradish.

Make ahead

The tongue can be cooked ahead, and the tongue and broth frozen, separately, for up to 1 month. The sauce, however, is best prepared at the last minute, because horseradish quickly turns it gray and bitter.

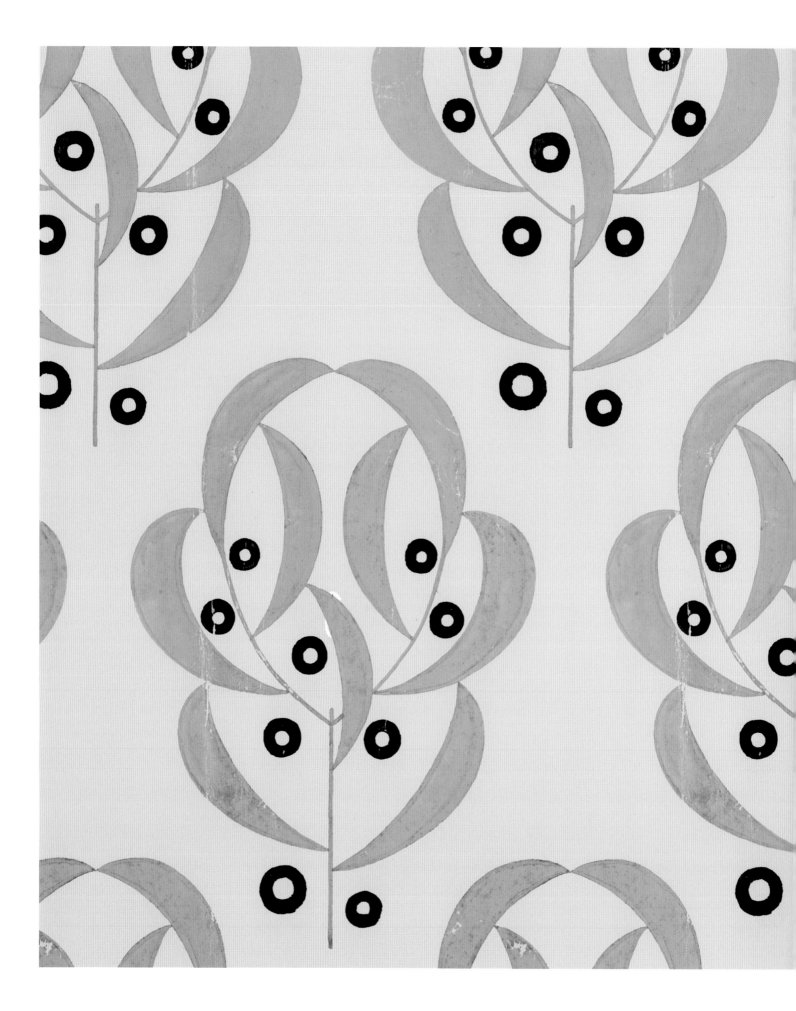

SIDE DISHES

MARINATED ZUCCHINI SALAD

Zucchini Salat

2 SERVINGS

1 pound zucchini, thinly sliced into ribbons
    on a mandoline
2 teaspoons sugar
4 teaspoons salt
1/4 teaspoon freshly ground pepper
1/4 cup extra-virgin olive oil
    Juice of 1/2 lime
    Small lettuce leaves, microgreens, and
    edible flowers, for garnishing (optional)

A salad can be a kind of condiment and contribute to the complexity of a meal, brightening the whole plate and adding a spark of unexpected flavor. Lightly marinated vegetable salads like this one are common on Austrian tables throughout the summer. I slice the zucchini on a mandoline into extra-thin ribbons to soak up the citrusy dressing.

1 In a large bowl, combine the zucchini with the sugar and salt and toss to coat. Add the pepper, olive oil, and lime juice and toss to coat.

2 Mound the salad on plates or a platter, garnish with lettuce leaves, microgreens, and edible flowers, if desired, and serve.

Tip

A mandoline is very sharp and can be tricky to use. Keep your fingertips at least 1/2 inch away from the blade when slicing the zucchini or use a guard.

Serve with

Make this dish part of a large summer antipasto buffet, along with other salads like Marinated Heirloom Tomato Salad (page 86). It's also a nice accompaniment to a grilled piece of fish.

Make ahead

The flavor of the salad deepens if left to marinate for at least 30 minutes. It can be refrigerated for up to 2 days.

Austria's lineup of specialty oils and vinegars goes beyond the familiar to make a dizzying assortment of salads including Marinated Zucchini Salad.

GREEN ASPARAGUS WITH ROASTED BEETS

Grüner Spargel mit gebratenen roten Rüben

4 SERVINGS

4 medium beets (about 1 ½ pounds total)
   Sea salt
2 teaspoons caraway seeds
1 pound medium green asparagus
   (16 spears)
2 tablespoons unsalted butter
½ cup extra-virgin olive oil
¼ cup fresh lemon juice
1 teaspoon Dijon mustard
¼ cup microgreens (optional)

Most people think vegetables can't be sexy. Outside of summer especially, you have to think about them differently. It's important to look at seasonal ingredients and treat them with a little more imagination. This bright and colorful spring dish with a pinch of caraway shows how amazing the rewards can be. Plus, it's not complicated to prepare.

1 Heat the oven to 350 degrees. Wrap each beet in foil, with ½ teaspoon of salt and ½ teaspoon of the caraway seeds. Set the packages on a baking sheet and roast until the beets are tender when pierced with a knife, about 1 ½ hours. Remove from the oven and let cool completely.

2 Meanwhile, bring a large saucepan of salted water to a boil. Fill a medium bowl with ice water. Add the asparagus to the boiling water and cook until just tender, 4 to 5 minutes. Drain and transfer to the ice water to cool as quickly as possible, 1 to 2 minutes. Drain again and pat dry.

3 Peel the beets and slice them lengthwise ¼ inch thick.

4 In a large skillet, melt the butter over medium-high heat. Add the asparagus and 1 teaspoon of salt and cook, stirring the asparagus to coat, for 1 to 2 minutes. Remove from the heat and let cool.

5 In a small bowl, whisk the olive oil with the lemon juice, mustard and ¼ teaspoon of salt.

6 Spread the slices of 1 beet on each plate and arrange 4 asparagus spears on top. Garnish with 1 tablespoon of the micro-greens, if desired. Drizzle with the lemon dressing, and serve.

Tip
This dish should be served at room temperature.

Serve with
The salad is delicious with Roasted Leg of Lamb (page 133) or a roast chicken.

Variation
For extra flavor and color, spoon a little basil oil on each plate before adding the beets and asparagus. See the Variation following Halibut with Cucumber-Dill Sauce and Chanterelles (page 104) for how to make basil oil.

Make ahead
Since it's best at room temperature, this salad is a great dish to prepare in advance. In addition, the blanched asparagus and roasted beets can be prepared ahead and refrigerated, separately, overnight.

ROASTED SUMMER VEGETABLES WITH HERBS

Sommer Gemüse mit frischen Kräutern

4 SERVINGS

- 2 tablespoons canola oil
- 2 ounces haricots verts, cut into thirds
- 2 ounces wax beans, cut into thirds
- 1/3 cup shelled fava beans (optional)
- 2 ounces baby carrots, preferably multicolored heirloom varieties, diced
- 1 tablespoon unsalted butter
- 4 baby zucchini, sliced 1/4 inch thick
- 1/2 bunch of scallions, thinly sliced
- 1 garlic clove, minced
- 1 teaspoon salt
- 1 tablespoon chopped mixed herbs, such as chervil, parsley, basil, and thyme
- 1 teaspoon fresh lemon juice
- 1/2 teaspoon freshly black pepper

This is a great way to showcase all the gorgeous produce available in the market at the height of summer. The vegetables are first lightly browned on top of the stove, then cooked in the oven until al dente and tossed with herbs and lemon juice for a hit of freshness.

1 Heat the oven to 350 degrees. In a large ovenproof skillet, warm the oil over medium-high heat until shimmering. Add the haricot verts, wax beans, and fava beans, if using, and cook, stirring, for 1 minute. Add the carrots and cook, stirring occasionally, until the vegetables are lightly browned, 1 to 2 minutes. Stir in the butter, zucchini, scallions, and garlic and season with the salt.

2 Transfer the skillet to the oven and roast the vegetables just until they are al dente, about 3 minutes. Remove the skillet from the oven and stir in the herbs, lemon juice, and pepper. Transfer to a warmed platter, and serve.

Variation

This is one of those dishes where, really, anything goes. Experiment with other vegetables, using, cauliflower or broccoli florets, for instance, or snap peas.

Serve with

Try these roasted vegetables with roast chicken or other poultry dishes, or serve alongside Roast Pork Loin with Armagnac-Prune Sauce (page 132). The roasted vegetables can be refrigerated for up to 1 day.

BAKED MARIZPAN-STUFFED APPLES

Bratäpfeln

6 SERVINGS

6 ounces marzipan (see Tips, page 202)

2 teaspoons rum

6 apples, preferably Boskoop or Gala, cored

¾ cup dry white wine

1 tablespoon unsalted butter

Baked apples are usually served as a cozy dessert, but they also make a great fall or winter side dish for poultry or pork instead of the usual roasted or boiled potatoes.

1 Heat the oven to 375 degrees. Blend the marzipan with the rum in a medium bowl.
2 Stand the apples in a large gratin dish and spoon the marzipan filling into them.

Add the wine and butter to the dish. Bake the apples, basting occasionally, until they are tender but still hold their shape, about 45 minutes. Serve warm.

Serve with

I like to serve these savory baked apples alongside Christmas Goose (page 110), Roasted Pork Shanks with Sauerkraut (page 131), or Roast Pork Loin with Armagnac-Prune Sauce (page 132).

Wiener Werkstätte Postcard Number 8A by Mela Koehler, Girl with Apple, 1910. Leonard A. Lauder Collection, Neue Galerie New York.

GREEN CABBAGE WITH GRANNY SMITH APPLES

Weisskraut mit grünen Äpfeln

6 SERVINGS

1 large green cabbage (about 3 pounds), halved, cored, and coarsely shredded (12 cups)
1 cup Riesling
2 tablespoons fresh lemon juice
1 ½ tablespoons sugar
¼ cup extra-virgin olive oil
1 large onion, thinly sliced
2 Granny Smith apples, peeled, cored, halved, and sliced ⅛ inch thick
Salt and freshly ground pepper

This simple blend of shredded cabbage, sliced green apples, and Riesling is a wonderful accompaniment to pork and game dishes, especially in the fall and winter.

1 In a large bowl, toss the cabbage with the wine, lemon juice, and sugar. Let marinate for 1 hour, tossing often.

2 In a large deep skillet, heat the olive oil. Add the onion and cook over medium heat until golden, about 8 minutes. Add the cabbage and its marinade and cook over medium-high heat, tossing, until wilted, about 5 minutes. Cover and cook over medium-low heat, stirring occasionally, until almost tender, about 20 minutes.

3 Add the apples and toss well. Cover and cook, stirring occasionally, until the apples are just tender, about 10 minutes. Season with salt and pepper, and serve.

Tip
If you toss the apples with lemon juice after slicing them, they will stay whiter longer. The lemon juice also adds a nice tartness to the sauté.

Serve with
I like this with either simple pan-seared pork chops or Christmas Goose (page 110).

Variation
Adding crispy bacon or pancetta gives the dish a heartier flavor.

Make ahead
The cabbage can be prepared through Step 2 and refrigerated overnight.

BRAISED RED CABBAGE

Geschmortes Rotkraut

4 SERVINGS

1 medium red cabbage (about 2 pounds),
　　quartered, cored, and thinly sliced

2 tablespoons salt

$1/4$ cup sugar

1 cup dry red wine

1 cup port

1 large onion, finely chopped

$1/2$ cup goose fat (see Tip) or canola oil

3 tablespoons red wine vinegar

$1/3$ cup honey

$1/2$ cup lingonberry preserves

1 apple, cored and grated (with skin)
　　Juice of 2 oranges
　　Juice of 1 lemon

Red cabbage is a traditional winter vegetable, which makes it an excellent partner for Christmas Goose (page 110). Adding goose fat to the cabbage as it braises helps blend the flavors together, while the slight acidity from the red wine and vinegar provides a nice foil for the rich goose.

1 In a large bowl, toss the cabbage with the salt.

2 In a large casserole, heat the sugar over medium-high heat until it forms a light brown caramel, about 4 minutes. Remove the casserole from the heat and carefully add the red wine and port. Return to the heat and cook, stirring to dissolve the hardened caramel, for 1 minute. Add the onion and fat, bring to a boil, and cook until the mixture has reduced by half, about 5 minutes.

3 Add the cabbage, vinegar, honey, lingonberries, apple, and orange and lemon juice, reduce the heat to medium, and cook, stirring occasionally, until the cabbage is tender, 40 to 45 minutes. Serve.

Tip
Goose fat is available at Schaller & Weber in New York City (schallerandweber.com). Or use the rendered fat from Christmas Goose (page 110), if you're roasting it at the same time.

Serve with
The cabbage is also great with duck, pork, and, really, any other type of braised meat, such as Venison Goulash (page 137) or Braised Venison Shoulder with Red Wine and Root Vegetables (page 140).

Variation
I like this cabbage as is, but at Christmastime, it's nice to add a pinch of ground cinnamon or cloves.

Make ahead
The cabbage can be refrigerated for up to 1 week.

CELERY ROOT PUREE

Selleriepüree

4 SERVINGS

2 pounds celery root, thickly peeled and
   cut into chunks (see Tips)
2 cups heavy cream
1 cup beef or chicken stock
1 large onion, cut into chunks
1 garlic clove, crushed
1 tablespoon fresh lemon juice
1 teaspoon salt
$\frac{1}{2}$ teaspoon freshly ground pepper
$\frac{1}{4}$ teaspoon freshly grated nutmeg

Bulbous white celery root, also called celeriac, is a common ingredient in Austrian cooking. Its flavor is much subtler than that of the pungent dark green celery stalks. Like most root vegetables, it keeps very well. Many families, including mine, used to store barrels of them in cellars to cook throughout the coldest months in everything from soups and stocks to purees. This is a creamy, light beige puree with an earthy taste.

1 In a large saucepan, combine all of the ingredients and cook, uncovered over medium-high heat, stirring occasionally, until the celery root is very soft, 20 to 25 minutes. Remove the pan from the heat and let cool for 7 to 10 minutes.

2 Working in batches, puree the mixture in a food processor or a blender at high speed until smooth. Reheat if necessary. Serve.

Tips

The skin of the celery root can be quite tough, so peel it thickly—down to the white flesh—using a paring knife rather than a vegetable peeler. You might want to cut it into quarters so it's easier to hold and peel.

Save the celery root peel to make stock or soup. It gives great flavor and color and, really, there is no reason to throw it out. In Austria, we are strong believers in wasting as little as possible.

Serve with

This puree is lovely with red meats, venison, and game birds such as squab and quail. At Wallsé, I serve it alongside Rib-Eye Steaks with Crispy Onion Rings (page 128).

Make ahead

The puree can be refrigerated for up to 2 days.

CREAMED SPINACH

Cremespinat

4 SERVINGS

Salt

1 ½ pounds spinach, large stems removed

5 tablespoons unsalted butter

⅓ cup all-purpose flour

2 ½ cups milk

Freshly grated nutmeg

Freshly ground pepper

This silky spinach dish is buttery and delicious—and the bright green color really stands out on the table. It's a classic side to boiled beef, soft-boiled eggs, or roasted whole trout. My customers often order one as a side for the table, then end up ordering more, maybe two or three extras. They just love it!

1 Bring a large pot of salted water to a boil. Fill a large bowl with ice water. Add the spinach to the boiling water and cook until it begins to wilt but is still bright green, 30 seconds to 1 minute. Drain in a colander and transfer to the ice water to cool as quickly as possible, 1 to 2 minutes; drain again. Spread on a kitchen towel or paper towels and roll up to remove most of the excess water.

2 In a small saucepan, melt the butter over medium-high heat. Add the flour and cook, stirring, until smooth, about 1 minute. Stir in the milk, season with nutmeg, salt, and pepper, and bring to a boil. Immediately reduce the heat to medium-low and cook, stirring occasionally, until the sauce thickens slightly, about 10 minutes. Remove the pan from the heat and let the sauce cool completely.

3 In a blender or food processor, puree the spinach with the sauce until smooth. In a medium saucepan, reheat the spinach gently, and taste for seasoning. Serve hot.

Tip

Take care to dry the spinach leaves well with a towel. Any excess water will make the creamed spinach separate.

Serve with

At Wallsé, this rich spinach is always served with Boiled Beef Shoulder with Vegetables and Fresh Horseradish (page 138).

Variation

While traditionally this spinach is passed at the table as a side dish, I also like to use it as a creamy bed for many entrées. I spread it under sautéed trout fillets, because the colors go together beautifully. For how to cook trout, see Brook Trout with Cauliflower, Raisins, and Almonds (page 98).

Make ahead

The creamed spinach can be refrigerated for up to 2 days. Also, it's an ideal recipe to freeze and then serve when you have people over; transfer it to the refrigerator to thaw the night before.

TABLEWARE ACCESSORIES

The Wiener Werkstätte stated in its 1905 *Working Program* that one of its objectives was to produce useful and well-made objects for the home. Many of these were intended for the table. In October 1906, the firm held an exhibition *Der gedeckte Tisch* or "The Laid Table." The show included sixty different tables artistically laid-out with cutlery, glassware, and ceramics designed by members of the firm.

Each table had a theme—a lady's tea table, a wedding table, an anniversary table, and an artist's table, among others. Floral settings were chosen to match, making certain no colors clashed. The children's table had a bowl of brightly colored decorative candies instead of flowers. Koloman Moser even designed pastries for the occasion.

The firm was most innovative with its metalwork designs. The *Gitterwerk*, or latticework, pieces by Josef Hoffmann and Koloman Moser from the founding years of the Wiener Werkstätte rank as icons of early twentieth-century design. While the simple aesthetic of these works suggests machine production, they were in fact handmade, often in very limited numbers. Record books confirm that the silver objects were typically produced in fewer than a dozen copies, and often far less than that. Sometimes only one item was crafted for a specific client.

A detail that is special about Wiener Werkstätte objects is how they are marked. Each piece typically bears the firm's hallmark but in addition, the monograms of the artist who designed it and of the maker who crafted the work are often included. This is one way in which the firm highlighted the importance of both the artist and the craftsman.

The Neue Galerie's 1914 wood-paneled dining room is again the setting for
a turn-of-the-century repast. Bertold Löffler's 1907 poster for the Fledermaus theater
and cabaret hangs on the wall beneath a jewel-like Josef Hoffmann sconce.
Hoffmann's 1907 steam-bent beechwood chairs surround a table adorned with his
1905 wine coaster and 1923 silver stopper. Karl Sedelmayer's 1810 silver spicecasters,
Heinz Weingarten's 1912 leaf-patterned damask napkins tucked into Biscaye Frères
2009 sterling silver napkin cuffs, and Benedikt Ranninger's 1817 silver candlesticks
add decorative touches. All items provided by Neue Galerie Design Shop.

POTATO AND CUCUMBER SALAD

Erdäpfel-Gurkensalat

4 TO 6 SERVINGS

1 English cucumber,
    sliced paper-thin on a mandoline
Salt
2 pounds Austrian Crescent or other
    fingerling potatoes (see Tips)
    Pinch of caraway seeds
    Freshly ground pepper
½ cup chicken stock
¼ cup finely chopped onion
1 tablespoon Dijon mustard
¼ cup cider vinegar, or to taste
2 tablespoons mild extra-virgin olive oil
1 tablespoon canola oil
2 tablespoons sour cream, crème fraîche,
    or plain yogurt (optional)
2 tablespoons finely chopped dill
    Borage flowers, for garnishing
    (see Tips; optional)

There is great teamwork in this classic Austrian potato salad, the crunchy cucumbers and the tender potatoes playing off each other. I love the pairing, because the cucumber makes the salad fresher and lighter than if it were made only with potatoes. The dressing includes cider vinegar—or white wine vinegar, if you prefer—and an oil that is fairly light but helps tie everything together. A little mustard gives it some bite.

1 In a medium bowl, toss the cucumber slices with 2 teaspoons of salt.

2 In a large saucepan, cover the potatoes with water. Add the caraway seeds and season with salt. Bring to a boil and cook until the potatoes are just tender, about 15 minutes. Drain the potatoes, peel, and thin slices into a large bowl while still warm. Season with salt and pepper.

3 In a small saucepan, bring the stock and onion to a boil. Add to the potatoes and toss gently until lightly thickened (see Tips). Fold in the mustard, vinegar, and oils.

4 Drain the cucumbers well, squeezing out the liquid. Fold the cucumbers into the potatoes. Season with more salt, pepper, and vinegar, if needed. Add the sour cream, if using it. Fold in the dill, garnish with the flowers, if desired, and serve.

Tips

I like to use fingerling potatoes for salads because you get beautiful little round slices. You absolutely must cook them unpeeled so they hold their shape. Then peel, slice, and dress them while they're still warm so they absorb the seasonings. Their natural starch will help them thicken the dressing and make it milky, and that won't happen if they've cooled.

Save the flavorful cucumber liquid; it can be used in soups or sauces.

If you can find them, periwinkle-blue borage flowers, with their cucumber-like taste, are the perfect garnish here.

Serve with

This salad is the traditional partner for Veal Schnitzel (page 122). Having such a cool and fresh salad to accompany it really balances the meal.

I also like to serve this with the golden fried chicken called *Backhändl*, as well as with various sausages.

Variations

Do you want a touch of raw or roasted garlic, or maybe some freshly grated horseradish? They're fine, providing you don't overdo it. Keep tasting as you go.

Adding a little mayonnaise and paprika to the salad will make it slightly richer.

Make ahead

The salad can be refrigerated for up to 3 days, but it's best at room temperature.

GOLDEN KOHLRABI-POTATO GRATIN

Erdäpfel-Kohlrabi Gratin

4 SERVINGS

Unsalted butter, for brushing

2 *medium kohlrabi (1 pound total), peeled and thinly sliced*

1 *pound russet (baking) potatoes, peeled and thinly sliced*

1 *teaspoon salt*

½ *teaspoon freshly ground pepper*

¼ *teaspoon freshly grated nutmeg*

1 ½ *cups heavy cream*

½ *cup milk*

1 *garlic clove, crushed*

Kohlrabi, sometimes called German turnip, is part of the cabbage family. (*Kohl* means "cabbage" in German.) But its texture is like a root, and the taste falls somewhere between that of a broccoli stem and a potato. It is easy to cultivate, so Austrians often grow it in their vegetable gardens. You see people starting to play around with kohlrabi in the U.S. these days, but in Europe—mainly Austria, Switzerland, and Germany—it's long been used as a component in side dishes or served by itself, boiled. I love to eat it raw with a little bit of sea salt. It's like a fresh turnip—a little crunchy and sometimes even a little sweet. In this recipe, I layer thinly sliced kohlrabi with potatoes and bake them in cream, as for scalloped potatoes, until tender and browned on top.

1 Heat the oven to 350 degrees. Lightly brush a gratin dish with butter. In a large bowl, toss the kohlrabi and potatoes with the salt, pepper, and nutmeg. Stir in the cream, milk, and garlic.

2 Spread the mixture in the gratin dish and bake until the top is golden brown, 45 to 50 minutes. Serve.

Tip

For another simple, traditional recipe, thinly slice the kohlrabi and cook it over low heat with a little butter, water, and chopped onion until softened but not browned.

Serve with

Try this creamy dish alongside Roasted Leg of Lamb (page 133) or Rib-Eye Steaks with Crispy Onion Rings (page 128).

You could also serve the gratin with a light green salad for lunch.

Variations

As an extra indulgence, sprinkle ½ cup of grated Emmentaler cheese on top before baking.

Adding some sliced and sautéed cremini mushrooms or cubed Bavarian ham lends more flavor and texture to this dish.

Make ahead

The gratin can be refrigerated for up to 3 days.

CLASSIC POTATO RÖSTI

Erdäpfelrösti

6 SERVINGS

Salt

2 *pounds russet (baking) potatoes, scrubbed*

½ *teaspoon freshly ground pepper*

Pinch of freshly grated nutmeg

Canola oil, for frying

Small herb sprigs and edible flowers,
*   for garnishing (optional)*

Similar to American hash browns, this traditional Austrian side dish is made by pressing shredded grated potatoes into a cake and frying it so it's soft on the inside and crunchy on the outside.

I like to make individual rösti in small cast-iron skillets, but a larger family-style size could easily be made in a 9- or 10-inch cast-iron pan.

1 Bring a large pot of salted water to a boil. Fill a large bowl with ice water. Add the potatoes to the boiling water and cook until starting to soften but still almost raw in the middle, about 10 minutes. Drain and transfer to the ice water to cool as quickly as possible, 1 to 2 minutes.

2 Drain the potatoes and peel them. Using the large holes of a box grater, shred them into a large bowl. Season with 1 teaspoon of salt, the pepper, and nutmeg and toss well to mix.

3 Film a 5-inch cast-iron skillet with oil. Press 1 to 1 ½ cups of the potatoes into the skillet, spreading them to the edges. Fry over medium heat, turning once, until crispy and golden brown, 3 to 4 minutes per side. Transfer to a baking sheet and keep warm in a low oven. Repeat with the remaining potatoes to make 6 rösti. Garnish with herbs and flowers, if desired. Serve as soon as possible.

Tips

A heavy cast-iron skillet is better than nonstick for making rösti because it heats evenly.

Pressing the potatoes into the skillet helps the rösti stick together so it doesn't fall apart when flipped.

Serve with

This dish often accompanies hearty meat entrées that come with a bit of sauce, such as the Boiled Beef Shoulder with Vegetables and Fresh Horseradish (page 138), but my customers like to order a couple of these for the table no matter what they're eating.

Variations

Grated Emmentaler cheese can be sprinkled on top of the finished rösti and melted under a broiler just before serving.

Stirring 1 tablespoon of raw chopped onions or bacon into the shredded potatoes adds extra flavor.

You can create a fun appetizer by cutting the rösti into small pieces and topping it with a dollop of crème fraîche and some Matjes herring, smoked salmon, or even a small slice of beef carpaccio.

Make ahead

Rösti are best when served hot and crispy, right off the stove, but they can be prepared up to 2 hours ahead and reheated in a low oven.

BREAD DUMPLINGS IN A NAPKIN

Serviettenknödel

4 SERVINGS

3 tablespoons unsalted butter

1 medium onion, chopped

5 ½ cups ½-inch cubes crustless bread,
    preferably baguette or brioche

Salt

¼ teaspoon freshly ground pepper

⅛ teaspoon freshly grated nutmeg

1 tablespoon finely chopped parsley

1 tablespoon finely chopped chervil
    (optional)

4 large eggs, lightly beaten

½ cup milk, at room temperature

1 tablespoon canola oil

These classic, homey dumplings are a brilliant way of using leftover bread. First bread cubes are softened in a blend of eggs, milk, and herbs and shaped into a fat sausage. Next, the mixture is wrapped in a napkin and poached in water, and then the dumpling is sliced for serving.

Using a linen napkin to make these dumplings is traditional. It works like a casing, keeping the dumplings from falling apart as they cook. The dumpling napkin is washed only by hand and never starched. The softer it is, the better it molds itself to the dough, and the smoother the dumplings.

1 In a large skillet, melt 1 tablespoon of the butter. Add the onion and cook over medium-high heat, stirring occasionally, until lightly browned, 7 to 10 minutes.

2 In a large bowl, combine the bread cubes with the onion, ½ teaspoon of salt, the pepper, nutmeg, parsley, chervil, eggs, and milk. Using a wooden spoon or your hands, press the mixture together lightly. Let it stand for 20 minutes. It should resemble a very moist stuffing mixture.

3 Bring a large pot of salted water to a boil. Dampen a large linen napkin and spread it on a work surface. Lightly brush with the oil. Transfer the bread mixture to the napkin about 2 inches from the bottom edge. Shape it into an 8-inch-long sausage about 2 ½ inches thick, leaving a border on either end. Tightly roll up the dumpling in the napkin. Tie the ends with kitchen string.

4 Add the dumpling to the boiling water and cook until it is firm and floats to the surface, 12 to 15 minutes. Fill a medium bowl with ice water. Transfer the dumpling to the ice water to cool it as quickly as possible, 1 to 2 minutes. Remove to a platter and refrigerate until completely cool and firm enough to cut, at least 30 minutes.

5 Transfer the dumpling to a cutting board and carefully remove the napkin. Cut the dumpling into slices 1 inch thick and transfer to a platter.

6 In a large skillet, melt the remaining 2 tablespoons of butter over low heat. Add the dumpling slices, without crowding (cook them in batches if needed), and cook, turning once, until lightly browned on both sides, 5 to 7 minutes. Transfer to a warmed platter, pour the butter in the skillet over the dumplings, and serve.

Tip

If one large 8-inch dumpling is too big to fit into your pot, use two napkins and make two 4-inch dumplings instead.

Serve with These dumplings are delicious alongside a hearty stew, such as Beef Goulash (page 134) or Braised Venison Shoulder with Red Wine and Root Vegetables (page 140). They would also go nicely with a hearty vegetarian chili or Roasted Leg of Lamb (page 133).

Variation

The dumplings can be varied endlessly. You could add some chopped cooked mushrooms or vegetables to make a substantial vegetarian dumpling. Or add ½ cup diced ham for extra flavor.

Make ahead

The recipe can be made through Step 5 and refrigerated for up to 1 day.

RAMP SPÄTZLE

Bärlauchspätzle

4 SERVINGS

Salt
1/4 *pound ramps, leaves only (see Tips)*
3/4 *cup quark cheese (see Tips, page 162)*
2 1/4 *cups all-purpose flour*
2 *large eggs*
2 *tablespoons unsalted butter*

Ramps, wild leeks, pack a great deal of garlicky flavor into any dish, and this one is no exception. I love this variation on classic Fresh Herbed Quark Spätzle (page 162), because of the taste and the beautiful bright green color.

1 Bring a large saucepan of salted water to a boil. Meanwhile, in a blender, combine the ramps and quark and puree until smooth.
2 In a large bowl, whisk the flour with 1/2 teaspoon of salt. Add the eggs and ramp puree and beat until smooth. The batter will be very soft and wet.
3 Fill a large bowl with ice water. Working in batches, press the dough through a spätzle maker into the boiling water, or use a colander with large holes and a rubber spatula. Cook until the spätzle float to the surface, 2 to 3 minutes. Using a fine sieve, transfer the spätzle to the ice water for 1 to 2 minutes to cool, then remove to a colander to drain.
4 In a large skillet, melt the butter. Add the spätzle and cook over medium-high heat, stirring occasionally, until lightly browned. Season with salt, and serve.

Tips
You can save the ramp roots and whites for pickling. See Tuna with White Asparagus, Citrus Marinade, and Pickled Ramps (page 101).
This recipe doubles easily.
Ramps need to be cleaned well to remove any dirt between the tight layers.

Serve with
I like this spätzle alongside something meaty, like grilled lamb, or next to a hearty fish such as Monkfish with Chanterelles and Jerusalem Artichokes (page 102).

Variations
Fresh basil can replace the ramps. Add 3/4 cup of chopped leaves.

Make ahead
If you toss the boiled spätzle with a little olive oil, it can be refrigerated for up to 2 days.

FRESH HERBED QUARK SPÄTZLE

Topfenspätzle mit frischen Kräutern

4 SERVINGS

Salt

2 *cups all-purpose flour*

Freshly ground pepper

$\frac{1}{8}$ *teaspoon freshly grated nutmeg*

2 *large eggs, lightly beaten*

1 *cup quark cheese (see Tips)*

$\frac{1}{3}$ *cup heavy cream*

2 *tablespoons unsalted butter*

2 *tablespoons mixed chopped herbs,
    such as parsley, basil, chervil,
    and tarragon*

Recipes travel. Spätzle, similar in texture to gnocchi, is found all across central Europe. At my restaurants, this fresh pasta, which is boiled and then sautéed in butter until golden and crisped in spots, is easily one of the most frequently ordered side dishes.

1 Bring a large saucepan of salted water to a boil. Meanwhile, in a large bowl, whisk the flour with $\frac{1}{2}$ teaspoon of salt, $\frac{1}{4}$ teaspoon of pepper, and the nutmeg. Add the eggs, quark, and cream and beat until smooth.

2 Fill a large bowl with ice water. Working in batches, press the dough through a spätzle maker into the boiling water; or use a colander with large holes and a rubber spatula.

Cook until the spätzle float to the surface, 2 to 3 minutes. Using a fine sieve, transfer the spätzle to the ice water for 1 to 2 minutes to cool, then remove to a colander to drain.

3 In a large skillet, melt the butter. Add the spätzle and cook over medium-high heat, stirring occasionally, until lightly browned. Season with salt and pepper, sprinkle the herbs over the top, and serve.

Tips

Quark is a soft, tangy fresh cheese with a consistency similar to that of Greek-style yogurt or sour cream. In Austria and Germany, it is often served as a topping for fruit, smeared on bread, or incorporated into dishes such as this creamy spätzle.

Spätzle makers come in different styles, but the two most common are the standard spätzle maker, which consists of a grater-like perforated surface with an adjustable attachment for pressing the dough through the grater, and the potato press, which does not work well for moist doughs like this quark spätzle. Both machines are easier to use than a colander and produce more uniformly shaped pasta.

Serve with

This simple staple is a wonderful accompaniment to all sorts of dishes, most notably hearty stews like Beef Goulash (page 134). It's also a terrific garnish in soups like Oxtail Consommé (page 83).

Make ahead

If you toss the boiled spätzle with a little olive oil, it can be refrigerated for up to 2 days.

An image of Max Beckmann's 1938 *Self-Portrait with Horn* (detail) is a provocative surface for Fresh Herbed Quark Spätzle, served in a Trude Petri *Urania* bowl designed for KPM, from Neue Galerie Design Shop.

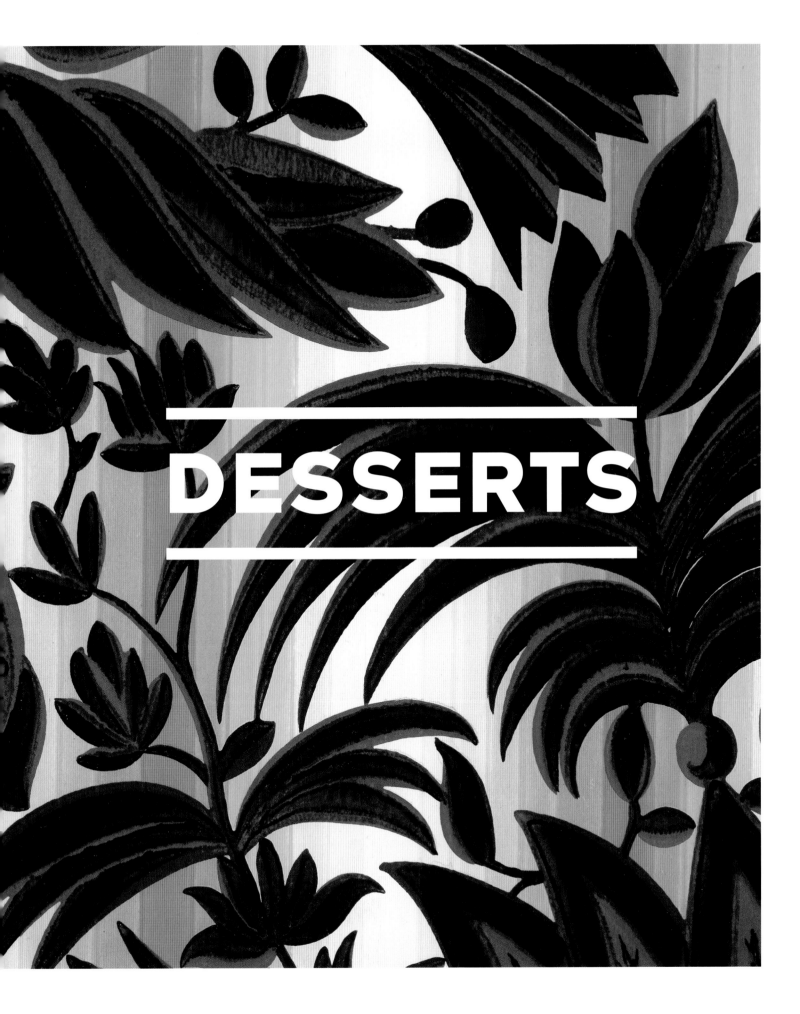

DESSERTS

DUMPLING SOUFFLÉ WITH WARM BERRIES

Salzburger Nockerl

4 SERVINGS

Unsalted butter, softened, for brushing

½ cup granulated sugar, plus more for coating

1 pint raspberries

Juice of ½ lemon

6 large eggs, separated

¼ teaspoon vanilla paste (see Tips)

4 large egg whites

½ cup all-purpose flour, sifted

Confectioners' sugar, for dusting

For me, the most wonderful Austrian dessert at Wallsé is the puffy vanilla mountain of a soufflé called *Salzburger Nockerl*. Traditionally three of them are baked together, one for each of the heights around Salzburg: Gaisberg, Mönchsberg, and Nonnberg. With their thick dusting of confectioners' sugar, they look like snow-covered peaks. This dessert bakes quickly and turns a crunchy, golden brown on the outside, while the inside is creamy and light. As with any soufflé, serve it at once!

1 Heat the oven to 350 degrees. Brush four 8-inch gratin dishes with butter. Add a little granulated sugar to the dishes and turn to lightly coat the bottom and sides, tapping out any excess.

2 In a medium bowl, toss the raspberries with the lemon juice. Slightly mound the berries in the center of the prepared dishes.

3 In a medium bowl, whisk the egg yolks with the vanilla paste.

4 In a large bowl, using an electric mixer, beat the egg whites at medium speed until slightly thickened and foamy, about 2 min-utes. Gradually add the granulated sugar and beat until the whites hold a soft peak. Using a rubber spatula, stir one-third of the beaten egg whites into the yolk mixture to lighten it. Fold this mixture into the remaining egg whites. Fold in the flour.

5 Carefully scoop the mixture on top of the berries, creating 3 large mounds on each gratin dish. Transfer to the oven and bake until the peaks are golden brown, 12 to 15 minutes.

6 Remove from the oven, dust with confectioners' sugar, and serve immediately.

Tips

Vanilla paste, a condensed paste made of pure vanilla extract and vanilla seeds, is readily available at specialty food markets.

The dishes must be well buttered, including the rim, and sprinkled with sugar so the mixture doesn't stick.

I use oval gratin dishes because I think they look pretty, but round ones, or even ovenproof plates, would be fine. What you're really making here is a soufflé, without using a soufflé dish. As long as you beat your egg whites prop-erly—the key to any soufflé—you won't have difficulty with *Salzburger Nockerl*. Beating the whites for a longer time at medium speed, rather than a shorter time at high speed—you must not rush it—gives much better results. You want the whites to be creamy, glossy, and smooth, more like softly whipped cream than stiff egg whites.

You should be able to see traces of your beaters in the whipped whites.

Variations

You can substitute any other berry, such as blackberries, huckleberries, or blueberries, for the raspberries. When fresh berries aren't in season, try ¼ cup of lingonberry jam or cranberry sauce. They all give a nice acidity that cuts the rich, sweet creaminess of the soufflé. I wouldn't vary it beyond that and go off the deep end with passion fruit or banana or something. Finding the fruit when you eat the soufflé is exciting.

Make ahead

The berries can be tossed with lemon juice and refrig-erated for up to 5 hours.

A Paul Renwick-designed cushion, inspired by Dagobert Peche's 1914 *Rom* (Rome) pattern, seems like a natural resting place for pillowy Dumpling Soufflé with Warm Berries. *Rom* cushion from Neue Galerie Design Shop.

QUARK SOUFFLÉS

Topfensouffles

6 SERVINGS

Unsalted butter, softened, for brushing

¼ cup granulated sugar, plus more
    for coating

⅓ cup quark cheese (see Tips, page 162)

1 small egg, separated

4 small egg whites

3 tablespoons all-purpose flour, sifted
    Confectioners' sugar, for dusting

¼ cup plus 2 tablespoons mixed berries

These little airy soufflés take less than half an hour to prepare—perfect if you're running behind on a dinner party menu. Tangy quark cheese is folded into sweetened whipped egg whites, then baked for just minutes, until slightly golden. I dust the tops with confectioners' sugar, then poke a hole in the soufflés and fill them with a spoonful of seasonal berries.

1 Heat the oven to 375 degrees. Lightly brush six 4-ounce ramekins with butter. Add a little granulated sugar to each ramekin and turn to lightly coat the bottom and sides, tapping out any excess.

2 In a medium bowl, whisk the quark with the egg yolk.

3 In a large bowl, using an electric mixer, beat the egg whites at medium speed until slightly thickened and foamy, about 2 minutes. Gradually add the granulated sugar, and beat until the whites hold a soft peak. Using a rubber spatula, stir one-third of the beaten egg whites into the quark mixture to lighten it. Gently fold this mixture into the remaining whites just until smooth. Fold in the flour.

4 Scrape the mixture into the prepared ramekins, filling them to the rim. Gently tap the ramekins on the counter to settle the contents, and wipe the rims.

5 Set the soufflés on a large baking sheet. Transfer to the oven and bake until the soufflés are puffed and slightly golden, about 9 minutes.

6 Remove from the oven and dust the soufflés with confectioners' sugar. Using a spoon, poke a hole in the top of each soufflé, and add 1 tablespoon of the berries. Serve immediately.

Tip
This recipe can easily be doubled to serve 12.

Serve with
I like to add a scoop of vanilla ice cream to the plates.

Variation
When fresh berries aren't in season, spoon lemon curd into the soufflés.

AUSTRIAN DOUGHNUTS

Krapfen

1/2 cup milk
* 1 envelope active dry yeast*
* 3 tablespoons granulated sugar*
1/2 teaspoon salt
1 3/4 cups all-purpose flour, plus more
*   for dipping*
*   Grated zest of 1 lemon*
* 3 large egg yolks*
3 1/2 tablespoons unsalted butter, softened
*   Canola oil, for deep-frying*
3/4 cup apricot jam, at room temperature
*   Confectioners' sugar, for dusting*

These delicious fried pastries filled with apricot jam are traditionally eaten during Carnival, or *Fasching* Tuesday, in Austria, but you can pretty much find them year-round in any good pastry shop or bakery. I like to serve them warm as part of a pastry basket for breakfast.

1 In a small saucepan, heat the milk to lukewarm (100 to 110 degrees). Remove the pan from the heat, stir in the yeast, and let stand until foamy, about 5 minutes.

2 In a bowl of a stand mixer, combine the granulated sugar with the salt, flour, and lemon zest. Add the milk with yeast, yolks, and butter. Using the hook attachment, knead at low speed for 4 minutes. Increase the speed to medium and knead until the dough is smooth and forms a ball, about 2 minutes.

3 Turn the dough out onto a work surface. Divide into 12 equal pieces. Using the palm of your hand, roll each piece on the work surface into a ball. Lightly dip one side of each ball in flour and transfer, flour side down, to a baking sheet. Cover loosely with plastic wrap and let rise in a warm spot until the balls are doubled in bulk and spring back when touched, about 45 minutes.

4 In a large deep skillet, heat 1 1/2 to 2 inches of oil to 350 degrees. Gently drop a few of the balls into the oil, without crowding the pan, and fry, turning once, until golden on both sides, about 2 minutes total. Using a slotted spoon, transfer the doughnuts to a rack to drain. Continue frying the remaining balls.

5 Using a pastry bag fitted with a plain needle tip or a small plain tip, pipe 1 tablespoon of the apricot jam into each doughnut. Dust with confectioners' sugar, and serve.

Tips
The rising time in Step 3 will vary depending on how hot the room is. A spot near the stove or a clothes' dryer helps speed the process.
Be careful when dropping the dough balls into the hot oil. Gently add them close to the surface to avoid splashing and burns.

Serve with
These are fantastic served still slightly warm with a cup of coffee and juice for breakfast.

Variation
The doughnuts can be filled with many other sweet options, including chocolate or vanilla custard or raspberry jam.

POACHED APRICOT DUMPLINGS

Marillenknödel

8 SERVINGS

- 1 large russet (baking) potato, peeled
- 8 ripe apricots
- 8 brown sugar cubes
- ¾ cup all-purpose flour, plus more for sprinkling
- 4 teaspoons semolina flour
- 1 large egg yolk
- 1 teaspoon unsalted butter, melted
  Confectioners' sugar, for dusting (optional)
  Edible flowers, for garnishing (optional)

Sweet bread crumbs

- 2 tablespoons unsalted butter
- 2 tablespoons sugar
- ¾ cup coarse dry bread crumbs, such as panko

Apricot compote

- 12 apricots, pitted and coarsely chopped
- ½ cup sugar
- 1 vanilla bean, split
- 1 thyme sprig

For these unusual dumplings, whole apricots are stuffed with sugar cubes and wrapped in a potato-and-flour dough. The dumplings are poached, then rolled in sweetened bread crumbs for a buttery crunch. Immigrants from Bohemia in the Czech Republic brought this recipe when they came to Vienna. Today it is served in coffeehouses and restaurants all over Austria.

1 Make the sweet bread crumbs: In a small saucepan, melt the butter over medium heat. Add the sugar and cook, stirring occasionally, until it dissolves, 2 to 3 minutes. Add the bread crumbs and cook, whisking constantly, until they are nicely coated and there are no clumps, 2 to 3 minutes. Remove the pan from the heat and spread the crumbs in a thin layer on a baking sheet to cool, then transfer to a bowl.

2 Make the apricot compote: In a small saucepan, combine the apricots with the sugar, vanilla bean, and thyme and cook over high heat until very soft, about 20 minutes. Discard the thyme sprig. Remove the vanilla bean and reserve for another use.

3 Meanwhile, add the potato to a medium saucepan of water, bring to a boil, and cook until tender, about 20 minutes. Drain and let cool slightly.

4 Use a needle-nose pliers to pit the apricots: Carefully insert the tip of the pliers into the bottom of each apricot and remove the pit. Push 1 sugar cube into the space where the pit was.

5 Using a ricer, mash the potato into a medium bowl. Beat in both flours, then add the egg yolk and butter and beat to make a pliable, sticky dough.

6 Bring a large pot of water to a boil. Sprinkle a sheet of parchment paper with all-purpose flour. Divide the dough into 8 equal pieces. For each dumpling, roll 1 piece of dough into a 3- to 4-inch round, depending of the size of the apricot, wrap it around an apricot, and pinch the edges to seal.

7 Reduce the boiling water to a bare simmer, then carefully add the dumplings and poach until they float, about 4 minutes. Using a slotted spoon, one at a time, remove the dumplings from the water and roll in the sweet bread crumbs to coat, then transfer them to the parchment paper.

8 Spoon some of the compote onto each plate and set a dumpling on top. Dust with confectioners' sugar and garnish with flowers, if desired, and serve.

Tip
The pits are easy to remove if the apricots are just ripe. If they are overripe, the operation is trickier, since the fruit tears easily.

Serve with
A scoop of vanilla ice cream added to each plate makes a luscious sauce as it melts.

Variation
Substitute another type of fruit compote, such as cherry or strawberry.

Make ahead
The sweet bread crumbs can be refrigerated in an airtight container for up to 1 month. The compote can be refrigerated for up to 2 weeks or frozen for up to 2 months.

Poached Apricot Dumplings coordinate with Dagobert Peche's fawn-colored *Antinous* wallpaper, designed in 1922 for the Wiener Werkstätte.

CRÈME FRAÎCHE PANNA COTTA WITH STRAWBERRIES

Panna Cotta mit frischen Erdbeeren

4 SERVINGS

2 gelatin sheets (see Tip)
Cooking spray
¼ cup plus 2 tablespoons sugar,
*   plus more for coating*
1 cup heavy cream
⅛ teaspoon vanilla paste (see Tips,
*   page 166)*
¾ cup crème fraîche
1 ½ cups strawberries, sliced ¼ inch thick
*   Squeeze of fresh lemon juice*

What is panna cotta doing in the repertoire of an Austrian cook? The creamy molded dessert originated in Piedmont, Italy, which was under Austrian rule until 1861 My version has a tangy crème fraîche base, and with the addition of sweetened fresh strawberries, it makes a summer evening treat.

1 Fill a small bowl with ice water. Add the gelatin sheets and let soak for 15 minutes. Spray four 4-ounce ramekins with cooking spray. Add a little sugar to each ramekin and turn to lightly coat the bottom and sides, tapping out any excess.

2 Meanwhile, in a small saucepan, combine the cream with ¼ cup of the sugar and the vanilla paste and heat over medium-high heat, stirring often, until the sugar dissolves. Pour into a medium bowl.

3 Remove the gelatin from the water and squeeze dry. Add the gelatin to the cream mixture and whisk until frothy. Let cool.

4 Add the crème fraîche to a medium bowl. Add one-quarter of the cream mixture and whisk until smooth. Whisk in the remaining cream mixture. Scrape into the prepared ramekins, filling them to the rim. Transfer to a baking sheet and refrigerate until set, 3 to 4 hours, or overnight.

5 In a small bowl, toss the strawberries with the remaining 2 tablespoons of sugar and the lemon juice. Let macerate in the refrigerator for 30 minutes.

6 Run a knife around each panna cotta to loosen it. Invert a dessert plate over each ramekin and, holding the plate and ramekin together, quickly invert them. Tap the bottom of the ramekin to loosen the panna cotta, and lift off the ramekin. Spoon the marinated strawberries over the top, and serve.

Tip

Pastry chefs like to use sheet gelatin because it yields a better texture than the powdered variety. Sheet gelatin is available in the baking section of specialty markets. However, powdered gelatin can be used here instead. In a small saucepan, sprinkle 1 ½ teaspoons of powdered gelatin over ¼ cup of the cream, and let stand until softened, about 5 minutes. Add the remaining ¾ cup of cream, ¼ cup of the sugar, and the vanilla, and cook over low heat, stirring often, until the gelatin and sugar dissolve. Pour into a large bowl, and proceed with Step 4.

Make ahead

We make the panna cotta ahead and refrigerate it overnight, but you can prepare it early in the day you will be serving it. In three to four hours, it will be chilled and sufficiently set in time for dessert for that evening.

Small, sweet strawberries from the farmer's market fill Dagobert Peche's glazed stoneware bowl, designed in 1922 for the Wiener Werkstätte. Stoneware bowl from Neue Galerie Design Shop.

STRUDEL SECRETS

Strudel is something I take for granted. In Austria, it is used for both desserts and savory dishes. I love its flexibility. I can fill the flaky pastry with whatever I want, which fits perfectly with my kitchen philosophy of marrying the classic and the contemporary. I've even done a strudel week at Blaue Gans, stuffing the dough with everything imaginable. When I worked in a restaurant in Vienna, we always made our own strudel dough, rolling out layer after paper-thin layer; however, store-bought phyllo works very well. Here are my pointers for making the most successful strudels ever.

While the pastry's superlight, crunchy texture is fantastic in all sorts of recipes, store-bought dough can be tricky to work with, because the sheets dry out quickly once thawed and separated. Melt the butter—actually, I clarify it (see below)—before removing the defrosted dough from the package, then butter each sheet as quickly as possible. Find a big brush so the job goes fast, but take care when brushing the sheets with butter—too much will make the strudel soggy.

I clarify the butter for brushing the phyllo—that is, remove the milk solids—so the butter does not burn when the strudel bakes. And, after melting the butter, I cook it for 10 minutes to evaporate the water, which would make the strudel soggy instead of crispy.

To clarify butter, melt it in a small heavy saucepan over medium-high heat. Bring to a simmer and cook over low heat for about 10 minutes, taking care not to brown or burn the butter. Remove the pan from the heat and, using a spoon, skim off the foam. Pour the remaining butter into a bowl, leaving behind the whitish milk solids at the bottom. (Discard the milk solids.) Clarified butter is easy to prepare if you start with at least $\frac{1}{2}$ pound. It can be refrigerated for up to 1 month, so you can make more than you need and have some on hand for another use. If the clarified butter has solidified, melt it before using.

When assembling a strudel, you want to roll the dough very tightly around the filling, or the dough may crack and the filling leak out.

These strudels can be assembled ahead and refrigerated for up to 5 hours. Brush with more clarified butter before baking. They can also be frozen for up to 1 month, then thawed and baked.

After a strudel is baked, it should be eaten right away. It gets soggy if cooled and stored.

APPLE STRUDEL

Äpfelstrudel

6 SERVINGS

¾ cup sour cream

1 tablespoon dark rum

4 large apples, preferably Granny
    Smith—peeled, cored, halved,
    and thinly sliced

½ cup granulated sugar

¾ cup coarse dry bread crumbs,
    such as panko

½ cup dark or golden raisins

¼ cup dried currants

½ cup finely chopped walnuts

5 frozen phyllo sheets, thawed

6 tablespoons clarified unsalted butter
    (see Strudel Secrets, page 175)
    Confectioners' sugar, for dusting

Sweet bread crumbs

4 tablespoons unsalted butter

¼ cup sugar

1 ½ cups coarse dry bread crumbs,
    such as panko

Strudel-making dates back to the Habsburg Empire, and strudel is found in pastry shops all across Germany, Austria, and central Europe. Apple is by far the most popular filling and, in my opinion, the best. We've had this buttery, flaky version on our menus for years; it's an excellent finish to a meal or a late-afternoon indulgence with a cup of coffee.

1 Make the sweet bread crumbs: In a small saucepan, melt the butter over medium heat. Add the sugar and cook, stirring occasionally, until it dissolves, 2 to 3 minutes. Add the bread crumbs and cook, whisking constantly, until they are nicely coated and there are no clumps, 2 to 3 minutes. Remove the pan from the heat and spread the crumbs in a thin layer on a baking sheet to cool.

2 Heat the oven to 450 degrees. Line a baking sheet with parchment paper.

3 In a large bowl, using a rubber spatula, stir the sour cream with the rum. Fold in the apples. Fold in the granulated sugar, sweet bread crumbs, dry bread crumbs, raisins, currants, and walnuts.

4 Spread 1 phyllo sheet on a work surface with a long side in front of you. Brush it lightly with clarified butter and dust with confectioners' sugar. Top with the remaining 4 sheets, brushing each with butter and dusting with confectioners' sugar.

5 Mound the apple filling across the lower third of the phyllo stack, leaving about 3 inches of space at the bottom. Roll up the strudel tightly, tucking in the ends. Brush with clarified butter and transfer to the prepared baking sheet, seam side down. Dust with confectioners' sugar.

6 Bake the strudel in the center of the oven until golden brown, 15 to 20 minutes. Remove the baking sheet from the oven and let the strudel cool for 5 to 7 minutes.

7 Dust the strudel with confectioners' sugar, slice, and serve warm.

Tips

Granny Smiths are the best apples to use here, but any relatively tart variety will do.

The sweet bread crumbs absorb moisture and keep the strudel firm. If the sugar were added separately, it would make the fruit—and strudel—soggy.

Serve with

I like my strudel the traditional Austrian way: dusted with confectioners' sugar, with a dollop of *Schlag* (sweetened whipped cream) added to the plate.

Variation

Substitute thinly sliced Bosc pears for the apples.

A slice of Apple Strudel pairs with a tumbler of Austrian dessert wine. The blown, hand-polished muslin crystal is a form dating from 1820 and decorated with engraved clovers. A Martin Kippenberger drawing seems to match the pastry's delicacy.

CHERRY STRUDEL

Kirschenstrudel

6 SERVINGS

2 pounds (4 cups) sour or
    sweet cherries, pitted

½ cup coarse dry bread crumbs,
    such as panko

2 tablespoons sliced almonds, toasted
    (see Tips)

1 teaspoon cornstarch, sifted

½ teaspoon pure vanilla extract
    Splash of kirsch, cherry schnapps,
    or cherry liqueur

2 tablespoons unsalted butter, softened

5 frozen phyllo sheets, thawed

6 tablespoons clarified unsalted butter
    (see Strudel Secrets, page 175)
    Confectioners' sugar, for dusting

Sweet bread crumbs

2 tablespoons unsalted butter

2 tablespoons sugar

¾ cup coarse dry bread crumbs,
    such as panko

I especially like to make this strudel during the few weeks in summer when sour cherries are in season, but sweet cherries are a fine substitute.

1 Make the sweet bread crumbs: In a small saucepan, melt the butter over medium heat. Add the sugar and cook, stirring occasionally, until it dissolves, 2 to 3 minutes. Add the bread crumbs and cook, whisking constantly, until they are nicely coated and there are no clumps, 2 to 3 minutes. Remove the pan from the heat and spread the crumbs in a thin layer on a baking sheet to cool.

2 Heat the oven to 450 degrees. Line a baking sheet with parchment paper.

3 In a large bowl, using a rubber spatula, mix the cherries with the sweet bread crumbs, dry bread crumbs, almonds, cornstarch, vanilla, kirsch, and softened butter until well combined.

4 Spread 1 phyllo sheet on a work surface with a long side in front of you. Brush it lightly with clarified butter and dust with confectioners' sugar. Top with the remaining 4 sheets, brushing each with butter and dusting with confectioners' sugar.

5 Mound the cherry filling across the lower third of the phyllo stack, leaving about 3 inches of space at the bottom. Roll up the strudel tightly, tucking in the ends. Brush with clarified butter and transfer to the prepared baking sheet, seam side down. Dust with confectioners' sugar.

6 Bake the strudel in the center of the oven until golden brown, 15 to 20 minutes. Remove the baking sheet from the oven and let the strudel cool for 5 to 7 minutes.

7 Dust the strudel with confectioners' sugar, slice, and serve warm.

Tips

Small, juicy sour cherries are excellent for baking because, unlike sweet cherries, they retain their shape as they cook. To toast sliced almonds, heat the oven to 350 degrees. Spread the nuts in a pie plate and toast until golden and fragrant, 5 to 8 minutes. Let cool completely.

Serve with

This strudel is nice with a refreshing lemon sorbet or almond ice cream.

Hermann Nitsch's 1980 *Relic Sixty-Ninth Action* (detail) is the bloody backdrop for a slice of tangy-sweet Cherry Strudel, served with Josef Hoffmann's 1906–1907 *Rundes Modell* fork and knife, from Neue Galerie Design Shop.

QUARK CUSTARD STRUDEL

Milchrahmstrudel

6 SERVINGS

4 tablespoons unsalted butter, softened
²⁄₃ cup quark cheese
  Pinch of grated lemon zest
  Pinch of salt
2 large eggs, separated
1 large egg yolk
²⁄₃ cup sour cream
¹⁄₄ cup all-purpose flour, sifted
¹⁄₃ cup granulated sugar, plus more
    for sprinkling
5 frozen phyllo sheets, thawed
6 tablespoons clarified unsalted butter
    (see Strudel Secrets, page 175)
  Confectioners' sugar, for dusting

Royale sauce

5 large eggs
¹⁄₃ cup sugar
¹⁄₂ cup milk
¹⁄₂ cup heavy cream

This is another strudel found pretty much everywhere in Austria. The filling is made with a tangy quark cheese mixture, topped with a delicious sauce that turns into a sweet custard when baked. Since this strudel is served at room temperature straight out of the baking dish, it's a great dessert to take to a party.

1 Make the royale sauce: In a medium bowl, beat the eggs with the sugar. Add the milk and cream and beat until smooth. Refrigerate.

2 In a large bowl, using an electric mixer, cream the softened butter with the quark, lemon zest, and salt. Beat in the egg yolks, one by one, then beat in the sour cream. Fold in the flour.

3 In a medium bowl, using clean beaters, whip the egg whites at medium speed until foamy. Gradually add the granulated sugar, then whip until the whites hold a soft peak. Using a rubber spatula, gently fold the beaten egg whites into the quark mixture.

4 Line a 12-by-2 ¹⁄₂-inch terrine mold with plastic wrap, leaving a generous overhang on the two long sides. Pour in the quark filling. Fold the plastic over, and freeze until very firm, at least 8 hours.

5 Heat the oven to 350 degrees.

6 Turn out the frozen quark mold onto a cutting board and remove the plastic wrap. Wash and dry the terrine mold. Trim the slanted edges by about ¹⁄₂ inch to make straight sides.

7 Spread 1 phyllo sheet on a work surface with a long side in front of you. Brush it lightly with clarified butter and dust with confectioners' sugar. Top with the 4 remaining sheets, brushing each with butter and dusting with confectioners' sugar.

8 Set the quark mold across the lower third of the phyllo stack, leaving about 3 inches of space at the bottom. Carefully roll up the quark in the phyllo, tucking in the ends.

9 Brush the terrine with clarified butter and sprinkle with granulated sugar to coat lightly. Return the strudel to the terrine, seam side down, and set in a roasting pan or large gratin dish. Transfer to the oven and bake until light golden brown, about 30 minutes.

10 Remove from the oven and pour the royale sauce into the terrine; the strudel should be almost completely submerged. Pour 4 cups of cold water around the terrine. Reduce the oven temperature to 300 degrees and bake the strudel until the custard is set, about 30 minutes. Remove from the oven and let cool completely.

11 Run a knife around the edges of the terrine. Cut into slices in the terrine. Using a spatula, transfer each slice to a plate. Dust the top with confectioners' sugar, and serve.

Serve with
Rum-soaked raisins and crème anglaise (vanilla custard sauce) are traditional accompaniments. Vanilla ice cream and fresh berries would also be nice.

Make ahead
The quark mold needs to freeze for at least 8 hours, so plan ahead. It can be frozen for up to 1 month.

A painting by the Spanish-born artist Alejandro Garmendia is displayed behind a dish of creamy Quark Custard Strudel garnished with red currants and edible flowers.

THE EMPEROR'S PANCAKE

Kaiserschmarren

4 DESSERT SERVINGS
OR 2 BREAKFAST SERVINGS

2 large eggs, separated
½ cup all-purpose flour
1 ¼ cups milk
1 teaspoon dark rum
2 tablespoons granulated sugar
Pinch of salt
1 tablespoon unsalted butter
¼ cup golden raisins
Confectioners' sugar, for dusting
Fruit compote, for serving

The rustic *Kaiserschmarren*—one large pancake cut roughly into bite-size pieces—is named for Kaiser Franz Joseph. The story goes that he got hungry when traveling through the forest and met an old woman who offered him something to eat. She had nothing but flour, eggs, and raisins, so she prepared this dish. The Kaiser thought it was the most amazing thing he had ever tasted. "What, this *Schmarren* [rubbish]?" she protested. "Yes," he replied. "But it's the Kaiser's *Schmarren*."

Kaiserschmarren is typically eaten as a dessert or as an afternoon sweet with coffee, but I like to serve it for brunch, since, made with whipped egg whites, it is a lot like a big, fluffy pancake. We present it the traditional way—with fruit compote on the side.

1 Heat the oven to 325 degrees. In a medium bowl, beat the egg yolks with the flour and ½ cup plus 2 tablespoons of the milk until smooth. Beat in the remaining ½ cup plus 2 tablespoons of milk and the rum.
2 In another medium bowl, using an electric mixer, beat the egg whites at slow speed until frothy. Add 1 tablespoon of the granulated sugar and the salt and beat until the whites are thicker and whiter in color, about 2 minutes. Add the remaining 1 tablespoon of granulated sugar and beat until the whites hold a soft peak. Stir half the egg whites into the egg-yolk mixture, then carefully fold in the remaining egg whites.

3 In a 9-inch ovenproof skillet, melt the butter over medium heat. Swirl the butter around the skillet so it coats the bottom and sides. Using a rubber spatula, scrape in the batter and cook until it begins to pull away from the sides of the pan, about 2 minutes.
4 Transfer the skillet to the oven and bake until the pancake is golden brown and the center is set, about 15 minutes.
5 Immediately invert the pancake onto a round platter. Using 2 knives, cut the pancake into 1-inch pieces. Scatter the raisins on top, dust with confectioners' sugar, and serve. Pass the fruit compote separately.

Tip
Unlike crepe batter, which is often left to stand to thicken, this pancake gets its volume from whipped egg whites, so use the batter quickly before the whites collapse.

Variation
For a fresh taste, substitute blueberries or sliced strawberries for the raisins.

Make ahead
The pancake is best served straight from the pan.

In this photograph of Emperor Franz Josef I, the Kaiser does not appear
to have discovered his favorite pancake snack yet—or he might look a bit jollier.
Emperor Franz Joseph I, 1910. Photograph by H. Makart. Albertina,
permanent loan from Höheren Graphischen Lehr- und Versuchsanstalt.

QUARK CHEESE CREPES WITH PEACHES

Topfenpalatschinken mit Pfirsichen

8 SERVINGS

2 ripe peaches, peeled, pitted,
 and sliced $1/8$ inch thick

$1/8$ teaspoon pure vanilla extract

$1/2$ cup plus 1 teaspoon granulated sugar

$1/3$ cup all-purpose flour

$1/4$ teaspoon salt

1 cup milk

2 large eggs

2 tablespoons unsalted butter, melted,
 plus softened butter, for brushing

 Cooking spray

1 cup heavy cream

$3/4$ cup quark cheese (see Tip)

 Grated zest of $1/2$ lemon

 Confectioners' sugar, for dusting

Palatschinken—what Austrians call crepes—are easy to make and very versatile. Here the thin pancakes are filled with sweet, creamy cheese, then baked, and topped with macerated fruit, but I also like to use them in savory dishes, like Chilled Smoked Trout Crepes and Horseradish Crème Fraîche (page 58).

1 In a small bowl, stir the peaches with the vanilla and $1/4$ cup of the granulated sugar. Let macerate in the refrigerator for 1 hour.

2 Meanwhile, in a medium bowl, whisk the flour with the salt and 1 teaspoon of the granulated sugar. Whisk in the milk, eggs, and butter until the batter is smooth. Let rest for 15 minutes.

3 Strain the batter through a fine sieve set over a small bowl. Spray a 10-inch nonstick skillet with cooking spray and heat over medium-low heat. Add $1/4$ cup of the batter, tilting the skillet to coat the bottom evenly, and cook until the edges of the crepe are lightly browned, about 1 minute. Using a spatula, flip the crepe, and cook until lightly colored on the second side, about 30 seconds. Transfer the crepe to a plate. Repeat with the remaining batter, adjusting the heat as necessary so that the crepes don't burn,

and stacking the crepes as they're done. You need 8 crepes for this dish.

4 Heat the broiler. Brush a large gratin dish with butter.

5 In a medium bowl, whisk the cream with the remaining $1/4$ cup of granulated sugar until it holds a soft peak. Whisk a little of the whipped cream into the quark to lighten it. Add the quark and lemon zest to the whipped cream and whisk until smooth.

6 Spread 1 crepe at a time with a scant $1/4$ cup of the quark cream. Roll up and transfer, seam side down, to the prepared gratin dish. Dust with confectioners' sugar.

7 Broil the crepes until the top is slightly browned and the quark cream is melted, 1 to 2 minutes. Transfer the crepes to warmed plates and dust with more confectioners' sugar. Spoon the macerated peaches on top, and serve.

Tip

If quark cheese is unavailable, you can substitute mascarpone or crème fraîche.

Serve with

A scoop of vanilla ice cream or some softly whipped cream is all you need.

Variations

I love peaches, but whatever fruit is in season can be used. Plums, strawberries, and raspberries are all great.

Make ahead

The unfilled crepes can be covered with plastic wrap and refrigerated for up to 3 days.

CHOCOLATE-HAZELNUT CAKES

Mohr im Hemd

6 SERVINGS

Cooking spray

⅓ *cup sugar, plus more for coating*

1 ⅓ *cups semisweet chocolate chips*

4 *tablespoons unsalted butter, softened*

5 *large eggs, separated*

⅓ *cup hazelnut flour (see Tip), sifted*

¼ *cup all-purpose flour, sifted*

1 *tablespoon unsweetened cocoa powder*

½ *cup water*

⅓ *cup light corn syrup*

This exquisite dessert is a chocolate lover's dream: extremely moist little cakes, drizzled with warm chocolate sauce. Whisked egg whites provide the lift, without the aid of artificial leavening, such as baking powder or baking soda.

1 Heat the oven to 300 degrees. Spray six 4-ounce ramekins with cooking spray. Add a little sugar to each ramekin and turn to lightly coat the bottom and sides, tapping out any excess.

2 In a double boiler or a small bowl set over a saucepan of simmering water, or in a microwave, heat ⅓ cup of the chocolate chips until just melted. Remove from the heat and stir until smooth.

3 Add the butter to a medium bowl. Using a hand-held mixer, add the egg yolks, one at a time, beating after each addition until smooth. Scrape in the chocolate and beat until smooth.

4 In a large bowl, using clean beaters, whip the egg whites at medium speed until slightly thickened and foamy, about 2 minutes. Gradually add the sugar and beat until the whites hold a soft peak. Using a rubber spatula, stir one-third of the beaten egg whites into the chocolate mixture to lighten it. Gently fold this mixture into the remaining egg whites,

just until smooth. In a small bowl, whisk the hazelnut flour with the all-purpose flour, then fold into the chocolate mixture, in two batches.

5 Pour the batter into the prepared ramekins, filling them to just below the rim. Transfer to a small roasting pan or shallow baking dish and fill the pan with ½ inch of cold water. Transfer to the oven and bake until the cakes have risen significantly, 15 to 20 minutes. Remove from the oven.

6 Meanwhile, combine the cocoa powder and the remaining 1 cup of chocolate chips in a medium bowl. In a small saucepan, bring the water and corn syrup to a boil over high heat. Add the mixture to the chocolate and cocoa powder, stirring constantly until the chocolate is melted and the mixture is smooth.

7 Run a knife around each ramekin and unmold the cakes onto dessert plates. Pour the warm chocolate sauce over the tops, and serve.

Tip
Hazelnut flour, or finely ground hazelnuts, is available in the baking section of specialty food shops and online from kingarthurflour.com.

Serve with
A dollop of *Schlag* (sweetened whipped cream) and a scoop of vanilla ice cream make cool contrasts to the warm cakes.

Make ahead
The cakes should be served hot, right out of the oven.

LINZERTORTE

Linzertorte

12 SERVINGS

½ pound (2 sticks) unsalted butter, softened

1 ½ cups confectioners' sugar, plus more for dusting

1 ½ teaspoons ground cinnamon

½ teaspoon ground cloves

Grated zest of ½ lemon

3 large eggs

1 large egg yolk

1 teaspoon kirsch (see Tips)

4 teaspoons milk, at room temperature

1 ¾ cups hazelnut flour (see Tip, page 185)

1 ¾ cups cake flour, sifted

⅓ cup seedless raspberry jam

¼ cup all-purpose flour

¼ cup sliced almonds

I like to sprinkle sliced almonds over this classic lattice-topped torte for extra crunch. A dusting of confectioners' sugar makes it look especially appealing.

1 In a large bowl, using an electric mixer, beat the butter with the confectioners' sugar, cinnamon, cloves, and lemon zest until pale and creamy, 3 to 4 minutes. Add the whole eggs and egg yolk, one by one, beating well after each addition. Beat in the kirsch, then beat in the milk. Add the hazelnut flour and cake flour all at once and beat until smooth. The dough will be very soft.

2 Divide the dough into 2 pieces; one twice as large as the other. Cover the smaller piece with plastic wrap.

3 Line the bottom of a 10-inch springform pan with parchment paper. Spread the larger piece of dough evenly in the bottom of the pan. Cover with plastic wrap and freeze until firm, about 20 minutes.

4 Heat the oven to 325 degrees. Spread the raspberry jam over the chilled dough in the pan, leaving a ½-inch border all around.

5 Knead the all-purpose flour into the remaining dough. Scoop the dough into a pastry bag fitted with a #4 (medium) star tip. Pipe a ring of dough around the edge of the pan. Then pipe the remaining dough into a lattice pattern on the torte, making 5 lines in each direction.

6 Transfer the torte to a baking sheet and bake until golden brown, 25 to 30 minutes. Remove from the oven and let cool completely on a rack.

7 Remove the sides of the springform pan and remove the torte from the pan bottom; discard the paper. Dust the torte with confectioners' sugar and sprinkle with the almonds. Transfer to a cake plate, cut into wedges, and serve.

Tips

The dough for this torte is really soft, like room-temperature butter.

Other pastry tips are fine here, but a star shape produces the most authentic piping.

Kirsch is a type of cherry brandy often used in German and Austrian confections.

Variation

Light rum or fruit liqueur can be substituted for kirsch.

Serve with

A slice of Linzertorte is often eaten as in the afternoon with a dollop of *Schlag* (sweetened whipped cream) and a cup of coffee or black tea.

Make ahead

The assembled torte can be frozen for up to 1 month. Defrost before baking.

CHRISTMAS STOLLEN

Weihnachtsstollen

MAKES 2 LOAVES

¼ cup milk

2 envelopes active dry yeast

1 ½ cups all-purpose flour

½ cup cake flour

⅓ cup coarsely chopped dried apricots

¼ cup sliced almonds

3 tablespoons dried currants,
    coarsely chopped

2 tablespoons dried cherries,
    coarsely chopped

¾ teaspoon salt

½ teaspoon ground cinnamon

¼ teaspoon freshly grated nutmeg

¼ teaspoon ground cloves
    Finely grated zest of ½ lemon

1 tablespoon candied citrus (see Tips)

1 large egg

2 tablespoons dark rum

1 ½ tablespoons honey

¼ teaspoon pure vanilla extract

8 tablespoons (1 stick) unsalted butter,
    softened

8 tablespoons (1 stick) unsalted butter,
    melted
    Confectioners' sugar, for dusting
    (optional)

Weihnachtsstollen, or *Christstollen*, reaches back to medieval Prussia, when the shape of this superbuttery nut-and-dried-fruit-filled loaf was meant to represent the baby Jesus in swaddling clothes. It's still incredibly popular at Christmastime in both Germany and Austria. Since I bake loaves and loaves of it for customers who want to give it as a holiday gift, I know one loaf is never enough. This recipe makes two; the extra one can be refrigerated or frozen.

1 In a small saucepan, heat the milk over medium-high heat to lukewarm (100 to 110 degrees). Remove the pan from the heat, add the yeast, and let stand until foamy, about 5 minutes.

2 Meanwhile, in the bowl of a stand mixer, combine both flours with the fruits, nuts, salt, spices, and lemon zest. Add the milk with yeast, egg, rum, honey, vanilla, and softened butter. Using the hook attachment, knead at low speed for 4 minutes. Increase the speed to medium and knead for 2 minutes. Cover the bowl with plastic wrap and let the dough rise in a warm spot for 1 hour.

3 Refrigerate the dough overnight.

4 Divide the dough into 2 equal pieces. Using your hands, flatten each piece into a 6-by-9-inch rectangle. Starting with a short side, roll each one into a log shape. Transfer to a large baking sheet and cover loosely with plastic wrap. Let rise in a warm spot (near a stove is good) until the dough springs back when touched, about 30 minutes.

5 Heat the oven to 325 degrees. Remove the plastic and transfer the loaves to the oven. Bake until golden brown, about 30 minutes.

6 Remove the baking sheet from the oven. Generously brush the warm loaves with the melted butter, and immediately cover each one with plastic wrap. Let cool slightly on the baking sheet, then refrigerate.

7 Before serving, let the stollen come to room temperature. Lightly dust with confectioners' sugar, if desired. Using a serrated knife, cut into slices, and serve.

Tips
I refrigerate the dough overnight to develop the flavor and to let it firm up so it can be shaped.
Brushing the baked loaves with melted butter helps them stay moist, in addition to adding flavor.
Good-quality candied citrus is available in the bakery section of specialty food shops.

Variation
Feel free to vary the dried fruit and nuts in the loaves. For instance, try substituting dried blueberries, walnuts, or pecans.

Serve with
This loaf is excellent in the afternoon with a glass of schnapps or a cup of coffee or tea. I also love it in the morning, toasted, with marmalade.

Make ahead
The stollen can be refrigerated for up to 1 week or frozen for up to 6 months.

LEMON–POPPY SEED CAKE

Mohngugelhupf

12 SERVINGS

½ pound (2 sticks) unsalted butter,
  melted, plus more for brushing
½ cup all-purpose flour,
  plus more for dusting
⅔ cup granulated sugar
1 large egg
8 large egg yolks
1 ½ tablespoons finely grated lemon zest
  (from 2 lemons)
½ cup cornstarch
½ cup poppy seeds
  Confectioners' sugar, for dusting
  (optional)

In Austria, there is a time in the middle of the afternoon called *Kaffeejause*, a moment when you sit down with a friend at a café, eat a piece of cake, and drink a cup of coffee. This is one of the superclassic *Kaffeehaus* desserts for the occasion. It's baked in a small Bundt pan and has lots of tiny poppy seeds throughout for an Austrian crunch. It is buttery but not too sweet and perfect accompanied by a cappuccino—what we call a *Wiener Mélange*. As an extra bonus, it's really easy to make.

1 Heat the oven to 325 degrees. Brush an 8-inch Bundt pan with butter and dust with flour. Butter the dull side of a 10-inch piece of foil.

2 In a large bowl, using an electric mixer, beat the granulated sugar with the egg and egg yolks at medium-high speed until the mixture is pale yellow and very fluffy, about 8 minutes. Beat in the lemon zest.

3 Sift the flour and cornstarch over the egg mixture and fold in using a rubber spatula. At medium speed, gradually beat in the butter, then beat in the poppy seeds.

4 Pour the batter into the prepared pan and cover tightly with the buttered foil. Bake until the cake pulls away from the sides of the pan and a cake tester inserted in the center of the cake comes out clean, about 45 minutes. Remove the foil and let the cake cool in the pan on a rack for 15 minutes.

5 Invert the cake onto the rack and let cool completely. Transfer to a cake plate, dust with confectioners' sugar, if desired, and serve.

Tip
Poppy seeds can add lots of character to a dish, especially if you use a good quantity of them, not just a sprinkling like you find on a bagel. They give texture, a bit of dark contrast, and a smart element of nutty flavor.

Serve with
You can always add a dollop of *Schlag* (sweetened whipped cream) to the plate if you like. The cake is excellent with coffee or tea or a glass of dessert wine. And because it's not that sweet, a glass of Champagne also goes well.

Variation
This recipe will give you a white cake speckled with blue-black seeds, but in Austria the cake is often almost totally black. For this effect, whir the poppy seeds in a coffee grinder before adding them to the batter.

Make ahead
The cake can be covered in plastic wrap or foil and stored at room temperature for up to 3 days.

Albert Oehlen's two mixed-media paintings (detail) seem to glow behind golden Lemon-Poppy Seed Cake.

CHOCOLATE-CHERRY TORTE

Marie-Thérèse Torte

12 SERVINGS

Ganache

2 ⅓ cups milk chocolate chips (14 ounces)

1 cup heavy cream

2 tablespoons light corn syrup

6 tablespoons unsalted butter, cut into tablespoons, softened

Cake

Cooking spray

12 large eggs, 6 separated

1 ½ cups plus 3 tablespoons granulated sugar

1 ½ teaspoons pure vanilla extract

1 ½ cups all-purpose flour, sifted Confectioners' sugar, for dusting

Cherries and glaze

1 cup sweet cherries (about 6 ounces), pitted and coarsely chopped (see Tips)

1 cup milk chocolate chips

8 tablespoons (1 stick) unsalted butter

This is an intricate, elegant cake I developed with my pastry chef, Matthew Lodes, for a friend, Susan Nagel, who was writing a book about Marie-Thérèse, daughter of Marie Antoinette (she was an archduchess of Austria) and King Louis XVI. For the occasion of the launch party, I spread vanilla sheet cakes with chocolate ganache and sliced them into strips. Then I rolled up the strips end to end to make one large cake and covered it entirely with chocolate glaze. Cutting into a wedge of torte with your fork, you discover pieces of sweet cherries interspersed between the layers.

1 Heat the oven to 325 degrees. Lightly spray three 12-by-17-inch rimmed baking sheets with cooking spray. Line the bottom of the pans with parchment paper and spray it.

2 Make the ganache: In a large bowl set over a saucepan of simmering water, or in a microwave, heat the chocolate chips until just melted. Remove from the heat and stir until smooth.

3 In a small saucepan, heat the cream with the corn syrup over high heat until bubbles appear around the edges; remove from the heat. Using a rubber spatula, stir ⅓ cup of the hot cream at a time into the melted chocolate until the mixture is very thick and shiny. Let the mixture stand for 5 minutes, then stir in the butter until smooth.

4 Refrigerate the ganache for 20 minutes. Then let stand until spreadable before using.

5 Meanwhile, make the cake: In a large bowl set over a saucepan of simmering water, lightly whisk the egg yolks with the whole eggs to combine. Add 1 ½ cups of the granulated sugar and whisk over low heat until the mixture is frothy and lukewarm, about 1 minute. Remove from the heat and, using an electric mixer, beat in the vanilla, then beat at high speed until the mixture is thick and glossy, about 5 minutes.

6 In a large bowl, using clean beaters, beat the egg whites at medium speed until slightly thickened and foamy, about 2 minutes. Gradually add the remaining 3 tablespoons of granulated sugar, and beat until the whites hold a soft peak. Using a rubber spatula, stir one-third of the beaten egg whites into the yolk mixture to lighten it. Gently fold this mixture into the remaining egg whites just until smooth. Fold in the flour.

7 Using an offset spatula, spread one-third of the batter into each prepared pan. Transfer to the oven and bake until the cake is light brown, about 8 minutes. Remove from the oven and let cool completely on racks.

8 Lightly dust the cakes with confectioners' sugar. Run a knife around the inside of each pan and gently lift out the cake onto a work surface.

9 Using an offset or rubber spatula, spread a ⅛-inch-thick layer of ganache onto the sides (not the bottom) of a 9-inch springform pan. Freeze until set, about 5 minutes.

10 Meanwhile, spread about one-quarter of the remaining ganache on each cake. Scatter the cherries over the top. Cut each cake lengthwise into four 3-by-17-inch strips. Carefully roll up 1 strip, removing the paper as you go. Set the end of the roll against the end of a second strip and roll up. Continue rolling, using as many of the remaining cake strips as needed, until you have one large cake roll that fits perfectly into the pan.

11 Spread just enough of the remaining ganache around the roll to hold it together. Gently press the cake into the pan. Trim the cake flush with the top of the pan. Spread the remaining ganache on top of the cake, and freeze until set, about 1 hour.

12 Using a blowtorch, heat the sides of the pan to release the cake and remove the sides of the pan. Smooth the sides and top of the cake, and freeze the cake until the ganache sets.

13 Make the glaze: In a double boiler or a medium bowl set over a saucepan of simmering water, or in a microwave, heat the chocolate chips with the butter until just melted. Remove from the heat, stir, and let cool slightly. Remove the cake from the freezer.

14 Pour the glaze over the top and sides of the cake, then spread it evenly over the cake. Refrigerate the cake until the glaze is set, 5 to 10 minutes.

15 Transfer the cake to a cake plate, and serve.

Tips

For the ganache, if you have a candy thermometer, heat the chocolate in Step 2 to about 95 degrees.

If you don't have a blowtorch, rub your hands against the sides of the pan to warm it until the cake releases. Or use a hairdryer, but be careful because the heat won't be as narrowly focused as a blowtorch.

You can sprinkle brandied cherries on the top of the cake as a decoration.

Variations

You can omit the cherries. Or substitute chopped brandied cherries or another fruit, such as fresh or frozen raspberries.

Make ahead

The cake can be refrigerated for up to 3 days or frozen for up to 6 months.

The chocolate glaze can be refrigerated for up to 3 days. Heat to just melting on the stove and stir until smooth before using.

Josef Hoffmann No. 135 Pastry Server, in silver, on a hand-loomed placemat of mercerized cotton inspired by the Wiener Werkstätte. Neue Galerie Design Shop.

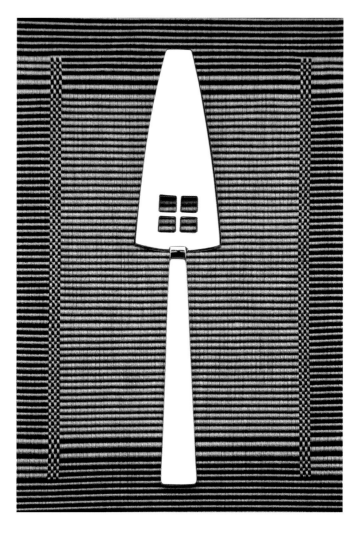

HAZELNUT TORTE WITH CHOCOLATE GANACHE

Klimttorte

12 SERVINGS

Ganache

1 ½ cups semisweet chocolate chips
     (9 ounces)
  ½ cup milk chocolate chips
   2 cups gianduja (about 1 pound)
     (see Tips)
1 ¼ cups heavy cream
  10 tablespoons (1 ¼ sticks) unsalted
     butter, cut into tablespoons,
     softened

Hazelnut cake

    Cooking spray
  14 ounces (3 ½ sticks) unsalted butter,
     softened
  22 large eggs, separated
2 ½ cups sugar
6 ½ cups hazelnut flour (see Tip,
     page 185)
   1 cup fine dry bread crumbs

Glaze and gold leaf

   6 ounces bittersweet chocolate,
     chopped (1 cup)
   8 tablespoons (1 stick) unsalted butter
     Gold leaf, for garnishing (optional)

I created this rich, dense cake in honor of one of Austria's most famous artists, the Vienna Secession painter Gustav Klimt. Decorated with crumbled gold leaf, it recalls Klimt's "Golden Phase," illustrated by such paintings as the portrait *Adele Bloch-Bauer I*, which is in the Neue Galerie's collection.

The torte is the one I make at Café Sabarsky. It is elaborate—you'll need three large bowls and six baking sheets to make the many layers of hazelnut cake—but the individual components are not complicated. The ingredients for the cake batter are divisible by two, so when making the recipe at home, it may be easier to bake the cakes in two batches.

Gustav Klimt, *Adele Bloch-Bauer I* (detail), 1907, oil, silver, and gold on canvas.
Neue Galerie New York. This acquisition made available in part through the generosity
of the heirs of the Estates of Ferdinand and Adele Bloch-Bauer.

1 Heat the oven to 325 degrees. Lightly spray six 12-by-17-inch rimmed baking sheets with cooking spray. Line the bottoms of the pans with parchment paper and spray it.

2 Make the ganache: In a large bowl set over a saucepan of simmering water, or in a microwave, heat the semisweet and milk chocolate chips with the gianduja until just melted. Remove from heat and stir until smooth.

3 In a small saucepan, heat the cream over high heat until bubbles appear around the edges; remove from the heat. Using a rubber spatula, stir $1/3$ cup of the hot cream at a time into the melted chocolate until the mixture is very thick and shiny. Let the mixture stand for 5 minutes, then stir in the butter until smooth.

4 Refrigerate the ganache for 20 minutes. Then let stand until spreadable before using.

5 Meanwhile, make the hazelnut cake: In a large bowl, using an electric mixer, beat the butter at medium speed until creamy, about 3 minutes. Add the egg yolks, two at a time, beating after each addition until smooth. Continue beating until the mixture is pale yellow and creamy.

6 In another large bowl, using clean beaters, beat the egg whites at medium speed until slightly thickened and foamy, about 2 minutes. Gradually add the sugar, and beat until the whites hold medium peaks, about 5 minutes. Using a rubber spatula, stir one-third of the beaten egg whites into the yolk mixture to lighten it. Gently fold this mixture into the remaining egg whites just until smooth.

7 In another large bowl, whisk the hazelnut flour with the bread crumbs. Fold into the wet ingredients until smooth.

8 Using an offset spatula, spread one-sixth of the batter in each prepared pan. Transfer to the oven and bake until the cake is light brown, about 12 minutes. Remove to racks and let cool completely in the pans.

9 Using a plate or a pot lid as a guide, cut each cake into two 8 $1/2$-inch rounds. Set one of the cake rounds on the bottom of a 9-inch springform pan. Using an offset spatula, spread about $1/8$ inch of ganache on top (the same thickness as the cake). Set another round on top and repeat layering with the remaining ganache and cake rounds, finishing with a layer of ganache. Refrigerate overnight.

10 Using a blowtorch, heat the sides of the pan to release the cake and remove the sides of the pan. Freeze until the ganache sets again.

11 Make the glaze: In a double boiler or a medium bowl set over a saucepan of simmering water, or in a microwave, heat the chocolate with the butter until just melted. Remove from the heat, stir until smooth, and let cool slightly. Remove the cake from the freezer.

12 Pour the glaze over the top and sides of the cake, then spread it evenly all over the cake. Refrigerate the cake until the glaze is set, 5 to 10 minutes, before serving.

13 Transfer the cake to a cake plate. Crumble the gold leaf on top, if using, and serve.

Tips

Gianduja is a smooth paste of chocolate and hazelnuts available in the baking section of specialty markets.
If the whisked hazelnut flour and bread crumbs form clumps in Step 7, work the mixture through a sifter or medium sieve.

Variation

A great use for leftover ganache is to make truffles. Form tiny balls using a melon baller and freeze until set. Remove the ganache balls from the freezer and roll in unsweetened cocoa powder before serving.

Make ahead

The cake can be refrigerated for up to 3 days.

SACHERTORTE

Sachertorte

12 SERVINGS

6 tablespoons unsalted butter, softened,
   plus more for brushing
   All-purpose flour, for dusting
½ cup semisweet chocolate chips
¼ cup confectioners' sugar
⅛ teaspoon ground cinnamon
4 large eggs, separated
1 large egg yolk
½ cup granulated sugar
¾ cup cake flour, sifted

Rum syrup and jam

½ cup sugar
½ cup water
2 tablespoons dark rum
1 ½ cups smooth apricot jam (not preserves)

Glaze

6 ounces bittersweet chocolate,
   chopped (1 cup)
8 tablespoons (1 stick) unsalted butter

Tip
European cakes are often brushed with syrup because
they tend to be dry.

Serve with
I present this cake in the classic fashion, with a dollop
of *Schlag* (sweetened whipped cream) on the side and
nothing else.

Variation
Instead of apricot jam, substitute another flavor—for example, seedless red currant or strawberry jam. You can
use any type as long as it is smooth and spreadable with
no chunks of fruit.

Make ahead
The cake can be refrigerated for up to 3 days. The syrup
can be refrigerated almost indefinitely.

The Sachertorte is one of the most disputed confections in culinary history; still, everyone agrees on its origins. The dense chocolate cake with a layer of apricot jam running through the middle was concocted by a sixteen-year-old pastry apprentice named Franz Sacher for Prince Klemens von Metternich. The torte was a success with the prince and then with all Vienna. In 1876, Sacher's son, Eduard, opened the celebrated Hotel Sacher. Eventually his son, Eduard Jr., sold the recipe to Demel, a famous pastry shop in Vienna. Both institutions then claimed to have created it, and the wrangling lasted seven years. In the end, the Hotel Sacher won the right to call its cake the "Original Sacher Torte," and any other cake made in the Sacher style is called a Sachertorte.

1 Heat the oven to 325 degrees. Brush a 9-inch round cake pan with butter and dust with flour. Line a baking sheet with parchment paper. In a double boiler or a medium bowl set over a saucepan of simmering water, or in a microwave, heat the chocolate chips until just melted. Remove from the heat and stir until smooth.

2 In a large bowl, using a hand-held mixer, beat the butter with the confectioners' sugar and cinnamon until pale and creamy, about 2 minutes. Add the egg yolks, one at a time, beating after each addition until smooth. Add the melted chocolate and beat until just combined.

3 In another large bowl, using clean beaters, beat the egg whites at medium speed until slightly thickened and foamy, about 2 minutes. Gradually add the granulated sugar, and beat until the whites hold a soft peak. Using a rubber spatula, stir one-third of the beaten egg whites into the yolk mixture to lighten it. Gently fold this mixture into the remaining egg whites just until smooth. Fold in the flour.

4 Using an offset spatula, spread the batter in the prepared pan. Transfer to the oven and bake until a toothpick inserted into the middle comes out clean, 35 to 45 minutes. Remove the cake from the oven and carefully flip it onto the prepared baking sheet. Let the cake cool for about 20 minutes.

5 Meanwhile, make the rum syrup: In a small saucepan, combine the sugar with the water and cook over medium heat, stirring occasionally, until the sugar dissolves. Stir in the rum, remove from the heat, and let cool.

6 Generously brush the cake all over with some of the rum syrup; reserve the remaining syrup. Cover the cake with plastic wrap and refrigerate overnight.

7 Cut the cake horizontally in half. Brush each cut side generously with the rum syrup. Spread ½ cup of the jam evenly over the bottom of the cake. Set the other half on top. Spread the remaining 1 cup of jam evenly over the top and sides of the cake. Refrigerate until set, about 2 hours.

8 Make the glaze: In a double boiler or a medium bowl set over a saucepan of simmering water, or in a microwave, heat the chocolate with the butter until just melted. Remove from the heat, stir until smooth, and let cool slightly. Remove the cake from the refrigerator.

9 Pour the glaze over the top and sides of the cake, then spread it evenly all over the cake. Refrigerate the cake until the glaze is set, 5 to 10 minutes, before serving.

10 Transfer the cake to a cake plate, and serve.

Gustav Klimt's nude is a voluptuous backdrop for a slice of rich Sachertorte with a spoonful of whipped cream on a Jutta Sika 1901–1902 / *Tondi* porcelain plate, from Neue Galerie Design Shop.

CARAMEL-CREAM LAYER CAKE

Dobostorte

12 SERVINGS

Cake

1 pound plus 2 tablespoons unsalted
   butter, softened

¾ cup confectioners' sugar
   Pinch of grated lemon zest

16 large eggs, separated

1 ¾ cups granulated sugar

2 ½ cups all-purpose flour, sifted

Caramel cream

¾ cup sugar

¼ cup water

3 ⅓ cups heavy cream

Caramel crown

2 cups granulated sugar

2 tablespoons water

2 tablespoons unsalted butter
   Cooking spray

Tips

The ingredients for the cake batter are divisible by two, so when making the recipe at home, it may be easier to bake the cakes in two batches. Add the cream slowly to the hot caramel in Step 6 to avoid splashing.

The layers of caramel cream should be about the same thickness as the rounds of cake.

Variations

To make my pinwheel decoration, pipe or spoon 12 evenly spaced mounds of whipped cream around the edges of the cake and lean a caramel wedge against each one.

Any extra caramel cream can be spread around the sides of the cake in Step 10. Refrigerate or freeze until set before adding the caramel wedges.

Make ahead

The caramel cream needs to be refrigerated overnight, so plan accordingly.

The *Dobostorte* (pronounced *"Doboshtorte"*) is a fancy Hungarian layer cake. The traditional recipe is made with chocolate buttercream, but my version is more of a caramel cream cake. For a dramatic presentation, I arrange twelve wedges of caramel (one for each slice) on top like a pinwheel, but they can also be laid flat in a round on the cake.

1 Heat the oven to 325 degrees. Line four 12-by-17-inch rimmed baking sheets with parchment paper.

2 Make the cake: In a large bowl, using an electric mixer, beat the butter with the confectioners' sugar and lemon zest until creamy. Add the egg yolks, one at a time, beating after each addition until smooth.

3 In another large bowl, using clean beaters, beat the egg whites at medium speed until slightly thickened and foamy, about 2 minutes. Gradually add the granulated sugar, and beat until the whites hold a soft peak. Using a rubber spatula, stir one-third of the beaten egg whites into the yolk mixture to lighten it. Gently fold this mixture into the remaining egg whites just until smooth. Fold in the flour.

4 Using an offset spatula, spread one-quarter of the batter in each prepared baking pan. Transfer to the oven and bake until the cake is very light brown, about 8 minutes. Remove to racks to cool completely. Using a plate or pot lid as a guide, cut each cake into two 8-inch rounds.

5 Make the caramel cream: In a medium saucepan, heat the sugar and water over high heat until the sugar dissolves, then cook, swirling the pan from time to time, until the caramel is dark brown and starts to bubble and smoke, 4 to 5 minutes. Remove the pan from the heat and slowly and carefully whisk in 1 ⅓ cups of the cream. Pour the hot caramel into a heatproof bowl and let cool, then refrigerate overnight.

6 In a large bowl, using an electric mixer, beat the remaining 2 cups of cream with the cold caramel until the cream holds a medium peak.

7 Line the bottom of a 9-inch springform pan with a round of parchment paper; line the sides with a long strip of parchment. Set one of the cake rounds in the prepared pan. Using an offset spatula, spread about ¾ cup of the caramel cream on top. Set another round on top and continue layering with the remaining caramel cream and 5 of the cake rounds, finishing with a layer of cream. Refrigerate the cake until set, 1 to 1 ½ hours, or freeze for about 30 minutes.

8 Make the caramel crown: Set the remaining cake round on a sheet of parchment paper. In a small saucepan, heat the sugar and water over high heat until the sugar dissolves, then cook, swirling the pan from time to time, until the caramel is golden brown, 4 to 5 minutes. Remove the pan from the heat and whisk in the butter. Pour over the cake and spread evenly.

9 Working quickly, spray a 10- to 12-inch chef's knife with cooking spray, and cut the caramel disk into 12 wedges; spray the knife again each time you make a cut. Let cool completely.

10 Remove the sides of the cake pan and discard the parchment. Transfer the cake to a cake plate. Arrange the caramel wedges on top to make a flat round, and serve.

A slice of Caramel-Cream Layer Cake rests on pages of my grandmother's handwritten recipes.

COFFEE AND TEA SERVICES

Vienna's School of Applied Arts (Kunstgewerbeschule) played a key role in the revitalization of the decorative arts around the turn of the last century. Josef Hoffmann and Koloman Moser both taught at the school, which instructed a new generation on novel ideas for form and decoration. Numerous women, who had recently gained the opportunity to pursue higher education in the Austro-Hungarian Empire, were among the students.

Hoffmann headed the architectural department, and Moser was responsible for the ceramics class, among others. Moser's notable students included Bruno Emmel, Gisela von Falke, Antoinette Krasnik, Jutta Sika, and Therese Trethan. With the support of Josef Böck, a porcelain decorating and manufacturing firm established in 1898, the works designed by these students were produced in Bohemia and marked "Schule Prof. Kolo Moser" (Prof. Kolo Moser's Class). The students designed practical objects for the home, including tea and coffee services, lamps, and vases. Most pieces had minimal decoration, and they were often geometric in design, which made them appear modern at the time.

One enduring design to come out of the venture was Jutta Sika's coffee and tea service from around 1901–1902, made of hard-paste porcelain. The shape is somewhat playful, with the tea spout resembling a bird's beak. The rectangular lid is pierced by a circle. The handle—also cut by a circle—mirrors the form of the lid. Overlapping circles are stenciled on the body of each piece. Different designs, both geometric and naturalistic, were printed on this form, but the circular motif remains the one most associated with Sika to this day. Sika may have been inspired in part by Japanese graphic design. The Sixth Vienna Secession exhibition held in 1900 was devoted to Japanese art, and the Secession journal, *Ver Sacrum*, had published an article on Japanese stencils in 1899. Certainly, the interest in patterns and the abstraction of nature was an idea that was increasingly explored in the West at the fin de siècle. In 1901, Koloman Moser published a pattern book, *Die Quelle: Flächenschmuck* (*The Source: Decorations for Flat Surfaces*), that showed ideas for decorating various surfaces.

Hoffmann also turned his hand to the design of tea and coffee services, and his approach varied over the years. Such designs as the *Merkur* (Mercury) service of around 1910 for Josef Böck reflected his training as an architect. The sides of the body are fluted and each is highlighted with luxurious black and gold glazes. Hoffmann's appropriately-named *Melon* mocha service of 1925 for Augarten also incorporated stripes. Tiny leaf finials add a whimsical flair.

Jutta Sika, *I Tondi* Tea Service, designed 1901–1902, porcelain
(clockwise: tea pot, cup and saucer, dessert plate, creamer).
Neue Galerie Design Shop.

QUARK CHEESECAKE

Topfentorte

12 SERVINGS

Sugar dough

8 tablespoons (1 stick) unsalted butter, softened

1 cup confectioners' sugar

1 large egg
Pinch of salt

2 cups all-purpose flour

Génoise

Cooking spray

3 tablespoons all-purpose flour, plus more for dusting

2 large eggs

2 large egg yolks

$\frac{1}{3}$ cup sugar

$\frac{1}{4}$ cup cornstarch

2 teaspoons unsalted butter, melted

Mousse

4 gelatin sheets (see Tip, page 172)

2 cups heavy cream

$\frac{1}{4}$ cup sugar

3 large egg yolks

1 tablespoon fresh lemon juice

1 cup quark cheese (see Tips, page 162)

Garnish

$\frac{3}{4}$ cup fruit preserves or jam
About 1 cup fresh berries

This light cake made with layers of spongy génoise, jam, and fluffy quark cheese mousse is a favorite of mine. It's an excellent springtime or brunch cake. I like it with fresh fruit, and I often arrange concentric circles of raspberries and blueberries on top.

1 Make the sugar dough: In a large bowl, using an electric mixer, beat the butter with the confectioners' sugar until creamy, about 3 minutes. Slowly add the egg and salt and beat at low speed until creamy. Add the flour and beat just until smooth.

2 Remove the dough and pat into a thick square. Cover with plastic wrap and refrigerate for 1 hour.

3 Heat the oven to 325 degrees. Line the bottom of a 9-inch springform pan with a round of parchment paper, line the sides with a long strip of parchment, and spray lightly with cooking spray. Cut the dough into 4 equal squares. Reserve 3 of the remaining squares for another use. Roll the remaining square into an 8 $\frac{1}{2}$-inch round, and transfer to the prepared pan. Bake the dough until golden brown, about 12 minutes. Transfer the pan to a rack to cool. Increase the oven temperature to 350 degrees.

4 Make the génoise: Spray a 9-inch springform pan with cooking spray and dust lightly with flour.

5 In a large bowl set over a saucepan of simmering water, whisk the eggs, egg yolks, and sugar until the sugar has dissolved and the mixture is frothy and very warm, but not hot, about 3 minutes. Remove the pan from the heat and beat at medium-high speed until the mixture has cooled slightly and doubled in volume, 3 to 4 minutes. Sift the flour with the cornstarch over the batter and fold in. Fold in the butter just until smooth.

6 Using an offset spatula, spread the batter in the prepared pan. Transfer to the oven and bake until the génoise is light brown and spongy, about 30 minutes.

7 Remove the pan from the oven and let cool completely on a rack. Remove the sides of the springform pan and carefully flip the génoise onto a cutting board.

8 Meanwhile, make the mousse: Soak the gelatin sheets in a bowl of ice water until softened, about 15 minutes. Drain, squeeze out as much water as possible, and put the gelatin in a small bowl.

9 In a large bowl, using an electric mixer, beat the cream until it holds a soft peak. Refrigerate.

10 In a large bowl set over a saucepan of simmering water, whisk the sugar with the egg yolks and lemon juice until tripled in volume and very shiny, about 4 minutes. Add the gelatin sheets and beat until dissolved. Remove the bowl from the heat and let the mixture cool completely.

11 Fold the quark into the egg-yolk mixture. Gradually fold in the whipped cream.

12 Using a long serrated knife, cut the génoise into 2 horizontal layers.

13 Spread a thin layer of jam on the sugar dough in the pan. Set the bottom layer of génoise on the dough, cut side up. Pour in the mousse and gently tap the pan on the work surface so that the mixture flows down the sides. Set the second génoise layer on top, cut side down, and gently press it. Freeze overnight.

14 Release the sides of the pan and remove the parchment paper. Spread a layer of jam on top of the cake. Transfer to a cake plate, decorate with the fresh berries, and serve.

Tips

Take care not to overwork the dough in Step 1, to avoid developing the gluten—which toughens the dough. When whipping the heavy cream in Step 8, don't beat until it holds a stiff peak. A soft peak is what you want when making a mousse.

Serve with

You can dollop some whipped heavy cream on the top of the cake before arranging the berries on it. Otherwise, just some additional berries on the side are nice.

Make ahead

The cake takes 1 day to prepare, so plan accordingly. The recipe makes more dough than you need; the remainder can be frozen for up to 6 months.

Wiener Werkstätte Postcard Number 62 by Moriz Jung, Conversation between Mutes, 1907. Leonard A. Lauder Collection, Neue Galerie New York.

CHOCOLATE-ALMOND LOAF CAKE

Rehrücken

The German name of this delicious chocolate cake means "venison saddle," referring to the color and shape of the cake, which resembles a saddle, or loin, of venison. It is traditionally baked in a *Rehrücken* pan, a long narrow pan with a rounded bottom, but a 12-inch terrine mold can be used instead.

12 SERVINGS

3 tablespoons unsalted butter, melted, plus more for brushing

All-purpose flour, for dusting

⅓ cup fine dry bread crumbs

¼ cup cake flour

3 tablespoons unsweetened cocoa powder

½ cup almond paste

3 tablespoons confectioners' sugar

6 large eggs, 5 separated

⅓ cup plus ¼ cup granulated sugar

¼ cup water

1 cup orange marmalade

2 ounces marzipan

Glaze

1 ⅓ cups semisweet chocolate chips (8 ounces)

8 tablespoons (1 stick) unsalted butter

Slivered almonds, for garnishing (optional)

1 Heat the oven to 325 degrees. Brush a 12-by-2 ½-inch terrine mold with butter and dust lightly with flour.

2 Sift the bread crumbs with the cake flour and cocoa powder into a large bowl.

3 In a large bowl, using an electric mixer, beat the almond paste with the confectioners' sugar at medium speed until the mixture is soft and creamy, about 3 minutes. Add the egg yolks and the whole egg, one at a time, beating after each addition until smooth.

4 In another large bowl, using clean beaters, beat the egg whites at medium speed until slightly thickened and foamy, about 2 minutes. Gradually add ⅓ cup of the sugar, and beat until the whites hold a soft peak. Using a rubber spatula, stir one-third of the beaten egg whites into the yolk mixture to lighten it. Gently fold this mixture into the remaining egg whites just until smooth. Gradually fold in the bread crumb mixture, then fold in the melted butter.

5 Using an offset spatula, spread the batter in the prepared terrine. Transfer to the oven and bake until a toothpick inserted in the center comes out clean, 30 to 35 minutes. Remove the cake from the oven and let cool completely on a rack.

6 Meanwhile, in a small saucepan, combine the remaining ¼ cup of granulated sugar with the water and cook over medium heat, stirring occasionally, until the sugar has dissolved. Remove from the heat and let cool.

7 Run a knife around the inside of the pan and carefully flip the cake onto a rack. Using a long serrated knife, cut the cake into 3 horizontal layers. Brush both sides of each layer with the syrup. Spread a thin layer of orange marmalade on the bottom and middle layers and reassemble the cake. Spread the remaining marmalade on the top and sides.

8 Using fingertips, roll the marzipan into a 12-by-¾-by-¾-inch rope; trim the edges. Arrange it down the center of the top of the cake.

9 Make the glaze: In a double boiler or a medium bowl set over a saucepan of simmering water, or in a microwave, heat the chocolate chips with the butter until just melted. Remove from the heat, stir until smooth, and let cool slightly.

10 Pour the glaze over the top and sides of the cake, then spread the glaze all over the cake. Refrigerate the cake until the glaze is set, 5 to 10 minutes, before serving.

11 Remove the cake from the refrigerator and decorate with the slivered almonds, if desired. Transfer the cake to a cake plate, and serve.

Tips

Rehrücken pans are available at some specialty food shops and online at surlatable.com.

Almond paste and marzipan are very similar. Both are made of ground blanched almonds and sugar, but marzipan is typically sweeter and smoother. In this recipe, you can substitute one for the other.

Serve with

This cake is an afternoon treat served with a mound of *Schlag* (sweetened whipped cream) and nothing else.

Variation

If orange marmalade isn't your favorite, substitute a jam like raspberry or strawberry.

Make ahead

The cake can be refrigerated for up to 2 days.

HAZELNUT CRESCENT COOKIES

Haselnuss Kipferl

MAKES ABOUT 2 DOZEN COOKIES

½ pound (2 sticks) unsalted butter,
    softened

1 cup confectioners' sugar

3 large egg yolks

1 ½ teaspoons pure vanilla extract

½ teaspoon salt

1 ¾ cups all-purpose flour

¾ cup blanched hazelnuts (see Tips),
    finely ground

These crumbly, sugar-coated cookies (photograph, page 205) are found everywhere in Austria at Christmastime, but I like to serve them year-round as petits fours after a nice meal.

1 In a large bowl, using an electric mixer, beat the butter with ½ cup of the confectioners' sugar at medium-high speed until pale and fluffy, about 1 minute. Add the egg yolks, vanilla, and salt and beat until blended, scraping down the sides of the bowl as needed. Beat in the flour and hazelnuts at medium speed until just incorporated.

2 Turn the dough out, pat into a thick disk, and cover with plastic wrap. Refrigerate until firm, at least 30 minutes.

3 Heat the oven to 350 degrees. Line 2 baking sheets with parchment paper.

4 Using about 1 ½ tablespoons of the dough for each cookie, roll the dough into cylinders 3 inches long, tapering the ends. Form the cookies into crescents and transfer them to the prepared baking sheets, spacing them 1 inch apart.

5 Bake the cookies until light golden, about 18 minutes. Remove from the oven and let the cookies cool on the baking sheets until just cool enough to handle, about 10 minutes.

6 Spread the remaining ½ cup of confectioners' sugar in a shallow bowl. Dip each warm cookie in the confectioners' sugar, turning to coat evenly. Transfer the cookies to racks and let cool completely.

Tips
Blanched (skinned) hazelnuts are available at some supermarkets and many specialty food shops.
Take care not to roll the dough into cylinders that are too thin, or the cookies may crack and fall apart when they are baked.

Serve with
These tender yet crisp cookies are perfect with a cup of coffee or hot tea.

Variation
If you can't find blanched hazelnuts, blanched almonds can be substituted.

Make ahead
The cookies can be stored in an airtight container at room temperature for up to 3 days.

LINZER COOKIES

Linzeraugen

MAKES ABOUT 6 ½ DOZEN COOKIES

10 ounces (2 ½ sticks) unsalted butter, softened

1 ½ cups confectioners' sugar, plus more for dusting

1 large egg

1 large egg yolk
Grated zest of ½ lemon

2 ½ cups hazelnut flour (see Tip, page 185)

2 cups all-purpose flour

1 teaspoon baking powder

1 teaspoon ground cinnamon

1 cup seedless raspberry jam

Translated literally as "Linzer eyes," these cinnamon-hazelnut sandwich cookies are a petite version of the famous linzertorte from the city of Linz in northern Austria. A thin layer of raspberry jam peeks out from a hole in the top of these cookies.

1 In a large bowl, using an electric mixer, beat the butter with the confectioners' sugar until pale and creamy, about 4 minutes. Add the whole egg and then the yolk, beating until creamy. Add the lemon zest, hazelnut flour, all-purpose flour, baking powder, and cinnamon and beat until incorporated, about 3 minutes. Turn the dough out, pat into a thick disk, and cover with plastic wrap. Refrigerate overnight.

2 Heat the oven to 325 degrees. Line 2 large baking sheets with parchment paper. Working in two batches, on a lightly floured work surface, roll out the dough ⅛ inch thick. Using a 1 ½-inch round cutter, cut out cookies and transfer to the prepared baking sheets. Using a ¾-inch round cookie cutter, cut holes in half of the cookies. Transfer to the oven and bake until golden brown, 10 to 12 minutes; keep in mind that the cookies with the holes will bake faster than the other cookies. Remove from the oven and transfer the parchment paper with the cookies to the work surface and let cool. Continue baking the cookies, lining the baking sheets with more parchment paper.

3 Dust the cookies with the holes with confectioners' sugar. Using a pastry bag fitted with a small plain tip or a spoon, mound 1 teaspoon of raspberry jam on each whole cookie. Sandwich with the dusted cookies, and serve.

Tip
The recipe can easily be cut in half.

Variation
A different fruit jam, such as apricot or strawberry, can be substituted for the raspberry.

Make ahead
The dough needs to chill overnight before baking, so plan accordingly. The cookie dough can be frozen for up to 2 months.

CHOCOLATE HAZELNUTS

Haselnüsse mit Weisser Schokolade

MAKES 4 CUPS

$\frac{1}{2}$ cup granulated sugar

2 tablespoons water

4 cups hazelnuts (about 20 ounces),
    toasted and skinned (see Tip)

1 cup milk chocolate chips

$\frac{1}{2}$ cup confectioners' sugar

I have served these delicious milk chocolate–covered hazelnuts as petits fours at my restaurants since I first opened. Along with our Dark Chocolate Almonds (opposite), they are a fantastic and simple way to end an elegant meal. A word of warning, though: they are ridiculously addictive, and once your friends try them, they will bug you to make them for years to come!

1 In a large saucepan, combine the granulated sugar with the water and heat over high heat until the sugar has dissolved and the mixture is bubbling, 2 to 3 minutes; do not let the syrup color. Add the hazelnuts and cook, stirring, until the sugar turns very white, about 1 minute. Remove the pan from the heat and spread the nuts on a rimmed baking sheet. Let cool completely.

2 In a double boiler or a small bowl set over a saucepan of simmering water, or in a microwave, heat the chocolate chips until just melted. Remove from the heat and stir until smooth. Let the chocolate cool until it reaches about 89 degrees on a candy thermometer.

3 Transfer the nuts to a large bowl. Add the melted chocolate and stir to coat until tacky, about 30 seconds. Sprinkle the confectioners' sugar over the nuts and stir to coat well.

Tip

You can buy toasted, skinned hazelnuts in specialty food shops, or make your own: Heat the oven to 350 degrees. Spread the hazelnuts on a rimmed baking sheet and toast until browned, 12 to 14 minutes. Let cool slightly, then transfer to a towel and rub to remove the skins.

Variation

In place of confectioners' sugar, use unsweetened cocoa powder.

Make ahead

The nuts can be stored in an airtight container at room temperature for up to 3 months.

DARK CHOCOLATE ALMONDS

Schokolade Mandeln

MAKES 4 CUPS

$^{1}/_{2}$ cup sugar

2 tablespoons water

4 cups almonds (about 20 ounces), toasted
(see Tip)

1 cup semisweet chocolate chips

$^{1}/_{2}$ cup unsweetened cocoa powder

Like our Chocolate Hazelnuts (opposite), these chocolate-covered almonds are a staple at my restaurants. Lightly caramelized in sugar and coated with dark chocolate and cocoa powder, they are simple to prepare and impossible not to love. I especially like them after dinner with coffee, but they also make a great snack.

1 In a large saucepan, combine the granulated sugar with the water and heat over high heat until the sugar has dissolved and the mixture is bubbling, 2 to 3 minutes; do not let the syrup color. Add the almonds and cook, stirring, until the sugar turns very white, about 1 minute. Remove the pan from the heat and spread the nuts on a rimmed baking sheet. Let cool completely.

2 In a double boiler or a small bowl set over a saucepan of simmering water, or in a microwave, heat the chocolate chips until just melted. Remove from the heat and stir until smooth. Let the chocolate cool until it reaches about 89 degrees on a candy thermometer.

3 Transfer the nuts to a large bowl. Add the melted chocolate and stir to coat until tacky, about 30 seconds. Sprinkle the cocoa powder over the nuts and mix to coat well.

Tip

You can buy toasted (or roasted) almonds in many supermarkets and specialty food shops, or make your own: Heat the oven to 350 degrees. Spread the almonds on a rimmed baking sheet and toast until browned, 8 to 10 minutes.

Variation

Instead of unsweetened cocoa powder, use confectioners' sugar.

Make ahead

The nuts can be stored in an airtight container at room temperature for up to 1 month.

AUSTRIAN WINES

I love wine and I especially love Austrian wine. It's a passion that began when I worked summers at a hotel in the Wachau wine region—and was not even drinking alcohol yet. But it was impossible not to be affected by what was happening around me: the serving of wine in the dining room, the work in the terraced vineyards along the Danube and in the cellars.

Over the years, I've gotten to explore the incredible variety of Austria's wines, many of them made from native grapes grown almost nowhere else. Austria is such a little place (it's the size of Maine), and not a tremendous amount of wine is produced there. Even less leaves the country—seventy percent of it is consumed locally. But what is available is often handcrafted on family estates following sustainable practices, regionally distinctive, and full of fresh character.

The country's most famous wine, Grüner Veltliner, is a crisp and minerally white with fresh notes of green apple. I love it as an aperitif, but, more important for me as a chef, it is remarkably easy to pair with food. This white wine goes as well with meat as it does with fish. And there isn't a vegetable that doesn't love the grape, including the notoriously difficult ones for wine, like asparagus and artichokes. Grüner Veltliner and the lesser known, rich yet snappy Neuburger—both from indigenous grapes—are probably my favorite matches for Veal Schnitzel (page 122). Grüner Veltliner's stylistic range is tremendous, from light to rich and powerful. Some from single-vineyard sites—for example, the Smaragd wines in the Wachau—can easily age for a decade or more.

Many Grüner Veltliner producers make Rieslings as well. What often surprises people about these wines is that they are dry, unlike German Rieslings. Other whites include Pinot Blancs with complexity and age-worthiness and world-class, mineral-rich Sauvignon Blancs.

If you like Pinot Noir for its bracing, food-friendly acidity, balance, fruitiness, and mellow tannins, you'll find Austria's light, mostly unoaked red wines just as alluring. In fact, St. Laurent, with its stewed berry and spice aromas, belongs to the Pinot family. Blaufränkisch has soft, smooth notes of blackberry and sometimes cinnamon, which makes it a good partner for robust stews like Venison Goulash (page 137). Zweigelt, a cross between these two grapes, has fruity aromas, ripe cherry notes, and light spiciness and goes beautifully with hearty meat dishes such as Roasted Leg of Lamb (page 133).

The sweet wines of Austria, including Beerenauslese and Trockenbeerenauslese, offer velvety fruit aromas and sugar balanced by fantastic acidity. I love them paired with a foie gras appetizer or with a cheese plate. They are the perfect finish to an elegant meal either before, or instead of, schnapps.

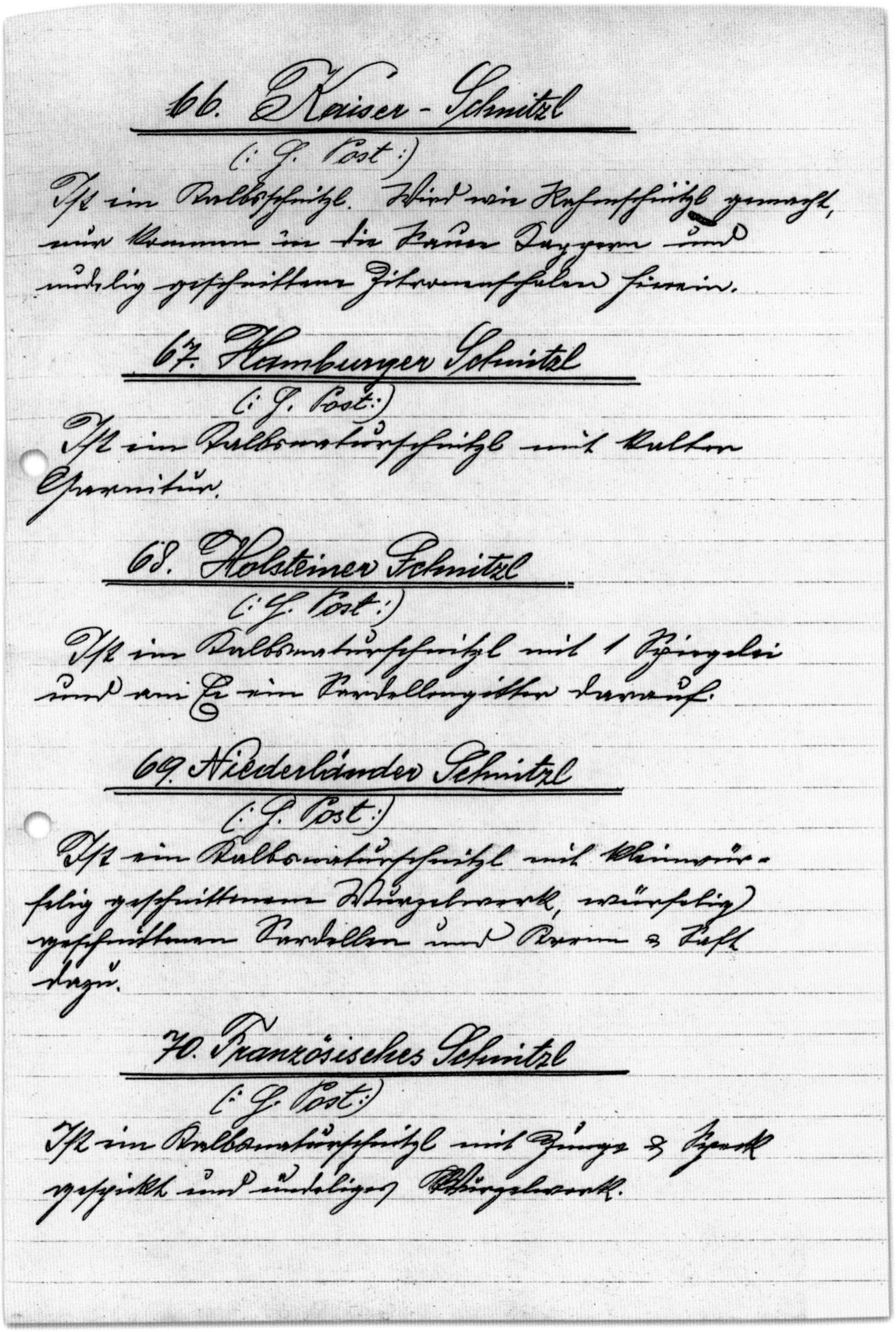

66. Kaiser-Schnitzl

(: G. Post :)

Ist ein Kalbsschnitzl. Wird wie Rahmschnitzl gemacht, nur kommen in die Sauce Kapern und nudelig geschnittene Zitronenschalen hinein.

67. Hamburger Schnitzl

(: G. Post :)

Ist ein Kalbsnaturschnitzl mit Butter Garnitur.

68. Holsteiner Schnitzl

(: G. Post :)

Ist ein Kalbsnaturschnitzl mit 1 Spiegelei und am Ei ein Sardellengitter darauf.

69. Niederländer Schnitzl

(: G. Post :)

Ist ein Kalbsnaturschnitzl mit kleinwürfelig geschnittenem Wurzelwerk, würfelig geschnittenen Sardellen und Rahm & Saft dazu.

70. Französisches Schnitzl

(: G. Post :)

Ist ein Kalbsnaturschnitzl mit Zunge & Speck gespickt und nudeligem Wurzelwerk.

Handwritten vintage cookbook from my collection.

U.S. AND METRIC CONVERSION CHARTS

All conversions are approximate.

WEIGHT CONVERSIONS

U.S./U.K.		Metric
½	ounce	14 g
1	ounce	28 g
1	ounces	43 g
2	ounces	57 g
2 ½	ounces	71 g
3	ounces	85 g
3 ½	ounces	100 g
4	ounces	113 g
5	ounces	142 g
6	ounces	170 g
7	ounces	200 g
8	ounces	227 g
9	ounces	255 g
10	ounces	284 g
11	ounces	312 g
12	ounces	340 g
13	ounces	368 g
14	ounces	400 g
15	ounces	425 g
1	pound	454 g

LIQUID CONVERSIONS

U.S		Metric
1	teaspoon	5 ml
1	tablespoon	15 ml
2	tablespoons	30 ml
3	tablespoons	45 ml
¼	cup	60 ml
⅓	cup	75 ml
⅓	cup plus 1 tablespoon	90 ml
⅓	cup plus 2 tablespoons	100 ml
½	cup	120 ml
⅔	cup	150 ml
¾	cup	180 ml
¾	cup plus 2 tablespoons	200 ml
1	cup	240 ml
1	cup plus 2 tablespoons	275 ml
1 ¼	cups	300 ml
1 ⅓	cups	325 ml
1 ½	cups	350 ml
1 ⅔	cups	375 ml
1 ¾	cups	400 ml
1 ¾	cups plus 2 tablespoons	450 ml
2	cups (1 pint)	475 ml
2	cups	600 ml
3	cups	725 ml
4	cups (1 quart)	945 ml
	(1,000 ml = 1 liter)	

OVEN TEMPERATURES

°F	Gas Mark	°C
250	–	120
275	1	140
300	2	150
325	3	165
350	4	180
375	5	190
400	6	200
425	7	220
450	8	230
475	9	240
500	10	260
550	Broil	290

RECIPE CONTENTS

WIENER WERKSTÄTTE Nº 408

Wiener Werkstätte Postcard Number 408 by Gustav Kalhammer,
National Railway Station Restaurant, Vienna X, Josef Pohl, 1911.
Leonard A. Lauder Collection, Neue Galerie New York.

INDEX

216

ACKNOWLEDGMENTS

Neue Cuisine would not exist without the dedication, support, and hard work of many great people. To begin, I want to thank publisher Charles Miers and Rizzoli International Publications, Inc., for sharing my love of food, art, and culture and making that love come to life on these pages. Thanks goes to the book's editorial team—Marilyn Flaig, William Loob, Hilary Ney, and Judith Sutton—as well as to production manager Colin Hough-Trapp and publicist Nicki Clendening. Above all, I am indebted to project editor Sandy Gilbert Freidus, who first approached me about writing *Neue Cuisine* and whose wonderful ideas and tremendous dedication continue to impress me.

A tremendous thanks to Richard Pandiscio and Bill Loccisano for their brilliant art direction and graphic design, and to my amazing writer, Jane Sigal, for deciphering my foreign tongue and putting together my thoughts so eloquently.

I am eternally blessed with my wonderful staff, who work so hard every day. In particular, I want to give thanks to chefs Daniel Kill, Matthew Lodes, Rita Cazeras, and Jesus Vargas, who make these recipes daily in my restaurants with the same love, precision, and tireless effort that I have given to them over the years. Without your constant support, input, and diligence, this book would not have been possible. And to all of the other talented chefs I have had the pleasure of working with, and who carry these recipes with them today, it has been an honor—I would also like to mention that my former chefs Michael Stahler and Grayson Schmitz were particularly helpful in testing recipes for *Neue Cuisine*.

To Krissy Quinn, for her valued input and encouragement throughout this journey. Thank you to Helen Freund for countless hours spent researching, typing, and testing recipes, and to Victoria Langer for helping with their translation. My appreciation also goes to Leo Schneeman, my wine director, for his knowledgeable advice.

Heartfelt thanks to the Neue Galerie staff, and in particular for the great work of Scott Gutterman, Paul Landy, Ronald S. Lauder, Renée Price, and Janis Staggs.

Many thanks to photographer Ellen Silverman, for her beautiful imagery; to Kevin Norris, for his technical support; to stylists Noemi Bonazzi and Susie Theodorou; to Aaron Freidus and my son, Ben, for their assistance with the photography shoots; and to all the people, in particular Allison Power, who generously volunteered their time to participate in the Café Sabarsky photograph.

Finally, thank you to Jack Desario, Yvonne Gomez, Werner Matt, Hermann Rainer, Heinz Winkler, and David Bouley for their belief in me from the beginning—for that, I am forever grateful.

Neue Cuisine was produced in association with the Neue Galerie New York.

Neue Galerie New York is a museum devoted to early twentieth-century German and Austrian art and design. Located in a landmark mansion built in 1914 by the firm of Carrère & Hastings, the museum offers a strong program of exhibitions, lectures, films, concerts, and other events.

The award-winning Neue Galerie Design Shop, with its superb modern interiors line, Neue Haus, offers objects based on original designs from Biedermeier, Vienna 1900, and the Bauhaus.

Information on the Neue Galerie and its Design Shop is available at www.neuegalerie.org.

CREDITS

The Neue Galerie contributed works of art and design objects that capture the elegance of Vienna 1900, as well as informative text about this creative period.

The Neue Galerie Design Shop lent many superb tableware pieces (credited in the captions) for the book's original photography. Several companies graciously supplied additional elegant tableware accessories: namely, Riedel, stemware (pages 41, 48 [right], 61, 130, and 195); Rosenthal, dinnerware and serving pieces (pages 55, 59, 61, 63, 87, 97, 103, 105, 107, 111, 123, 135, 167, 171, 177, 179, and 181); and Nachtmann, cake stands and plate (pages 6, 11, 189, and 197). Zezé designed the magnificent flower arrangements.

Gustav Klimt print reproductions (details) were used as backdrops for the photographs on pages 6 and 195.

All of the book's photographs were taken by Ellen Silverman unless otherwise noted.
The photographs on pages 14 and 15 are courtesy of Peter Medilek.
Maike Paul took the photograph on page 21.
The photograph on page 224 was taken by Sebastiano Pellion di Persano.
The author photograph on the jacket flap is by Rainer Hosch.

CAPTIONS

PAGES 38–39: Dagobert Peche design *Antinous* (detail), 1922. Neue Galerie Design Shop.

PAGES 70–71: Dagobert Peche design *Der Spitz* (Point) (detail), 1922. Neue Galerie Design Shop.

PAGES 94–95: Dagobert Peche design *Butterfly* (detail), 1910. Neue Galerie Design Shop.

PAGES 142–143: Josef Hoffmann Fabric Design no. 5068 (detail), 1904. Courtesy of Johann Backhausen & Söhne Company Archive, Vienna.

PAGES 164–165: Dagobert Peche design *Viola* pattern (detail), 1922. Neue Galerie Design Shop.

Stonborough Apartment Dining Room 2006 reconstruction for the Neue Galerie New York.
Hoffmann created this luxurious dining room in 1905 for the Berlin apartment of Jerome and Margaret
Stonborough. The table is set with a combination of period and reproduction cutlery,
glassware, ceramics, and table linens. The small sideboard is decorated with the two orchid vases
by Koloman Moser, which had been originally placed there.

The "living wallpaper" of posters at Blaue Gans, plus a menu of sausages and beer, help create the atmosphere of an Austrian *Wirtshaus*. Photo by Sebastiano Pellion di Persano.